# RHOSNEIGR
## ~then & now~
## Series

volume three

# Rhosneigr ~ People & Places

Compiled & Edited by
T.T.M. Hale

13579108642

**Published by**
www.rhosneigrpublishing.co.uk
2 Roman Ridge Rd.
Sheffield, S9 1XG

ISBN 978-0956296214

Copyright © 2017 T.T.M. Hale or others as noted within.
All Rights Reserved. No part of this publication may be reproduced, stored in a retrieval system or utilised in any form or by any means, electronic or mechanical, including photocopying, recording, web publishing, or scanning, without the prior written permission from the copyright owner.

Meaning of 'Rhosneigr' from 'Enwau Lleoedd yn Mon' (Place Names in Anglesey) by R.T Williams, 1908.

Rhosneigr is a lively village in Llanfaelog parish, at the seaside, on the opposite side to Llyn Maelog, and recently, on account of the numbers who visit it in the summer, it has been given its own station on the edge of 'Towyn Trewan'. I imagine that the place bears the name of Saint Eneigr, the daughter of Cadrod Calchfynydd by his wife Gwrgon, the daughter of Brychan, at the beginning of the 5th century. Others try to make a connection with the word niger – the natural and permanent blackness of some of the outer parts of his bleak place.

('Rhos', of course is a 'moor').

## Foreword

1. Rhosneigr has been a lifelong passion and some of my oldest friendships were forged here. I hope my love for the village and its interesting and varied history shines through.

2. This book is probably way too long and detailed - my family (and therefore my strongest critics) say it's too weighty for a wide readership. Nevertheless, Rhosneigr does have a lot of interesting stories to tell.

3. Researching the stories has been challenging and frequently complicated. Where possible, I have tried to report from the original records of the time, rather than the sometimes more inventive 'legends' that other writers have on occasions created for dramatic effect. I'm pretty sure I haven't left too much out, or made too many mistakes, but if I have - please accept my apologies - and let me know what they are! All corrections will be updated on the website.

4. There's more to tell on just about every location you can think of - I have files full of things I wanted to include, but just didn't have the space or time for. I feel the next book assembling itself already ! If you have any stories to tell of other Rhosneigr 'People and Places', I would be thrilled to receive them.

5. Apologies for being unable to find a photo of the 'hole in the wall' fruit and veg shop; or a photo of Les 'Plas' and his horse drawn milk-cart; or an interior shot of Diana's, or Bon Marche, or Balkin's, or any of the shops I remember from my own youth - photos I was sure would be fairly easy to track down, but couldn't. I really did try. If you have one please send me a copy!

6. There are a small number of illustrations in these pages for which the current copyright holder has not been traced. A donation to the R.N.L.I. has been made in lieu of these.

7. Please don't throw away or burn your old photos or plans or maps or charts or tickets or flyers or ephemera - any such material gratefully received. One day, when I've retired, I'd love to empty numerous storage crates and open a Rhosneigr Heritage Centre so that the ongoing history of our charming little village may be enjoyed by all.

**Tim Hale**
January 2017

# Acknowledgements

Unless specifically noted in the text or captions, all the photographs, maps, postcards, prints, ephemera and illustrations are taken from the Editor's own collection.

The Editor is grateful for permission to use additional illustrations and extracts from publications as noted in the text, or in the bibliography.

Particular thanks must be made to 5 organisations which have proved particularly helpful when conducting research into a myriad of subjects, and without which our ability to research local history would be very much restricted:

The British Newspaper Archive (in partnership with the British Library & Findmypast.com). *[Images of newspapers from the archive are ©The British Library Board].*
The National Archives (nationalarchives.gov.uk).
The National Library of Wales (www.llgc.org.uk).
Anglesey Archives (archifdy@ynysmon.gov.uk);
Bangor University Library (archives@bangor.ac.uk).

Individuals and organisations who have been kind enough to offer support and assistance, over the several years it has taken to compile this book, include:

Anglesey Antiquarian Society; Anglesey Archive Service (Anne Venables, Amanda Sweet, Helen Lewis); Anthony Moore; Archives & Collections Society, Canada; archives@parliament.co.uk (Simon Gough); Arthur G. Owen; BAE Systems Heritage Centre, Brough (Steve Gillard); Barry Mason; BBC Antiques Roadshow (Heather Campbell, Hannah Ford); Beken of Cowes (Peter Mumford); Bernard Wellings (www.walesdirectory.co.uk); Bloomsbury Publishing (Claire Weatherhead); bnielsen@science.au.dk; Caernarfon record office (Angharad Jones); Charles Nugent; Charles Parsons; Charles Stephenson; Christopher Lees-Jones; Classic & Sportscar Centre (James Szkiler); Claydon House Trust Archives and the Verney Collection (Sue Baxter); Clive Farahar; Conway Publishing - Anova Books (Jon Lee, Alison Moss); Cowes Maritime Museum; David Baynham; David Cockram; David Wilde; Derek Bartley; Dilys Moore; East Cheshire Sub Aqua Club (Kevin Phillips); Elizabeth Young; Emily Hale; Ferens Art Gallery (Claire Longrigg, Kristen Simister); Francis Frith Collection (Julia Skinner); Gilly Llewelyn; G. Budenberg; G. Butterworth; Gwyn Williams; Holyhead Maritime Museum (Gerry Thomas); Huw Humphreys (huwmedia); Ian Gardner; Jenni Wyn Hyatt (Welsh Translations); Joan Goodhand; John Cowell; John Ingle; John Morrison; John Peel Centre for Creative Arts (Matthew Abercrombie); John Woodford; Judith Matthews; Keith Adams; Ken Rees; Leslie Ingram-Brown; Lisa Hale; Liver Sketching Club (David Brown); Liverpoolmuseums.org.uk (Charlotte Murray); London Metropolitan Archives - Captains Registers.; Margaret Durnford (nee Baynham); Martin Butler; Martyn Rees; Mary Roberts; Medici Society Ltd (Ewa Panak); Mike Doble; Mirrorpix.com (David Scripps); Mitchell Library, Glasgow (Lyn Crawford); Mr & Mrs L. Hughes; Mr & Mrs Paul Gasson; Mr & Mrs Peter Gasson; Mr D. Rowlands; Mrs Enid Jones (Paran); Mrs A. Ravenscroft; Mrs Claire Chivers; Mrs J. Yeoward; Mrs R. Bennett-Jones; Mrs R. McKenzie; Mrs Sandy Bingham; Mrs Sara Richards; Mrs V. M. Clancy; Ms Lizzie Owen; National Library of Scotland; National Library of Wales (Martin Riley, Linda Davies); National Maritime Museum, Liverpool (Helen Threlfall); National Museums Liverpool (Alex Kidson); National Piers Society (Martin Easdown); Nigel Bruce; Paul van Aardt (Gadlys Hotel); Peter Lacey; Peter Nahum; RAF Valley station records (at the National Archives); Rev. Dr. Dafydd Wyn Wiliam; Richard Joslin Fine Art; Richard Larn; RNLI.org.uk (Barry Cox); Roger Cockram; Roy Mearns; Royal Academy (Elizabeth King); Royal Cambrian Academy (Gill Bird, Cath Doney); Royal Collection Enterprises, London (Kate Heard, Karen Lawson); Royal Institute of Naval Architects (Trevor Blakeley); Sarah Robinson; Scotlandspeople.gov.uk; Scottishhistory.com; Sheila Ravenscroft; Shropshire Archives (Lorna Roberts); Simon Baynham; South Wales Maritime Heritage Society (David Clement); Stephen Crompton; Susan Cockram; Sylvia Williams; Tate Gallery (Laura McLardy, Claudia Schmid); The Baring Archive (Clara Harrow); The British Library; The British Newspaper Archive (www.britishnewspaperarchive.co.uk); The London Gazette (HMSO); Timpsons (Russ Sanders, John Timpson); Tony Rees; Trac Mon (Andrew Hughes); U.S.Naval Institute (Susan Brooks); Ventnor Local History Society (Fay Brown, E.D.G.Payne); Ventnor Heritage Museum; Wikipedia.com; Worsleydivers.com (Keith Snowden); www.246.dk/teamcgre.html; www.ajjcollection.co.uk (David Jackson); www.ancestry.co.uk; www.aviation-safety.net; www.bodorgan.com (Tim Bowie); www.clydesite.co.uk; www.daimi.au.dk (Birger Nielsen); www.dive.uk.net (Lindsey Fell); www.figureheads.co.uk (Richard Hunter); www.findmypast.com (Elizabeth Bundy); www.homefrontmuseum.co.uk (Adrian Hughes); www.menai-bridge.co.uk; www.nationalarchives.co.uk; www.normancourt-homestead.com; www.panix.com/~kendra/tea; www.pga.org.uk (David Wright); www.rafcommands.com; www.tea.co.uk; www.telegraph.co.uk.

With many apologies to anyone I've missed.

Last but not least, special thanks to my wife, Jane for her help, interest and enthusiasm for the whole project, despite mountains of files and paperwork which seem to occupy almost every room of the house. They will get tidied up soon - I promise!

## Contents

| | | |
|---|---|---|
| 1. | Introduction | 7 |
| 2. | The Crigyll Robbers & Shipwrecks | 11 |
| | 2a Loveday & Betty | 14 |
| | 2b The Trial of the Mob | 18 |
| | 2c Charming Jenny | 20 |
| | 2d The Earl of Chester Inquest | 23 |
| 3. | The Battle of the Atlantic & The Maelog Lake Hotel | 29 |
| 4. | John Peel & The Bungalow | 43 |
| 5. | Stewart Wood & The Crash of a Blackburn Botha | 51 |
| | 5a Awarded the George Medal | 60 |
| | 5b Obituaries | 61 |
| 6. | George Cockram, Artist & Gentleman | 63 |
| 7. | The Owens & Florence Nightingale | 87 |
| | 7a The Principles of Cooking | 95 |
| 8. | Ken Rees & The Sandymount | 97 |
| | 8a Eulogy | 102 |
| | 8b Prince William | 104 |
| 9.1 | Tea Clippers & The Norman Court | 107 |
| | 9a Norman Court Measurements | 115 |
| | 9b A Thrilling Lifeboat Story | 120 |
| | 9c The Judgement | 124 |
| | 9d Tracing McBride | 126 |
| | 9e Holyhead Lifeboat Concert | 128 |
| 9.2 | The Great Days of Sail (1927) | 133 |
| 9.3 | The China Clippers (1916) | 145 |
| 10. | The Paddle Steamer Rhos Neigr | 151 |
| | 10a Steamer Ashore Sensation | 160 |
| 11. | Rhosneigr - Then & Now Images | 163 |
| Bibliography | | 201 |
| Index | | 204 |

An Avro 'Cadet' Special, two-seater Biplane. "Taken June 10th 1934. On the beach, Rhosneigr." Addressed to 'Miss B.Griffiths, Ty Plant, Rhosneigr' but not posted.

Built by A.V.Roe & Co. Ltd of Manchester to the order of Douglas and the Hon. Mrs. Margaret Fairweather of Renfrew, and fitted with an in-line Cirrus Hermes IV engine. It was constructed in 1933 and destroyed in a crash on 22nd Dec.1935 at Thundersley, Essex.

1. Introduction

# 1. Introduction

Where the Atlantic surf crashes onto the rocks and the river Crigyll meets the sea, lies the village on the South West coast of Anglesey that we now know as Rhosneigr.

Back in the mid 18th century, Rhosneigr was just a small and scattered collection of whitewashed cottages, dotted here and there amongst the sand dunes. Too small to even be called a hamlet.

The inhabitants were principally fishermen and farmers, and then as now, fishing nets and lobster pots provided the main harvest of the sea.

Any surplus would have been taken by mule and cart to the nearest market town at Holyhead, following the sandy tracks that passed for 'roads' over the beaches at low tide, or across the sand dunes to reach the principal highways.

In addition to subsistence farming, the womenfolk would make besoms, and weave baskets and mats out of the reeds and marram grass, growing abundantly on their doorsteps.

An additional income might be had in plundering the wrecks that this part of the Anglesey coast was renowned for. Crigyll and Cymyran bay appear often in the early written records, due to their notoriety. The so-called "Crigyll Robbers" appearing as early as the mid-1700s, and continuing well into the late 1870s.

According to reports of the period:

"Cymyran is a dreadful place for Wrecks and God help the ships and sailors who may be driven there in a storm. It is a wild, savage part of the coast and the sand for miles around gives it the appearance of a desert"[1]

This book attempts to flesh out nine Rhosneigr-related stories, from the Crigyll Robbers in the mid 18th century, to a gallant schoolboy hero of the 20th century, and several others in between All have fascinating Rhosneigr connections.

In the late 19th century, the village was described by an eminent historian thus[2]:

"This place was a high sandy desolate place with only a few houses, and those few of remarkably ugly appearance, both inside and outside; where there was nothing but an appearance of barrenness, totally Arabian: the place was covered by sea sedge and fern, together with a little gorse here and there. There is also a river either side of Rhosneigr: the River Llifon on the southern side and the River Crigyll on the western side; so that it could be said that this place is a sort of small Mesopotamia[3], with its 'boundary towards the salt sea' in Crigyll rocks.

At around this time, Rhosneigr had a harbour or small landing place, where small ships came to pick up the agricultural produce of these neighbourhoods. There were also storehouses where much of this produce was stored.

By 1888 the place had become a public place for summer visitors; grand houses had been built for them; and recently an English service has been provided for them in the summer months each year."

**1.** North Wales Chronicle 15th March 1862
**2.** 'Hanes Methodistiaeth, Bryn Du, Mon', (The History of Methodism in Bryn Du, Anglesey). by John Watkin Hughes. Published 1912
**3.** The area around the Tigris and Euphrates river system in the Middle East.

THE ISLE OF ANGLESEA AS A HOLIDAY CENTRE IS KNOWN TO VERY FEW PEOPLE AND I WAS UNABLE TO OBTAIN ANY PERSONAL INFORMATION RESPECTING ITS POSSIBILITIES.  THE FEW PEOPLE I KNEW WHO HAD MADE THE JOURNEY TO HOLYHEAD IN THE NORTH OF THE ISLAND SAID IT WAS FLAT AND LOOKED UNINTERESTING. GUIDE BOOKS WRITE VERY GUARDEDLY OF IT AND ARE CONTRADICTORY.

THE MIDLAND RAILWAY, HAD, HOWEVER CHOSEN A SIGHT AT RHOSNIGRE ON THE WEST COAST OF ANGLESEY FOR ONE OF THEIR CARAVANS — THAT WAS SUFFICIENT FOR US. WE TOOK THE RISK OF DISAPPOINTMENT AND BOOKED A STAY OF 14 DAYS IN EARLY MAY 1936.

WE TRAVELLED VIA CHESTER, LLANDUDNO AND THE MENAI BRIDGE. KATHLEEN, WHO TRAVELLED UP FROM LONDON JOINED AT CHESTER WHERE WE HAD TEA.    IT WAS A DELIGHTFUL JOURNEY.

RHOSNIGRE PROVED TO BE A TINY VILLAGE OF 1000 OR LESS INHABITANTS THERE ARE MILES OF GOLDEN SANDS, ROCKS AND LITTLE BAYS TO EXPLORE. LOW SANDHILLS UPON WHICH SHEEP GRAZE ROLL DOWN TO THE BEACH.

A LITTLE STREAM CROSSED BY TINY BRIDGES GENTLY FINDS ITS WAY INTO THE SEA AT ONE END OF THE VILLAGE AND A LAKE ¾ MILE LONG BORDERS THE OTHER END.

IT IS A DELIGHTFUL SPOT FOR HAPPY PEOPLE WHO CAN MAKE THEIR OWN AMUSEMENTS.         WE WERE CHARMED.

The village continued to grow as we moved into the 20th Century.

One visitor's holiday photo album from 1936 reveals the innocent delights of this charming little village - as this extract, and the illustration opposite, show:

"The village of Rhosnigre (sic) is small and quite unspoiled. There are no promenades or miles of concrete. And the sands alternate with little rock pools and splashes of vivid green sea weed."

"The Isle of Anglesea as a holiday centre is known to very few people and I was unable to obtain any personal information respecting Its possibilities. The few people I knew who had made the journey to Holyhead in the north of the island said it was flat and looked uninteresting. Guide books write very guardedly of it and are contradictory.

The Midland Railway, had, however chosen a sight (sic) at Rhosnigre on the West coast of Anglesey for one of their caravans[4] — that was sufficient for us. We took the risk of disappointment and booked a stay of 14 days in early May 1936.

Rhosneigr proved to be a tiny village of 1000 or less inhabitants.

There are miles of golden sands, rocks and little bays to explore. Low sandhills upon which sheep graze, roll down to the beach.

A little stream crossed by tiny bridges gently finds its way into the sea at one end of the village and a lake 3/4 mile long borders the other end.

It is a delightful spot for happy people who can make their own amusements. We were charmed."

The latter half of the 20th Century saw Rhosneigr continue its development and the Rhosneigr Guide[5] from c1958 summed up the situation well:

"There is always a danger in inviting the general public, through the pages of a guide book, to spend a holiday at an attractive little seaside resort. The invitation might be too readily accepted and the peaceful village invaded by so many holiday-makers that the intangible part of its charm which lies in its seclusion and quietude will be lost."

Some might say that paragraph is as relevant today as it was then.

Rhosneigr in the 21st Century has become one of the most popular holiday destinations in North Wales. It attracts boating aficionados of all types - water-skiers, kayakers, dinghy sailors, paddle-boarders and wind and kite surfers to its windswept shoreline. And it still provides clean beaches and sparkling waters, where children's sandcastles and rockpooling offer activities for the very young, and the young at heart.

There can be no pleasanter place to be than on the sands in the evening, watching one of Rhosneigr's legendary sunsets with friends or family.

Rhosneigr has a fascinating history - and a bright future. Is it any surprise that we love it so?

---

**4.** Railway Caravans (or Camping Coaches) were introduced in the 1930s as a way of utilising old passenger coaches, to take advantage of the new demand for camping as a holiday activity.
**5.** The Official Guide to Rhosneigr published for the Rhosneigr Advertising Association by Ed. J. Burrow & Co Ltd.

# Chapter 2
# The Crigyll Robbers & Shipwrecks

Extract from the Anglesey quarter session court papers of January 1740.

"The Examination of George Jackson of Liverpool in the County of Lancaster – Master of the ship called the Loveday and Betty taken upon Oath before William Lewis Esq one of his Majestys Justices of the Peace for this County of Anglesey on Tuesday the 13th day of January 1740."

[Source: Great session Gaol file, National Library of Wales ref 4/251/1].

## 2. The Crigyll Robbers & Shipwrecks

The coastline of Anglesey, with its long sandy beaches, windswept acres of dunes and gorse, deceptively dangerous rocky islands, and many cliffs and coves, provided a perfect setting for Wreckers and Smugglers during the 18th & 19th centuries. Its stormy seas and treacherous waters merely adding to the attraction.

Robbing and 'salvaging' from shipwrecks was a widespread pastime on the Anglesey & North Wales coastline. Times were hard and many people were on the borderline of starvation, so it is little wonder that they took advantage of a ship's cargo released by providence, even if it was technically against the law.

As Britain became a World trading nation, developing links with its trading partners and Colonies, its seafaring activities flourished, and the incidences of Maritime crime - Wrecking, Smuggling, Piracy and Common Theft - flourished alongside.

In fact, the plundering of wrecked ships had been a specific crime on the statute book for decades when one of the most notorious of these groups, The Crigyll Robbers (Lladron Crigyll) first came to the attention of the authorities.

The Lladron Crigyll were infamous Brigands of the first order. They were so named after the wider Crigyll area, drawing from the South West coastal villages and focussed on the Llanfaelog and Rhosneigr area, where the Cymyran straits and the Crigyll river meet the sea.

At that time, Rhosneigr was barely a settlement, merely a handful of houses on the coastal periphery of Llanfaelog. Crigyll Bay however was well known to seafarers as a place full of dangerous reefs, to be avoided if at all possible. The "Crigyll Robbers" was clearly a name chosen to strike fear into the hearts of those concerned.

### Loveday and Betty

The earliest written report which notes their activities, was in 1741 with the detailed diary entries of William Bulkeley, an Anglesey JP, who recorded the loss of a ship on the rocks at Crigyll, called the 'Loveday and Betty' and the merciless plundering of the wreckage that followed, with little regard for helping the crew.

Four of the robbers were caught and summoned to appear at Beaumaris Assizes in front of William Chapple, the Chief Justice of Anglesey and a very well respected man. However, as he was away, Justice Thomas Martyn, renowned for being drunk in court, presided over the case. Due to his total incompetence, the men were acquitted and released. Naturally this caused outrage in the community.

The Reverend Dr. Dafydd Wyn Wiliam conducted original research in the early 1980s on the court documents held at the National Library of Wales and his excellent report on The Loveday and Betty (translated from the original in Welsh) is shown by kind permission in panel 2a overleaf.

Lewis Morris, the Anglesey scholar and poet, wrote a poem which became famous, on the subject. The Trial of the Mob (Trial y Mob) describes the whole court case as a shambles, and the Anglesey village of Rhosneigr - the scene of many of the Crigyll Robbers' exploits - as a "Godless, good for nothing hideout for pirates and thieves".

The full poem has been re-imagined in panel 2b on p18 and the original Welsh and a literal translation are shown on p19.

## The Story of the Loveday & Betty
by Dafydd Wyn Wiliam

### The Weather
On the morning of Thursday, the last day of December in the year 1740, a terrible storm raged over land and sea in this part of the world. The diarist, William Bulkeley, of Brynddu (Blackhill) in Llanfechell Parish, took particular notice of the weather and this is how he recorded his observations about the storm:

Extract from the diary of William Bulkeley for December 31st 1740. [Bangor University Archives].

"Dec. 31 (1740) The Wind W. and by S. with a Brisk gale, fair & dry all day after sun rise, but made very heavy rain from 5 in the morning till 7 or 8, yet the snow is not quite melting yet."

### The Shipwreck
In the teeth of the storm was a ship which was known as the Loveday and Betty.

It belonged to John Smith, Thomas Washington the Younger and Samuel Seacome, all three from Liverpool. Early that morning their ship was hurled mercilessly ashore near the estuary of the River Crigyll. The ship was not smashed up, however, and, apart from some minor holes in its hull it was not much damaged. The sails and the ropes were, amongst other things, intact. The captain, George Jackson, from Liverpool, secured the ship with an anchor and a rope five inches thick and 90 fathoms long[1], to prevent further damage to it. He then went away to seek further help to secure the vessel.

[panel 2a]

### The Robbers
Very quickly, news of the shipwreck spread and, under cover of darkness, thieves flocked to the spot. By eight o'clock in the evening they were busy plundering the ship with their axes and knives. It is not known who was the first of the robbers to arrive but Samuel Roberts, of Ceirchiog Parish, was one of them. He unfastened one of the smaller sails, folded it neatly and took it ashore. Then, with the help of William Griffith Hughes of Llanbeulan, he threw heaps of ropes which had been cut away from the ship into the hands of Rowland Humphrey, who stood on the sand.

At the request of his fellow-robbers, the last-named went away to round up horses to carry the spoil away. Before long he returned with his brother-in-law, William Roberts, and three horses. By the time they arrived a large sail had been brought to the beach. It was all loaded onto the horses and taken to the house of Rowland Humphrey. Then the big sail was cut into smaller pieces by Samuel Roberts and William Hughes and shared among Samuel Roberts, William Griffith Hughes, Hugh Griffith Hughes of Llanfaelog, Rowland Humphrey and William Roberts.

William Griffith Hughes took the small sail for himself and gave the others sixpence each for the bargain. Then everyone took his share of the spoil home. Two other robbers who were very busy at about the same period were Gabriel Roberts from Ceirchiog Parish and his brother Thomas Roberts from Llanfaelog. The former cut a pile of ropes from the ship and threw them at the feet of his brother who was standing on the sand. They too took their spoils home. It appears that a man by the name of Evan Owen had been paid to guard the ship. He abrigated his responsibility because he was heard encouraging the thieves. These are his exact words: 'If you don't make a hundred pounds tonight, you'll never make it." By this time the deck of the ship was completely bare.

1. Metric measurements: 5" = 12 ¾cm. 90 fathoms = 164 ½m

The next day, the first of January, Owen John Ambrose from Llanfihangel-yn-Nhowyn and John Pritchard from Llanfaelog came to the ship. The first had ridden his horse there. They each took a portion of the five-inch rope which secured the ship to the land.

## The Capture
After they had gone away, the Captain returned to the ship. The previous day he had gone to Aberffraw Parish and there he had got hold of Peter Hughes, the toll official. At seven o'clock the two of them came to the Loveday and Betty and discovered the mess that the thieves had made. Edward Ellis came by on horseback and informed them that parts of the rope which secured the ship to the land had only just been taken away.

Without delay, off they went on the trail of the thieves at a gallop across the sand-dunes. The two robbers had half a mile's start on them but, after a three-mile race, John Pritchard was caught. On seeing their pursuers gaining on them, he and Owen John Ambrose flung their portions of the rope to the ground and tried to escape. Owen John Ambrose succeeded in staying ahead and hid out of sight at the base of a hedge-bank. His pursuers went past his hiding place to the house of William Thomas in the parish of Llanfihangel-yn-Nhywyn, not far from the thief's hiding place. They asked the man of the house if he was the man they had seen fleeing in front of them. He denied it. Then Edward Ellis announced audibly that Owen John Ambrose was the one who had fled in front of them.

On hearing his name being spoken the latter came out of his hiding place and said, 'In the name of God what shall I do?' The ready answer was, 'You'd better take the rope back to the ship, brother.' That was done and they returned to the ship, picking up the rope which had been thrown down on the way. The other thieves were caught too, and much to their consternation they were brought before the judge.

## The Courts
A fortnight after the shipwreck Rowland Humphrey, toll collector, and George Jackson, Captain of the Loveday and Betty, appeared before William Lewis, Justice of the Peace, to give their evidence under oath about what had happened. Then on 22nd January, Owen John Ambrose, Gabriel Roberts, Thomas Roberts and Hugh Griffith Hughes gave their evidence under oath.

It is noted that neither William Griffith Hughes nor Samuel Roberts was questioned. The two had fled and I do not believe they were caught. At least, five years later the hunt for them was still going on. The Clerk of the Court read their names in public from court to court. That was done in the Court of Great Sessions in Beaumaris on 24th April 1746, adding that they:

"... Doth Strole and Wander up and Down in Contempt of us and prejudice to the Crown ..."

Following the preliminary questioning, everything was ready for the trial which was held in Beaumaris between 7th and 10th April 1741.

William Bulkeley of Brynddu was present in the court because he was a Justice of the Peace and observed:

"10th (April) tho this is the last day of the sessions the Court sat to try causes till 3 in the Evening; a thing never known before in the memory of man. Martyn the Judge being every day drunk deferred all business to the last, when they were hudled (sic) over in a very unbecoming manner..."

*[panel 2a continued]*

**The Trial of The Mob**
It is a fact that, during this period, the courts of Anglesey did not serve justice and a drunken judge did not promote justice at all. Lewis Morris yearned for a judge like William Chapple. He was the Chief Justice of the Anglesey Great Sessions during the period 1728 – 37. The poet says:

Oh for Chapple in Anglesey
To hang the Crigyll Robbers.

Defending the robbers was Morus (Morris Owen) 1698 – 1759, who was an attorney) and the poet suggests that he blamed the Captain for deliberately running the ship aground:

Morus, loud as the sea,
Was for saving the dogs standing there,
He gave the captain many a rebuke
With head-shaking and sidelong glances
For deliberately taking his ship
Onto the harmless rocks of Crigyll.

If the robbers were not going to be hanged, Lewis Morris would have liked them to spend time in the service of the Admiral Edward Vernon (1684 – 1757). He had been a great hero since 1739 because of his work in capturing Portobello, and John (1706 – 40), Lewis's brother, had died in his service. A period in Vernon's fleet would have been an excellent punishment for the thieves:

Give them to Vernon of great renown
And (let them use?) their tricks to break castles...
It is not known in detail what happened in the court in Beaumaris but there is a hint at the bottom of one of the documents of the case in connection with the names Hugh Griffith Hughes, Owen John Ambrose, Thomas Roberts and Gabriel Roberts, which is 'all discharged paying fee'.

[panel 2a continued]

From the title of Lewis Morris's poem we get a suggestion that a 'mob' or crowd of the robbers' supporters had gathered in Beaumaris at the time of the trial and had had an influence on the verdict. The poet was not happy with this and he was completely dissatisfied that some of the robbers had escaped. If they were caught he wished to see them hanged:

This stanza is too difficult to translate word for word but expresses the poet's desire to see them strung up on twin gallows.

**Editor's notes:**
1. The Reverend Dr. Dafydd Wyn Wiliam first published this article in 1983 in his Welsh language book 'Llwynogod Mon ac Ysgrifau Eraill' (The Foxes of Anglesey and other Essays). The extracts above have been translated from Welsh for this book, by Jenni Wyn Hyatt and are included here by kind permission of Dr Wiliam.

2. Dr Wiliam notes that all the above details about the robbers were obtained from the Anglesey Court of Great Sessions which is now kept in the National Library of Wales in Aberystwyth.

3. There is a small complication over the exact date of this event. The ship was washed up on December 31st 1740 and the trial took place in April 1741. However the first page of the court record (shown on page 14) records the date as 'Tuesday the 13th January 1740. At that time (until 1752) the Julian calendar was being used, which started the new year on March 25th[2]. The historic day calculator, Julian style[3], calculates January 13th 1740 to be a Sunday and in 1741 to be a Tuesday. Clearly the trial could not take place before the event, so it is easier to think of it as December 1740 with the trial in April 1741.

**2.** British Calendar Act 1751
(http://www.webexhibits.org/calendars/year-text-British.html)
**3.** http://5ko.free.fr/en/jul.php?y=1740 and http://www.dayoftheweek.org/

**Bark, barkentine.** — *Bark.* — Generally speaking a three-masted vessel square-rigged on the fore and main masts and fore-and-aft rigged on the mizzen.

BARK.

The following definition is given by Denham Robinson :—" *Bark* or *barque* (Low Lat., *barca*). A term applied rather vaguely to square-rigged merchant vessels. A bark has three masts which do not rake; but beyond this there appears to be no special mark to distinguish it from any other large merchantman. A bark, however, is never a steamer." But among coasters the *bark* is distinguished from the *barkentine*, a merchant vessel having three masts, the foremast square-rigged like the bark, but the main and mizzen masts fore-and-aft rigged. These are occasionally called three-masted schooners or jackass rig; but here again a distinction must be made, the barkentine having a brig foremast (*i.e.*, foremast, fore-topmast, and fore-top-gallant), while the three-masted schooner

BARKENTINE.

has the schooner foremast (foremast and fore-top-mast only). (*See also* under SCHOONER.)

The Earl of Chester was a Barque (or Bark) and the Norman Court - see chapter 9 - was converted to a Barque in her later years. With less rigging, the ship needed less crew to sail her. [Definition: from Anstead's Dictionary of Sea Terms, 1919].

## Trial y Mob (The Trial of the Mob) by Lewis Morris
On robbing of a Liverpool Brigantine, stranded at Crigyll in Anglesey; and of the Proceedings thereon at Beaumares Assizes, 1741. To the Tune of Leave Land[4].

Honest people love the light -
fires and candles therefore;
in their hovels crooks plot crimes -
that's what dark is rare for;
as for me, to see them swing
high is what I care for.

Crigyll, worthless, Godless hole -
wrecking's all their tillage;
there loot's hidden under cloaks
when those devils pillage.
God keep kind hearts from the rocks
of that vicious village!

If a good ship runs aground
where their false lights lure it
Crigyll's men on Gwyndraeth beach,
watch their rocks ensure it.
Catch and hang them, Men of Môn -
why should we endure it?

Taken off to Court to pay
for their axe-work dearly
all those merry Crigyll men
joked with daggers merely -
just how pure the best of them
were, this world saw clearly!

Gold coin crossed the lawyer's palm -
thoughts of retribution
vanished: like a trout he leapt,
for that contribution,
gulping all he ought - to earn
(God grant!) execution!

Great the greed of lawyers - some
play as children paddle;
honest local folk keep mum
(even good eggs addle)
All Môn longs for honest Judge
Chapple in the saddle.

Noisy Morus backed the rats,
shook his robes and ranted,
blamed the ship and blessed the rocks
(all he said was slanted)
for to smear the Captain bold
was what Morus wanted!

But God sent a judge who's wise -
he will give no quarter
to the robbers and their chicks -
every son and daughter -
all the Crigyll-born who stole -
hang them at high water!

God will pay the vermin back
for their filthy revel,
pillaged ships and harried men
when the sea was level,
Crigyll wives deserted all
moaning to the Devil.

'Blow up, powder in their guns!' -
that's the the sailors praying -
hags all scabs shall bake within
dirty tents and fraying;
Crigyll, watch from birth to death
all your children paying!

If, come summer, they're not all
hanged for unrepented
crimes, let Vernon have the whole
rotten, unlamented
gang - to Crigyll, two by two
then we'll go contented,

or should they to Arfon flee,
clutching willows to them,
apple-branch and withy-noose
collars will undo them -
or a sailor-jury from
Môn put stoppers to them!

**Editor's note:**
Never before translated into English as poetry, and bearing the same rhythm and meter as the original, this poem was specially commissioned for this book from Tony Rees, retired academic and poet.

Tony was born in Machen, Gwent, of Welsh-speaking parents, but had to learn the language for himself. He is fascinated by the language and by Welsh history.

[panel 2b]

[4]. The 'Leave Land' tune has unfortunately not been identified.

## The original Welsh and literal translation

Gwych gan Bobl onest lân, Oleuni Tân a Channwyll
Gwych gan Wylliaid fod y Nos, Mewn Teios yn y Tywyll;
Gwych gan inneu glywed son, Am grogi, Lladron Grigyll.

Pentref yw di Dduw, di dda, Lle'r eillia llawer Ellyll,
Mor-yspeilwyr, Trinwyr trais, A'u Mantais dan eu Mentyll;
Cadwed Duw bob Calon frau, Rhag mynd i Greigiau Grigyll.

Os Llong a ddaw o draw i drai, I Draethau'r Bobl drythyll,
Tosturi rhain sydd fal y Tân, Neu'r Gwyndraeth a'i gwna'n gandryll;
Goreu Gwaith a wnae Wŷr Mon, Oedd grogi Lladron Grigyll.

Pan ddoed â'r Gwylliaid at y Bar, A beio ar eu Bwiyll,
Ni wnaethant hwy â'r Cyrt (Myn Mair), Ond cellwair gyd a'u Cyllyll;
Cae'r Byd weled yno ar fyr, Mor lân goreugwyr Grigyll.

Hwy roent, ar Law'r Attwrnai, Groes, Yn sydyn troes yn Sidyll;
Am Aur melyn mae'r Dŷn du, Yn brathu fal y Brithyll;
Mae'n ol i hwnnw a wnelo hyn, Ei grogi yn Nhywyn Grigyll.

Rhai Cyfreithwyr, mawr eu Chwant, Yn chware Plant mewn Pistyll;
A rhai gonest ar y Cwest, Am guddio'r Orchest erchyll;
Och am Siappel yn Sir Fon, I grogi Lladron Grigyll.

Morus oedd, fal Mor ei Swn, Am safio'r Cwn yn sefyll,
Fe roe i'r Cadpen aml Sen, Ac ysgwyd Pen ac Esgyll,
Am fynd a'i Long â Meddwl drwg, I Greigiau diddrwg Grigyll.

Fe yrr Duw ini Farnwr doeth, I safio'n Cyfoeth sefyll,
I ddistrywio Gwylliaid Mon, A'u Cywion yn eu Cewyll;
A ddygodd Gortyn, daed i'w ran, I'w grogi ar Orllan' Grigyll.

Fe dâl yr Arglwydd i'r Yspred, A wnaeth y Weithred dywyll;
Yspeilio'r Llong, a gwylltior Gwŷr, Yn dostur yn y Distyll;
Gweddwon oll, ac oer eu tôn, Fo Gwragedd Lladron Grigyll.

Gweddi ffyddlon Dynion Dw'r, Y Powdwr dan eu Pedyll;
Na weler Gwrach heb grach, neu gri, Yn pobi yn eu Pebyll;
Bo eisiau Bwyd, o'r Bais i'r Bedd, Ar Eppil Gwragedd Grigyll.

Ac oni chrogwch cyn yr Haf, Ddihiraf Dyrfa derfyll,
Rhowch nhwy' i Fernon, fawr ei fri, A'u castiau i dorri Cestyll;
Ac yno down o fesul dau, Yn rhydd i Greigiau Grigyll.

Os dont i Arfon rhag y grog, Ac ergyd Rog i Irgyll,
Ni fynnwn Wdyn yn eu hoed, I'w difa ar Goed Efyll;
Neu Gwest o Longwyr o Sir Fon, I grogi Lladron Grigyll.

Respectable law-abiding People, Rejoice in the Light of Fire and Candle
Brigands rejoice in the Night, In Hovels in the Dark
I myself rejoice in hearing, About hanging the Robbers of Crigyll.

A Godless, worthless Village, Where many a Fiend pillages,
Sea-looters, Users of violence, With their Loot under their Cloaks;
May God keep every tender Heart, From going on the Rocks of Crigyll.

If a Ship comes from afar to the low tide To the Beaches of the wanton People,
Their mercy is like Fire, Or the Gwyndraeth beach wrecks it;
The best Work Anglesey Men would do, Was to hang the Thieves of Crigyll.

When the Robbers were brought to the Bar, And their Axes were censured,
They did nothing with the Court (By Mary) But jest with their Knives;
The World could quickly see there, How pure were the best men of Crigyll.

They placed, on the Attorney's Hand, a Cross,
He suddenly performed a complete turnabout; For yellow Gold the black - gowned Man, Bites like the Trout; There remains for Whomever does this, To be hanged on the Strand of Crigyll.

Some Lawyers, full of Greed, Play about like Children;
And some honest people at the Inquest, Want to conceal the dreadful Exploit;
Oh for a (Judge) Chapple in Anglesey To hang the Thieves of Crigyll.

Morus as noisy as the Sea Wanted to save the Dogs who stood
He cast several Affronts on the Captain, and shook Head and Wings,
For taking the Ship with ill Intent, Onto the innocent Rocks of Crigyll.

God sends us a wise Judge, To save our standing Wealth,
To destroy the Anglesey Robbers, And their Chicks in their Cages;
Who stole even a Cord, just as well for him, To be hanged at the high water mark at Crigyll.

The Lord will pay the Vermin, Who did this dark Deed;
Pillaging the Ship, and harrying the Men, Grieviously in the Low Water,
Widows all, moaning dismally, Be the Wives of the Robbers of Crigyll.

The Seamen's devout Prayer, May their Pans be blown up;
May no Hag be seen without scab, or cry, Baking in their Tents;
May Hunger, from the Petticoat to the Grave, Befall the Offspring of the Women of Crigyll.

And if, before the Summer, You do not hang the most knavish obstinate Crew, Give them to the renowned Vernon, with their wiles enough to break down Castles And there we'll come two by two, Freely to the Rocks of Crigyll.

If they come to Arfon to avoid hanging, With a Rogue's stroke to hazel Saplings,
We will demand Nooses of mature Withies, To destroy them on Apple Trees;
Or an Inquest by Anglesey Sailors, To hang the Robbers of Crigyll.

*[panel 2b continued]*

2. The Crigyll Robbers & Shipwrecks

## Charming Jenny

> IRELAND.
> Dublin, Sept 13. The Charming Jenny, William Chilcot, bound from this Port to Waterford, was wrecked lately near Holyhead, when every Person on board, except the Captain, perished, and the whole Cargo, save one Cask of Geneva, and two Puncheons of Rum, was lost. The neighbouring Inhabitants, instead of assisting the unfortunate Survivor, plundered whatever escaped the Fury of the Waves, even to cutting away the Pockets from the Captain's Wife, whose Corpse was driven ashore on that inhospitable Coast.

[panel 2c.1. First report of the wreck of the Charming Jenny. Derby Mercury, 1st October 1773]

There are only a handful of well-documented cases of shipwrecks and the plundering of stricken vessels from this period. These include the 'Charming Jenny' in 1773, where the crew were attacked whilst defenceless in the sea, and the corpse of Captain Chilcot's wife was found in the pounding surf, half-naked and bereft of her belongings.

Because of the reluctance of the Anglesey magistrates to deal promptly with the case, it was transferred to Shrewsbury in England to be dealt with.

Reports of the wreck were reported nationally and several of these, bringing together the whole chilling story, are detailed in panels 2c on these pages.

The wide reporting of the case intensified the pressure on the authorities to bear down more firmly on such activities across the country, not just on Anglesey. Coastal policing was eventually improved and gradually, more moral emphasis began to be placed on saving life and helping victims. However it was by no means a quick process.

> Bills of indictment were preferred at the last Shrewsbury assizes by Capt. Chilcot, late of the Charming Jenny, against three opulent inhabitants of the isle of Anglesea (one of whom is said to be possessed of a considerable estate, and to have offered £5,000[5] bail) in order to their being tried at the next assizes on a charge of piracy, &c. when the bills were found. It appeared, in the course of the depositions, that on the 11th of September last, in very bad weather, in consequence of false lights being discovered, the Captain bore for the shore, when his vessel, the cargo of which was valued at £19,000[6] unfortunately went to pieces, and all the crew, except the Captain and his wife perished, whom the waves had brought on shore upon part of the wreck. Nearly exhausted they lay for some time, till the savages of the adjacent places, more ravenous than the devouring element from which they had just escaped, rushed down upon the devoted victims. The lady was just able to lift a handkerchief up to her head when her husband was torn from her side. Eager to make the quickest dispatch, they cut his buckles from his shoes, and deprived him of every covering. Happy to escape with life, he hasted to the beach, in search of his beloved wife; when, horrid to tell, her half-naked and plundered corpse presented itself to his view - A dismal spectacle!
>
> What to do, the unfortunate Capt. Chilcot was at a loss: Providence, however, conducted him to the roof of a venerable pair, who, in a short space, had been reduced from affluence to a most deplorable state, and who bestowed on him every assistance his hard case required. The Captain's wife, it seems, at the time the ship went to pieces, had two bank bills of considerable value, and 70 guineas in her pocket.
>
> There are five others concerned, who, it is hoped, will soon be taken, and brought to condign punishment[7].

[panel 2c.2. Kentish Gazette, 6th April 1774]

5. £5000 bail in 1774 equivalent to appx £562,000 today. www.measuringworth.com
6. £19000 cargo in 1774 equivalent to appx £2.1m today. www.measuringworth.com
7. condign punishment = appropriate to the crime.

> At the same assizes, on three several indictments, came on the trials of John Parry, Wm. Williams, and William Roberts, natives of the Isle of Anglesea, for plundering a vessel wrecked upon that coast.—The facts that came out on evidence were as follow, viz.—William Chillcot, commander of a vessel called the Charming Jenny, being in a hard gale of wind driven on the above coast, his wife and all the sailors were washed overboard: the captain continuing on board till the wreck parted, with great difficulty reached the shore, where the dead body of his wife lay; when many of the natives, among whom were the prisoners, flocked to the Beach, and instead of performing the rites of humanity, by assisting the distressed, devoted themselves wholly to plunder; they cut away the pockets from the dead body of Mrs. Chilcot, in which was a large sum of money, and also the buckles from her shoes.—By the spirited endeavours of some gentlemen of Anglesea, the prisoners, though men of property, have been brought to justice; and Parry and Roberts being both found guilty of a capital offence, are to receive sentence next assizes.

[panel 2c.3. Bath Chronicle, 11th August 1774]

William Roberts and John Parry were found guilty, and William Williams was acquitted. Roberts and Parry had to wait until the next assizes to hear their fate confirmed. However, a legal objection was raised, and subsequently overruled as invalid, which further slowed the progress of the sentencing. It was not until the following year that Parry was executed.

> SHREWSBURY, *April 8.*
>
> On Saturday last John Parry was Executed at the Old-Heath near this Town, pursuant to his Sentence, at our last Assizes, for plundering the Wreck of the Ship, Charming Jenny, on the Coast of Anglesea, Sept. 11, 1773.

[panel 2c.4. Shrewsbury Chronicle, 8th April 1775]

William Roberts, who had also been condemned to death at the last assizes, had his sentence "respited during his Majesty's pleasure" but was not mentioned in the ruling and "must remain till his fate is decided".

His sentence was later commuted.

---

Lawful salvage was of course fully permitted. Defined as: Property which is rescued from the sea and which is returned to its rightful owner for a reward.

## Earl of Chester

Eventually, after over a century of wrecks being plundered and ransacked off the coast, the last published report which mentioned the Crigyll Robbers by name, was of their merciless attack on the 493 ton Barque[8] the 'Earl of Chester' in 1867.

This ship had left Liverpool with a general cargo for India, under the command of Captain Nancollis, but was driven onshore by the appalling weather, at Cerrig y Defaid (Sheep Rocks) at the Southern end of Broad Beach.

So significant a National disaster was this, that a report was published in 'The Times' of October 1867 which noted that:

"The wreck is now prey to the notorious wreckers of the coast known to Welsh seafaring men as 'Lladron Crigyll' – 'The Wreckers of Crigyll'. Many hundreds of them were there yesterday, stealing whatever they could carry away."

Additional reporting commented that "The efforts of Captain Jones, Lloyd's agent and of the Coastguard were utterly inadequate to protect the property."

Even the Llanfaelog school log book[9] recorded that "Several of the bodies were brought to the school and many strangers called, in an attempt to identify the dead." In fact, several bodies were buried in Llanfaelog Parish Church and some of their headstones are still visible to this day.

The gravestone of Henry Brockell at St Maelog's church, Llanfaelog, from the Earl of Chester shipwreck.

**In memory of Henry Brockell aged 19 years who was lost with all hands on Sunday 27th October 1867 in the ship "Earl of Chester" in Anglesea Bay.**

A full report on the disaster was given at the inquest, which is shown in panel 2d.

As far as Rhosneigr is concerned, the impact of the 'Earl of Chester' disaster, essentially became the last straw. The Anglesey Lifeboat Institution, who already had a lifeboat at Rhoscolyn, noted at their March 1868 meeting that "some movement had been made as to placing a lifeboat at Rhosneigr... but the difficulty of obtaining a crew ready and willing to man a boat in those desolate regions rendered the utility of placing one there rather dubious".

So it was not until 1872 that Rhosneigr, by courtesy of a benefactor, Mrs Lingham, got its own lifeboat, the 'Thomas Lingham' and the plundering of wrecks started to draw to a close. By the time the 'Norman Court' sank in the bay, in 1883[10], the Rhosneigr and Holyhead lifeboats were quickly on the scene. Though completely wrecked and with two lives lost, the wreckage was stripped and salvaged without any appearance from the Crigyll Robbers.

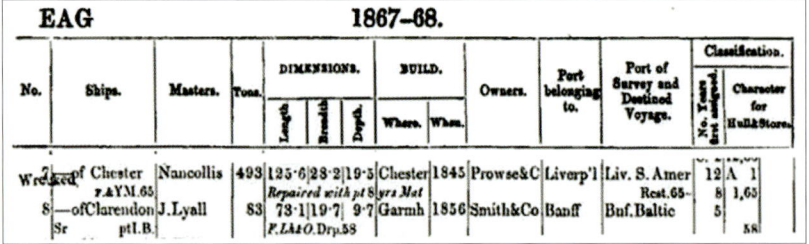

8. Barque - a sailing ship with less rigging than a full rigged ship.
9. Recorded as such from reputable sources but no longer in the archives.
10. Norman Court, see chapter 9.

# DREADFUL SHIPWRECK ON THE COAST OF ANGLESEY. EIGHTEEN LIVES LOST.

### THE INQUEST.

On Tuesday afternoon an inquest was held on the bodies of Captain V. B. Nancollis, his wife and twelve unknown persons who perished with the Earl of Chester which left Liverpool on Friday last, and foundered at Rhosneigr, nine miles from Holyhead, at about half-past seven o'clock on the morning of Sunday last, eighteen souls being then aboard. The bodies, fourteen in number, were lying in the National school-room, of Llanfaelog, where also the inquest was held.

There were present - Mr William Prowse, part proprietor of the Earl of Chester; Captain Chrisholme, of the Underwriters' Association, Liverpool; Mr W. B. Taylor, Liverpool (Son-in-law of the captain); Mr Hall, North Richmond Street, Dublin, (the mate's father); and several persons locally connected.

A jury of twelve was empanelled; the Rev. R. Williams rector of Llanfaelog (the parish in which the ship wreck took place) being foreman.

The first witness called was John Williams, Cefndu, Llanbeuno, who said - I live on the beach at Rhosneigr. Last Sunday morning about 6 o'clock, I saw a ship opposite the spot where I live. At the time it was rather dark. She struck about 8 am. on a rock, and became a total wreck in half an hour. My house is about a quarter of a mile from the scene of the wreck. There were several people on the beach between 7 and 8 o'clock in the morning. The sea, and the breakers were so terrible they prevented any assistance. No signal of distress was given. No gun was fired from the ship. The nearest life-boat association is that of Rhoscolyn.

By the Coroner—Why did you not send to Rhoscolyn for the life boat?

Witness — I cannot say, indeed. It would be of no use sending to Rhoscolyn as no boat could survive in such a sea. That is the opinion of the most experienced sailors on the coast.

By Rev. R. Williams, (foreman of the jury) - It was your duty to send to Rhoscolyn even if that was the case. The responsibility of a failure would not have rested with you had the life-boat proved unsuccessful.

By Coroner - did anyone go there?

Witness - I do not think anyone went to Rhoscolyn.

Police-officer No. 18 - I examined the pockets of Capt. Nancollis, at 4 o'clock on Sunday afternoon when the body was found. I found on the body a certificate an well as the sum of £1 18s 9d in a pocket-book.

By the Foreman - A doubt has been raised whether a gold watch was on the Captain's body when first found. To have the question put to the witness would answer a good purpose.

The Coroner - I am also anxious that the question be put. Who were present when the body was found?

Witness — When the body was found I was on the beach about thirty yards from the body when it was discovered. It was impossible that the watch could have been extracted from the body during the time it was removed without my knowledge. I had my eye continually on the body, that nothing could be taken from him. The body had no waistcoat on when found. (continues)

[panel 2d]

(Panel 2d Continued)
Mr Edward Williams, Llanfaelog - I informed the Captain's son-in-law on the authority of a boy, that the Captain had a watch on when found.

The boy on being called to prove this assertion, said that he had been told on the beach that a boy from Llangwyfan had had a gold watch. On this a police-officer was sent for the boy.

Stephen Mummery, police-officer, said that he had found certain papers on the person of a man having moustachoes but no whiskers. He had also found a set of gold studs on the same person. He was described in the certificate found on his person as William Foreman, born at Boston in 1841. He was supposed to be the cook and was a Black man. He also had five pawn tickets on his person.

Richard Roberts, Tyn-y-llan, (churchwarden of the parish), certified that he had received two rings, which had been taken from the fingers of the Captain's wife. When discovered, she was in a nude state, with the exception of a chemise, a pair of stockings, and one boot.

A police-officer had found the supposed possessor of the Captain's gold watch who was brought forth. He was Owen Jones, Llangwyfan, who said he was 14 years of age. He then gave an account of himself. I was last Sunday afternoon on the sea beach near the scene of the wreck. There were other boys with me. I was told that some one had had a gold watch in the Captain's pocket, but I was not previously aware of this. No watch of any kind has been in my hand for months. I cannot account for the propagation of such a story.

The learned Coroner, (William Jones, Esq., Menai Bridge, the county Coroner), then summed up the evidence in a very lucid and able manner. He raised no objection as to the cause of death. In respect to the conduct of the Rhosneigr men not applying for the aid of the Rhoscolyn life-boat, he censured their neglect. He said that he had occasion before in the case of an inquest on the bodies of a whole crew drowned at Llanbadrig some years ago, where no one survived to relate the tale.

The foreman of the Jury (Rev. R. Williams, rector), returned the verdict of the Jury "Accidental Death by Drowning."

The inquest being over, the Rev. Robert Williams, M.A., Rector of the parish, invited all strangers to the rectory for luncheon, and our correspondent has been requested by the friends and relations of the deceased to tender publicly their thanks to the Rev. gentleman for his very great kindness, assistance, and sympathy towards strangers. Ever since the first intelligence of the disaster, he has not spared any pains to render every aid in his power, and this is really valuable in such wild parts of the country as this, where houses are so distant, and public-houses unknown.

The following is a list of the persons on board on leaving Liverpool, last Friday: - Captain W. B. Nancollis and Mrs Nancollis;

Henry William Hall, mate, aged 26, Dublin (son of Mr Samuel Hall, North Richmond Street, Dublin) ;

Malcolm Service, second mate, (who was engaged at the last moment before sailing instead of Thomas Harvey, who was prevented by illness to go out with the Earl of Chester);

Hanrich Mathies, carpenter, 27, Hanover;

William Henry Fooman, steward, 24, Boston, America, and James Cross, Cork—both these men being black;

John Thompson, 29, Holland;

James Macdonald, 25, Edinburgh;

John Johnson, 23, Finland;

John Dean, 20, Chester;

George Bowen, 33, Guernsey;

John Campbell, 22, and John Macgravy, 19 - both belonging to Belfast.

There were four apprentices - John Berry, 15; Robert Fields, 16; J. Pringle, 14 ; and Henry Brockell, 15; - all of Liverpool.

(Panel 2d Continued)
There were therefore eighteen persons drowned. It was the captain's intention to retire from the sea after this voyage. James Pringle had only sailed to sea last Friday on his first voyage.

A piece of chest, with the letters "J. McDonald", painted thereon, was picked up on Tuesday. This belonged, it is supposed, to James McDonald, Edinburgh, 25 years of age.

The bodies of Captain Nancollis, and that of his wife, were taken, yesterday (Wednesday) to Birkenhead, where they will be interred. The remaining bodies - twelve - already found (up to 11 pm., Tuesday) will be buried at Llanfaelog churchyard, the rector of the parish, Rev R. Williams, officiating. The National Schoolroom of Llanfaelog presented an extraordinary appearance on Tuesday. In one end of it fourteen bodies were lying side by side - all bearing evident signs of distress and misfortune. In the other end of the schoolroom were as many coffins waiting being made use of. Between sat a jury to consider the cause of death. It was a sight without a parallel within the memory of the "oldest inhabitant" living on this rock bound coast, saving that ever-memorable inquest at Llanallgo, respecting the Royal Charter, when the same coroner had to hold an inquest on the bodies of 100 persons.

Apropos of the Royal Charter, that as well as the Earl of Chester, were stranded in October, and each on the night of the 26th.

Mr Hall, of Dublin, the mate's father, having come over to seek his son's body, failed to identify it in any of the dead. It must, therefore, be one of the four remaining ones not found. During a strolling ramble he made along the beach in search of his son, he came across a coat of his son's. With what haste he examined each pocket and the lining of the garment, I need not tell the reader. He was not, however, rewarded with the object of his search, and had with a gloomy heart to return to Holyhead, to wait the dawn of Wednesday to renew his search.

Within a stone's throw of the scene of the wreck of the Earl of Chester, Hugh Hughes, an old man, 79 years of age, a hardy fisherman, and father of the life-saving Evan Hughes, Cwmerran, informed our correspondent that he remembers other fearful shipwrecks on or close to this same spot.

The Oakland foundered here 13 years ago, and many lives were lost. The schooner, Sea King, foundered, and lost four lives. Thirty-one years ago The Sarah became a complete wreck, but had all lives saved; While in the case of Jane, of Liverpool, the result was a parallel to that of the Earl of Chester - all the crew perished.

The burial of the twelve bodies not yet (Wednesday) claimed, will take place this afternoon at Llanfaelog. There remains a duty. Mrs Capt. Jones, Hibernia Terrace, should be acknowledged for the sisterly kindness she bestowed this week as on similar occasions, to shipwrecked sailors and their captains.

Mrs Penny lent a shelter for the coastguard at the scene of the wreck, and our correspondent desires us to return our best thanks to the coast guard, particularly Martin, Lyons, and Sweeney, for the assistance they had given in arriving at correct information respecting the wreck. And likewise to Mr T. Owen, customs-officer, for much valuable aid rendered daily throughout the week, in obtaining a synopsis of news. Mr Owen being the only Customs-officer continually on the spot, the sobriety of the hundreds that were daily near the wreck is a proof that the Customs and Underwriters had able, vigilant and faithful servants.

In respect to the Coast-guard force, it was ridiculously small. Only three men to take charge of wreckage, strewn thickly over a mile and a half coast, open to wreckers (if there still be any at Crigyll). Surely the Coast Guard Station at Holyhead ought to be augmented in number, and in this instance the force was divided, with fifteen miles distance, guarding two valuable wrecks on two opposite shores.

The Cargo of the Earl of Chester is being conveyed per rail for Tycroes station to Liverpool, where it will be offered on sale by auction.

[North Wales Chronicle 2nd November 1867]

Cattle on the headland at Porth Trecastell (Cable Bay). Undated, postcard sized photo.

Following on from the Crigyll Robbers, came the Anglesey legend of 'Madam Wen' (White Lady) and her band of smugglers and thieves. The earliest written reference to her exploits, dates back to 1897 when the Methodist historian and writer, J.W. Huws records her as living at "the beginning of the 18th century". However, her legend was undoubtedly an oral tradition for many years prior to this date.

Rhosneigr solicitor and author William David Owen, who set the tale on paper for the first time in his eponymous romantic novel[11], attributes it even earlier - to the late 17th Century Jacobite uprising in Ireland (1690-1691). If true, this would put Madam Wen's gang several decades before the Crigyll Robbers themselves. Perhaps even implying that Madam Wen was the founder of the Crigyll Robbers dynasty!

Although the introduction of the lifeboats and the construction of the lighthouses helped, there are of course still shipwrecks to this day when the wind is strong and the seas are treacherous.

As a footnote, it is worth recording that despite the anecdotes of how Wreckers used to put lights around the necks of cattle in the fields on the cliff-tops, to simulate the gentle movement of anchored ships in a safe harbour, no one on Anglesey has ever been convicted of 'Wrecking'.

11. Madam Wen, see chapter 7.

Rhosneigr Lifeboat Station was founded in 1872 and its total cost of £680, including the lifeboat, *Thomas Lingham*, was the gift of Mrs Lingham, in memorial to her late husband, formerly of Worcester, but lately of Lower Norwood, London. The station had 4 lifeboats, (and one temporary boat) all subsequently named *Thomas Lingham*.

The earliest known photo in this group is No.3, which is an 1893 photo of the lifeboat being wheeled across the sands. It is likely that photo No.1 of the crew on the lifeboat also dates from around this time. The other photo, showing a different style of boat, is thought to be from c1916. [Photo No.2, A.G. Owen Collection.]

The station closed in 1924, having recorded 29 launches and 70 lives saved over the period.

# Chapter 3
# The Battle of the Atlantic and the Maelog Lake Hotel

September 1911.

Maelog Lake Hotel after its closure awaiting demolition. November 2010.

30   3. The Battle of the Atlantic and the Maelog Lake Hotel

# 3. The Battle of the Atlantic and the Maelog Lake Hotel.

Of all the innumerable individual battles of the Second World War, one of the most vital for Allied survival, let alone victory, was what Winston Churchill dubbed 'The Battle of the Atlantic.' It was, as he put it: '…the dominating factor all through the war. Never for one moment could we forget that everything happening elsewhere, on land, at sea, or in the air, depended ultimately on its outcome.'[1]

The German Navy too, knew the importance of the Atlantic and accordingly did everything possible to cut this critical line of communication. The strategy had been attempted once before, during the First World War, and came perilously close to success. It is then no surprise to note that the campaign was resumed almost immediately on the outbreak of war in 1939. Indeed on 3rd September, the very day Britain declared war on Germany, the British liner *Athenia* was torpedoed by a German submarine.

Submarines, the infamous U-boats, were the primary weapon with which Nazi Germany waged the battle, and they were, from 1 October 1939, under the command, of an officer who had served in them during the former conflict; Rear Admiral Karl Dönitz. Dönitz, after careful study of the earlier campaign, had evolved tactics for maximising the effectiveness of his U-boats. He grouped them in lines that were arrayed in the path of an approaching convoy, and upon one of them sighting the target the information would be radioed to U-boat HQ. All available U-boats would then be ordered to the target area, and the resultant 'Wolf Pack' would attack whilst surfaced during the hours of darkness; the whole operation being centrally controlled and coordinated by Dönitz.[2]

Max Horton features on the cover of the American popular magazine "Life", dated Aug 2nd 1943. A 6-page article by Richard Wilcox features inside.

**1.** Winston S Churchill, *Closing the Ring* (New York; Houghton Mifflin, 1951) p. 20.
**2.** David Syrett, *The Defeat of the German U-Boats: The Battle of the Atlantic* (Columbia SC; South Carolina University Press, 1994) p. 6.

These tactics were fearsomely effective and by November 1942, with 700,000 tons of shipping sunk that month alone, and the total for the year amounting to 1006 ships equating to 5,471,222 tons, the U-boats were close to achieving a stranglehold on Britain's Atlantic lifeline[3]. However, in an approach characterised as setting 'a thief to catch a thief,' on the 19 November 1942 an eminent British submariner was appointed to be Dönitz's direct opponent. He became head of Western Approaches Command based in Derby House, Liverpool, the headquarters where the day-to-day management of the battle was directed from the Allied side. That man was Admiral Sir Max Horton[4].

Early postcard (postmarked August 1904) captioned 'Maelog Lake with Hotel and Golf Links, Rhosneigr'. No photographer or publisher identified.

[3]. Winston S Churchill, *Their Finest Hour* (New York; Houghton Mifflin, 1949) p. 529.
[4]. John Winton, *The War at Sea: The British Navy in World War II* (New York; William Morrow, 1968) p. 364. See also: http://www.liverpoolmuseums.org.uk/maritime/collections/boa/derbyhouse.asp

Many readers must, by now, be wondering what all this has to do with Rhosneigr? The answer is this: some 58 years and 355 days before his appointment, on 29 November 1883, a boy, christened Max Kennedy Horton, was born to Esther Maud Horton and Robert Joseph Angel Horton at... the Maelog Lake Hotel. According to Max Horton's official biographer, Rear Admiral W S Chalmers, Horton senior was a member of the London Stock Exchange and his wife was the daughter of a stockbroker[5]. They thus belonged to the Victorian upper middle classes, meaning that they could be categorised as wealthy without being massively rich[6]. Quite what caused them to become involved with the Maelog Lake Hotel is unknown, and at this distance in time probably impossible to ascertain with any certainty. This is particularly so since tales concerning Max Horton's 'early days' came from D'Arcy Horton, his elder brother, who told them to Chalmers in the early 1950's following the admiral's death in 1951.

According to these seventy-year old recollections, shortly before Max was born Horton senior was 'hard hit by a slump' in his fortunes and, 'possibly for reasons of economy, but more likely for fishing and shooting, bought the Maelog Lake Hotel together with the shooting rights'[7] Indeed, when he registered the birth of his son on 24 January 1884, Robert Horton gave his place of residence as the Maelog Lake Hotel and his occupation as 'Hotel Proprietor'[8].

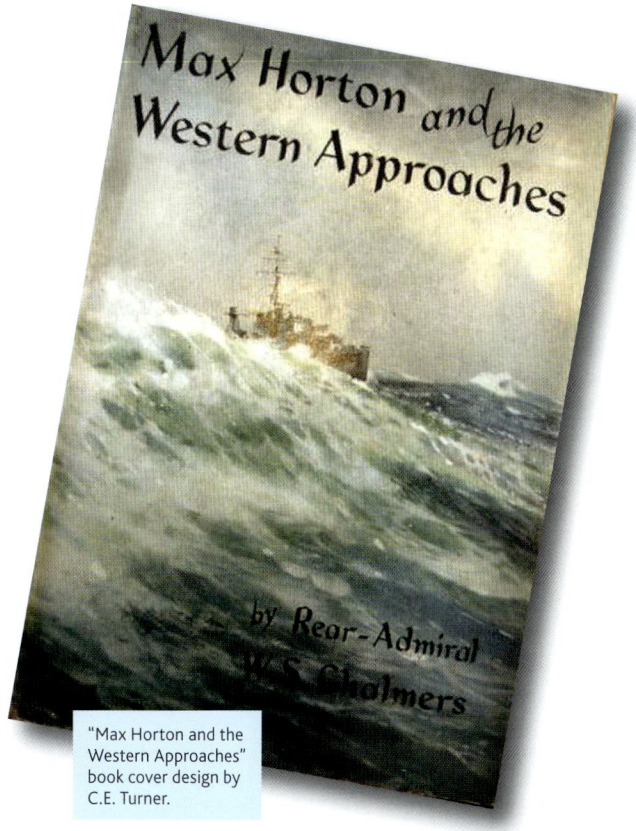

"Max Horton and the Western Approaches" book cover design by C.E. Turner.

**5.** W S Chalmers, 'Horton, Sir Max Kennedy (1883-1951)', rev., Oxford Dictionary of National Biography, Oxford University Press, 2004 [http://www.oxforddnb.com/view/article/34001] See also: W S Chalmers, *Max Horton and the Western Approaches* (London; Hodder & Stoughton, 1957) pp. 9-10.
**6.** F M L Thompson, *Gentrification and the Enterprise Culture: Britain 1780-1980* (Oxford; Oxford University Press, 2001); Ranald C. Michie, *The London Stock Exchange: A History* (Oxford; Oxford University Press, 1999).
**7.** Chalmers. *Western Approaches*. p. 10.
**8.** From a 'Certified Copy of an Entry of Birth.' Application Number COL 833541, obtained on 8 March 2008.

*3. The Battle of the Atlantic and the Maelog Lake Hotel*

H.M. Submarine A1. Real photographic postcard by the renowned Southsea photographer Stephen Cribb. Undated, Unposted, c1903. [Postcard: Cdre S.D. Whalley collection].

Chalmers quotes a letter written to Max Horton in 1914 by one Stanley Wood, of 'Dinglewood, Colwyn Bay.' This was in fact from Stanley Wood MA, headmaster of Dinglewood School and author of a number of booklets in the *Dinglewood Scripture Manuals* and *Dinglewood Shakespeare Manuals* series[9]. Wood's letter was congratulatory, and sent following the sinking of the Hela. It enquired if the heroic Lieutenant-Commander was one and the same as the Max Horton "that I had in my school some eighteen or nineteen years ago…" Horton's parents were, according to Wood, 'temporarily resident in Anglesey at the time'[10].

Given that the letter contains accurate information, it follows that whilst the Horton's residence might have been temporary it was not particularly brief if they were still there in 1895-6 when Max was twelve or thirteen[11].

Indeed, Dinglewood must have been one of the several small boarding schools his brother later remembered him attending. He also recollected that, as children they had few playmates, due to the language barrier, and that 'Max learned his ABC and the three 'R's' from the village postmaster.'[12]

9. These publications, consisting of questions and notes on the works under consideration, were intended for students preparing for examinations. *The Schoolmasters Yearbook and Directory: A Reference Book of Secondary Education* (London; Swan Sonnenschein & Co, 1903) p. 352. *Bibliotheca Celtica: A Register of Publications Relating to Wales and the Celtic Peoples & Languages* (Aberystwyth; National Library of Wales, 1932) p. 250.
10. Chalmers. *Western Approaches.* p. 9.
11. 'Robert J Horton' was entered in the electoral register for 1889 as still residing there. Esther Horton does not appear of course, as women did not have the vote at that time.
12. Chalmers. *Western Approaches.* p. 10.

34  3. The Battle of the Atlantic and the Maelog Lake Hotel

The implication here is that he did not attend the local school, and whilst the 1880 Elementary Education Act ('Mundella's Act') made it compulsory for children to attend school between the ages of five and ten at a cost of three pence per week, his parents, as persons of wealth, might have opted to have him privately tutored.[13]

Nothing more can be safely inferred, but, whatever determined his parents ownership of it, the boy born at the Maelog Lake Hotel was to achieve singular distinction in two world wars. He joined the Royal Navy in 1898 and seven years later he took charge of the submarine A.1, a vessel of 200 tons used for experimental work.

In 1912 he successfully commanded D.6 during manoeuvres in the Firth of Forth and his demonstrable skill propelled him to the front rank of what was a very small, and not much loved, fraternity. Indeed, Admiral Sir Arthur Wilson VC, who was also of the opinion that submarine crews should be hanged as pirates if captured, had condemned the submarine in 1902 as 'underhand, unfair and damned un-English.' It was not a lone view.[14]

War however provides its own dynamic, and the 'unwashed chauffeurs' soon proved they could strike.[15] The first such example was provided by Lieutenant Commander Max Horton in command of E.9, a new ocean-going submarine. On 13 September 1914 he torpedoed the German light cruiser *Hela* south of *Heligoland*; the first enemy warship ever to be sunk by a British submarine. It was following this event that Horton, perhaps in response to Admiral Wilson's opinion, instigated the tradition of hoisting the Jolly Roger upon returning to port. This convention was last displayed during the 1982 Falklands Conflict when HMS Conqueror returned home following the sinking of the *General Belgrano*.[16]

Further service followed in the Baltic where E.9 sank two destroyers and torpedoed a large German cruiser whilst, with other Royal Navy submarines, severely disrupting the

supply of iron ore from Sweden to Germany. It was a highly dangerous profession where only the most cunning and skillful could survive. As he put it: 'In submarines there is no margin for mistakes, you are either alive or dead'[17]. Horton ended the war with a clutch of decorations including the DSO and bar.

Having remained in the Royal Navy throughout the inter-war years, he was promoted to Admiral and made commander of home-based submarines in 1940. Horton, who was an intuitive individual, became convinced, despite official opinion being otherwise, that Germany would attempt an invasion of Norway and ordered all available Royal Navy submarines to concentrate in the approaches to the Norwegian coast. The German invasion started on 3 April and, though they could not directly influence the outcome of the campaign, his preparations allowed the British submarines to sink twenty-one enemy transports and supply ships as well as two cruisers.

**13.** Herbert Ward, *The Educational System of England and Wales and Its Recent History* (Cambridge; Cambridge University Press, 1935) p. 243, and Malcolm Seaborne, 'The Historical Background' in J W Tibble, *The Extra Year: The Raising of the School Leaving Age* (London; Routledge & Kegan Paul, 1970) p. 9.
**14.** Robert L O'Connell, Of Arms and Men: A History of War, Weapons, and Aggression (Oxford; Oxford University Press, 1989) p. 223; Richard Mackay, A Precarious Existence: British Submariners in World War One (Penzance; Periscope Publishing, 2003) p. 9.
**15.** Richard Compton-Hall, Submarines at War 1914-18 (Penzance; Periscope Publishing, 2004) p. 7.
**16.** W S Chalmers, Max Horton and the Western Approaches (London; Hodder & Stoughton, 1954) p. 27.
**17.** Richard Compton-Hall, *Submarines at War 1939-45* (Penzance; Periscope Publishing, 2004) p. 33.

One submarine, HMS Spearfish, almost blew the stern off the pocket-battleship *Lützow*, which, though she did not sink, took until spring of 1941 to repair and, in June, HMS Clyde damaged the battle cruiser *Gneisenau*. All in all, Horton's submarines savagely handled Hitler's surface fleet and he was commended for their efficiency: 'The high percentage of successful submarine attacks, and the low number of material failures, contributed a remarkable achievement.'[18]

"Submarine E9 & Lieut. Com. Max K Horton, Photos Cribb & West S'sea". Reverse states: "Postcard presented free with 'Yes or No' & 'Smart Fiction' weekly 1d." Undated, Unposted, c1914.

His most important appointment though was to Western Approaches Command, where he basically had to reverse his earlier order of priorities and inflict damage from above on German submarines. Though his predecessor, Sir Percy Noble, had laid the foundations of the eventual success, it fell to Horton, who was a much more ruthless and forceful character, to defeat the U-boats. Thanks to the decryption efforts of Station X at Bletchley Park he knew that more than a hundred U-boats were working in packs in mid-Atlantic where they were out of range of allied aircraft, aircraft being a deadly enemy as they forced the vessels to submerge where both their endurance and performance was limited. A fierce proponent of air-sea cooperation, Horton established a school of anti-submarine warfare at Larne, Northern Ireland, where fast naval support groups, increasingly including small aircraft carriers, learned their trade. It is a little known fact that many of the naval resources dedicated to the struggle were Canadian, and that Canada had by the end of the war the third largest navy, in terms of hulls, in the world.[19]

In April 1943 the resources husbanded and trained by Horton were unleashed, together with an additional air offensive to destroy U-boats as they crossed the Bay of Biscay en route to and from their bases. Among the support groups was one commanded by the legendary 'Johnnie' Walker, and the combined depredations inflicted on the German forces was such that at the end of May, Dönitz withdrew his U-boats from mid-Atlantic to regroup, stating 'we have lost the battle.' Though it was not final, it was nevertheless a great victory. As Churchill was to later put it: 'The only thing that ever really frightened me during the war was the U-boat peril.'[20]

There is perhaps added piquancy to Horton's victory over Dönitz. Horton's mother was related (her father, William, was a first cousin) to Sir Julian Goldsmid; 'English baronet, privy councillor, Member of Parliament, and philanthropist.' This 'Jewish blood,' according to the interpretation afforded it by the historian John Colvin, led him 'via cautiousness with authority, to the means of acquiring both power and independence.' The same source also argues that he inherited a speculative nature from his father, which manifested itself in a love of 'high-stakes poker and bridge.' More sinisterly, according to the Nazi's racial laws, this 'Jewish blood' categorised him as being a Jewish Mischling (half-breed) of the first degree. In other words, Dönitz, a convinced Nazi and devotee of his 'beloved Führer' (who named him as his successor), was bested by an opponent he would have regarded as sub-human (Untermensch).

18. W S Chalmers, 'Horton, Sir Max Kennedy (1883-1951)'
19. John Keegan, *Intelligence in War: Knowledge of the Enemy from Napoleon to al-Qaeda* (New York; Knopf, 2003) p. 281.
20. Winston S Churchill, *Their Finest Hour* (New York; Houghton Mifflin, 1949) p. 472.

Having gained the initiative the Allies were not to lose it again, and though the struggle continued until the very last days, the U-boat menace had at least been controlled. That the campaign was eventually successful, and decisively so, was unequivocally demonstrated on 14 May 1945. On that day Oberleutnant Klaus Hilgendorf formally surrendered the U-boat fleet (via a representative flotilla) at Lisahally in Northern Ireland to Horton in person[23].

It was a fearsome campaign fought in dreadful conditions and it's scale is difficult to comprehend; out of 185,000 personnel who served in the British Merchant Navy in the Atlantic, 32,952 lost their lives, a rate of some 17 per cent.

This is, in percentage terms, greater than that suffered by any of the three British armed services. However, to this number must be added a large, though unquantifiable, proportion of the *circa* 80,000 personnel of the Royal Navy who sadly perished between 1939-45, as well as casualties from Canada, the US, and many other nations.

Shocking though these figures are, they are, in percentage terms, dwarfed by the casualty rate amongst the U-boats; 785 German submarines were lost during the Second World War. The casualty rate for the crews of these vessels, numbering over 32,000, constitutes a loss rate of around 85 percent.[21]

These are horrendous figures, and it is sobering to consider how many brave men perished on both sides during this titanic struggle. It is though almost fantastic to note that the man who commanded the ultimately successful side, the original submarine 'pirate,' first came into this world in the Maelog Lake Hotel, Rhosneigr.

Perhaps the last word should go to Rear-Admiral Chalmers: 'One of the most jealously guarded traditions of the British Submarine Service is that a man should be judged by results. By this standard it is safe to say that Max Horton would be acclaimed the greatest authority on submarine warfare of his time.'[22]

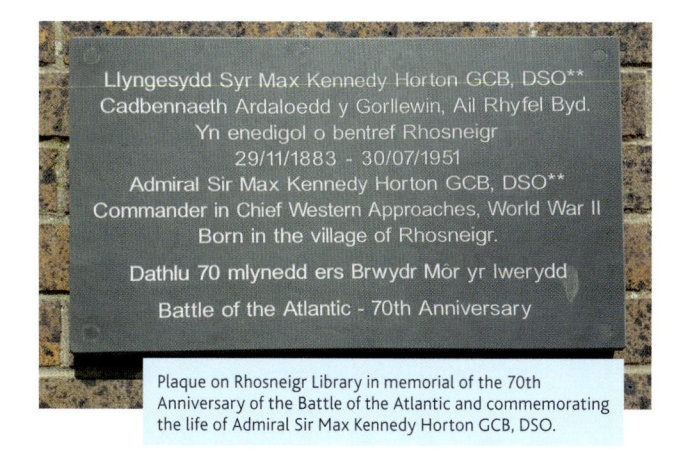

Plaque on Rhosneigr Library in memorial of the 70th Anniversary of the Battle of the Atlantic and commemorating the life of Admiral Sir Max Kennedy Horton GCB, DSO.

### Editor's Notes:

A memorial to Max Horton in Liverpool Cathedral was unveiled at a ceremony on 27th October 1957. On 14th April 2013, a plaque was unveiled at Rhosneigr Library, to commemorate Admiral Sir Max Horton, and the key role he played in the Battle of the Atlantic, which marked its 70th Anniversary in 2013.

The Plaque was unveiled in front of a small crowd of local residents & visitors, by Commodore Jamie Millar R.N. He was accompanied by council representatives and a Royal Navy contingent from HMS St. Albans, which had docked at Holyhead, along with representatives from the Sea Cadets, the Air Training Corps and the Universities Royal Naval Unit in Wales.

**21.** John Terraine, *Business in Great Waters: The U-Boat Wars 1916-1945* (London; Leo Cooper, 1989) p. 669. This book is one of the best accounts of the U-boat campaigns, but see also Dan Van Der Vat, *The Atlantic Campaign: The Great Struggle at Sea 1939-1945* (London; Hodder and Stoughton, 1988).
**22.** Chalmers. *Western Approaches*. Preface.
**23.** The U-boats were escorted by three warships, one each from the Royal Navy, the Royal Canadian Navy, and the US Navy. Also present at the ceremony was the head of Irish intelligence, Colonel Dan Bryan. This was a subtle acknowledgement of Ireland's contribution. See: 'Derry was Allies' best-kept secret in Battle of Atlantic' in The Derry Journal. http://www.derryjournal.com/news/derry-was-allies-best-kept-secret-in-battle-of-atlantic-1-5081660

**This Chapter Researched & Written by Charles Stephenson**

Charles Stephenson is a naval and military historian and is the author of several books including The Admiral's Secret Weapon: Lord Dundonald and the Origins of Chemical Warfare (2006), Germany's Asia-Pacific Empire: Colonialism and Naval Policy, 1885-1914 (2009), and (as Consultant Editor) Castles: A Global History of Fortified Structures: Ancient, Medieval & Modern (2011). He is also responsible for the two works that (thus far) comprise 'The Samson Plews Collection'; The Face of OO (2013) and The Niagara Device (2015).

Charles lives in Flintshire, North Wales but was brought up in Rhosneigr.

Commander Max Horton on the cover of 'The Great War' magazine from March 1916.

38    3. The Battle of the Atlantic and the Maelog Lake Hotel

Admiral Karl Donitz of the German Navy. Official Military photograph, unattributed photographer, c1943.

Admiral Sir Max Horton, official military photograph, Unattributed photographer, c1945.

3. The Battle of the Atlantic and the Maelog Lake Hotel 39

The Maelog Lake Hotel was demolished in the Autumn of 2011 to make way for The Oystercatcher Restaurant and Chef's Training Academy. [Photo: Anthony Moore].

The Maelog Lake Hotel was originally built in 1863 for Evan Thomas, one of the famous family of bone-setters from Liverpool. It was built on Towyn Llyn common and its construction caused such an outcry that it was burned down by a mob of local people in protest. Eventually the dispute ended and the hotel was built. In 1869, the hotel and its 70 acres of land, was sold and the 1871 census shows J.R.Arnold as proprietor. The 1881 census shows Robert J.A.Horton as the 'hotel keeper' in residence and in 1883, Max Horton, the subject of this chapter, was born there.

The 1891 census shows Samuel Withens 'Superintending' the hotel followed by T.J.Cotterell as proprietor (from an 1899 Advertisement) and remaining there through the 1901 census. He was followed by Thomas & Sarah Fagan showing in 1911 - the last census publicly available. The Fagans owned the hotel - and the 9-hole golf course on the duneland alongside - until 1944, following which it was sold to the J.W.Lees brewery.

**Over the courseof the next 60 years, The Maelog had 16 managers or tenants as follows (courtesy J.W.Lees archives):**

R Woodhead manager and then became the tenant 1st September 1949

John Joseph Norwood Thompson 10th December 1957 Manager

George Edward Jones 14th October 1958 Manager

William Henry Jones 26th September 1963 Manager

Dennis George Clutton 19th May 1971 Manager

Josephine Davies 28th February 1978 Tenant

Vernon Lord 21st November 1979 Tenant

Josephine Davies 17th November 1982 Tenant

George Alfred Davies 8th May 1984 Tenant

Clive Stuart Mayall 13th November 1985 Tenant

Marlene Lowry 9th April 1987 Tenant

Valerie Benyon 15th June 1988 Tenant

David S Turner 12th February 1991 Tenant

Holding Company as Tenants

Peter M Hannigan 1st April 1998 Tenant

David Williams 14th December 2001 Tenant

Jean Brown 5th July 2005

*3. The Battle of the Atlantic and the Maelog Lake Hotel*

In September 2008 the 12 bedroom Maelog Lake Hotel and its 70 acres of common land, river bank and lake frontage was put on the market by Lees Brewery and bought at auction by the Timpson family, (of key-cutting and shoe-repair fame) who also owned The White Eagle in Rhoscolyn.

Over the course of the next few years, The Maelog was totally demolished, rebuilt and rebranded 'The Oystercatcher'. It reopened in 2012 with a restaurant on the upper floor and 'Will's Bar' on the ground floor - 'supposedly' named as a tribute to Prince William who spent several years living on Anglesey whilst training at RAF Valley. The investment made was of the order of £3m and according to Timpson's own publicity,:

'Inspired by a visit to Jamie Oliver's 'Fifteen', they decided to use the land to build a chef academy, helping local aspiring chefs to fulfil their dreams under The Timpson Foundation. All profits made were put back into the training academy to train, mentor and support the trainees through their journey.'

'The Timpson's engaged Huf Haus, a German company famous for glass fronted, environmentally friendly properties to work in partnership with them to create a building fit for its stunning location. The glass structure has several energy efficient features, including a series of bore holes with a ground source heat pump to provide hot water and heating, and clever computers that keep energy use to a minimum.'

Both The Oystercatcher and The White Eagle were sold by Timpsons to 16 Hospitality in September 2015.

The Oystercatcher Restaurant and Chef's Training Academy.

# Chapter 4
# John Peel & The Bungalow

Lakeside bungalow - original postcard dated 1919, no publisher listed.

44   4. John Peel & The Bungalow

## 4. John Peel & The Bungalow

John Peel was born in 1939 in Heswall on the Wirral as John Robert Parker Ravenscroft, one of three sons of respected cotton merchant, Bob Ravenscroft and his wife, Harriet. He went to Woodlands boarding school in Deganwy, and then on to Shrewsbury Public School.

John used to spend many holidays in Rhosneigr in his youth, usually staying with his family at the Red House at Lion Rocks. His grandfather, Leslie Ravenscroft, lived at what is now called Lakeside Bungalow, (the first bungalow on the left as you enter Rhosneigr from the Llanfaelog end, originally built in about 1898).

John reminisced about his time in Rhosneigr in a short programme for Channel 4 entitled "Snapshots", which was first aired in January 1993.

"This bungalow", he said, "called rather amusingly 'The Bungalow', is the place where my grandfather lived when I was a child, and we came here with my dad and with my mum and various other relatives, but we were always a bit wary here, because my grandad didn't like children very much, and he particularly didn't like us we always got the impression, so when we did come here we tried to sneak off into the kitchen, where his excellent cook would look after us and make us even fatter little boys than we were already."

'Red House' at Lion rocks in 2006 (before the additional annexe was built) and in 2015.

Screen-Grab from 'Snapshots' showing John in front of 'The Bungalow' at Lakeside.

*4. John Peel & The Bungalow* 45

"My grandad was a fairly grumpy old fellow, he'd come out here in his flat hat and his bedroom slippers, and there was a stream down here *[the stream from Maelog Lake to Broad Beach]* - it was his obsession to keep the stream clear. I think my grandad would be quite pleased with the general standard of the stream now and its cleanliness – it seems to be flowing pretty well and rather less overgrown than it was in his day, so he'd give a thumbs up to the stream and whoever it is that's responsible for cleaning it."

Douglas Ravenscroft, (his father's cousin) also lived in Rhosneigr and with his second wife, Elizabeth, ran the Plas Club - one of several drinking clubs which thrived in the village, when there was no drinking on Sundays in the pubs - from the 1950s right up until the late 1970s. When the Plas was sold, they retired to White Gables just above the lake. John's memory of meeting his father for the very first time (he'd been away in the Army during his early childhood) was in Trearddur Bay at the age of 5 or 6 and it was clear that he wished he'd got to know him better. They went Cowrie hunting, with their favourite spot being the Island Church at Aberffraw, and his jam-jar full of Cowries remained a family "treasure" – as our own jam-jars full do to us.

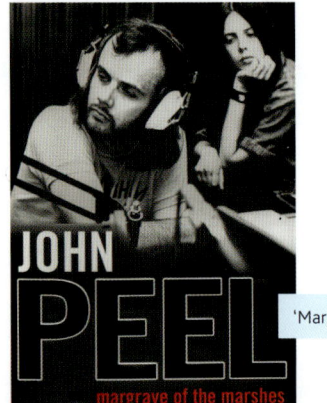

Plas Club advert from the 'Guide to Rhosneigr' c1953.

'Margrave of the Marshes' book cover.

The full story of the moment they met is also told in John's posthumously-published autobiography 'Margrave of the Marshes'[1] and John added the poignant comment:
"Years later I found myself standing in the same spot retelling this story for a television crew. As I told it, I could feel something ungovernable rising within me and fancied that I would have some sort of seizure at the completion of my account. In the event, I gave a rather theatrical low moan and slumped to the ground in tears. The television people mercifully edited this collapse from their film. I can only assume that their thoughtfulness was due to their lack of experience in the ways of television."

As a child, John was not a good swimmer:

"I blame my mother for lack of distinction in the pool and on the beaches, as she felt the very best way to teach a very young child to swim was to carry it out to sea and drop it into the waves. She had done this at Rhosneigr when I was four or five years old with frankly disastrous consequences. I had sunk from view in a trice and had been plucked from the sea a few seconds later determined never to allow my head below the surface of any water ever."

1. 'Margrave of the Marshes', Bantam Press 2005. Isbn 0-593-05252-8. Some 400 pages of interesting and amusing anecdotes including several stories about John's exploits at Ty Croes camp and in North Wales. A great read. Extracts used here by kind permission.

During a two-year spell of National Service in the army in the late 1950s John spent most of it at Ty Croes camp. He didn't like it much, and it featured in a BBC documentary, entitled 'Army of Innocents', which was broadcast in April 1997. Although nominally a Radar Operator in the Royal Artillery, he avoided activity wherever possible:

"I just drifted really from one radar set to another, drinking cups of tea in the back of the radar set 'cause you could plug a kettle into the back somewhere, or playing football. And if anybody came up to you and said 'can you take this message over to Captain Jones or something' I'd just say 'Officer, I am doing a job for someone else at the moment but I'll get back as quickly as I can' - and I did absolutely nothing!"
'Army of Innocents' was devised by a production company making a film about Servicemen who had subsequently become involved with the media. A researcher had told John that:

"All of the camps at which those chosen to appear on the programme had served had been demolished and the land returned to civilian use. In fact,' she said, 'there's only one such camp left anywhere in the country.' 'Oh, yeah?' I replied, only marginally interested. 'Where's that, then?' 'It's called Ty Croes. It's in Anglesey,' she replied."

"Thus, by default, I became the star of the programme, staying at the Maelog Lake Hotel, where my dad had drunk when we stayed in Rhosneigr as kids, sitting on the little footbridge over the river running from the lake into the sea - a river that my grandfather had devoted his declining years to keeping clear of weed, walking along the banks angrily swiping at the water with a cane - and waiting for Sheila to drive up from Suffolk with William, Alexandra and Thomas, then aged seven, five and three respectively.² Sitting on the bridge and reflecting that I had known this place as child, soldier and now husband, and could associate it with my father and grandfather, both of whom were dead, it all got too much and I sat in the sunshine in floods of tears, my feet dangling over the water."

John Peel on the beach at Rhosneigr. [photo: Sheila Ravenscroft collection].

2. John's wife & children.

4. John Peel & The Bungalow   47

"Sadly, the footage completed over that weekend was never used. No-one ever got to see me standing outside the cinema telling stories about the great fire and the skiffle group, or talking to the ancient locals looking after the Camp, all of whom pretended to remember me but couldn't possibly have done. The film people told me that every inch of the footage had been overexposed, but I knew differently. When I put the phone down after hearing the bad news, I told Sheila that it seemed I had been as crap an ex-soldier as I had been a soldier and we laughed."

One reason for John's posting to Ty Croes was because he would be closer to his younger brother Alan, who was at school at Trearddur Bay. His visits to see Alan were only intermittent though:
"... all I ever did was occasionally save money from the twenty-five shillings I was paid each week for protecting our island nation from her enemies and take him and his friend Anthony Holder, now classical records critic with the Observer, for tea at the Bay Hotel. Both boys have grown to be quite bulky chaps, but then they were whippet thin and on one celebrated occasion ate their way through the Bay Hotel's tea menu twice."

A very crucial moment for John occurred at Ty Croes camp, as it was there that he so unimpressed his Superiors by marching his squad of men across a flowerbed, that (he later learned) it was the exact moment his Commanding Officer decided NOT to put John forward for Officer Training. Had he done so, as John said, "I'd have become an Officer, stayed in Cheshire,...become an accountant and life would have been very different."

John Peel in around 1960, around the time he was demobilised from the Army, and left for the U.S. [photo: Sheila Ravenscroft collection].

And how different it would have been without the John Peel we knew - an inspirational broadcaster and a music legend who will be missed by millions. As John Ravenscroft though, he was a young Rhosneigr holidaymaker in the great tradition. We mourn his passing and extend our sympathies to his family – some of whom still stay in Rhosneigr.

[A shorter version of this chapter was first published in the RBA magazine, 2004/5.]

Aerial photo of Ty Croes camp c1970s. [Photo: Trac Mon collection].

Ty Croes camp after its closure. [Photo: Trac Mon collection].

4. John Peel & The Bungalow

# Chapter 5
# Stewart Wood & The Crash of a Blackburn Botha

Full page advertisement from 'The Aeroplane' magazine of June 13 1941.

52  5. Stewart Wood & the crash of a Blackburn Botha

## 5. Stewart Wood & the crash of a Blackburn Botha

R.A.F. Valley (originally called RAF Rhosneigr) First opened in February 1941 and, as this was in the middle of the Second World War, its early squadrons were Hurricanes and Beaufighters flying convoy patrols over the Irish Sea.

The new twin-engined Blackburn Botha I had only recently entered service with the RAF, to be used for reconnaissance, torpedo carrying or as a bomber. Unfortunately, the aircraft proved to be unstable and underpowered, resulting in several crashes. It was withdrawn from service in 1944.

On the morning of 25th August 1941, one of these planes, L6417, from No.4 Air Observers' School, West Freugh, Scotland, crashed into the sea off Rhosneigr in gale force winds, and a rescue by local villagers was attempted. Two of those were 17 year old Stewart Wood, aided by his friend Derrick Baynham. They received the George Medal for gallantry for their brave attempt to save the crew, along with Silver Medals awarded by the RNLI.

In addition, because one of the aircrew had been Polish, the Prime Minister of Poland, General Sikorski, later presented them with gold cigarette cases, engraved with his signature, together with a warm letter of appreciation.

Stewart later wrote a personal memoir about the tragedy for his parents Geoffrey and Kathleen Wood, at their request, some years after the rescue took place. This amazing story is included on the following pages, by kind permission of the late Stewart Wood, and his family.

There are still people living who were involved with, or lost members of their family, on that fateful day. The bravery of all those who lost their lives or put their lives at risk, was something that Stewart Wood humbly recognised throughout his life. The fourteen who died in the disaster were:

PC George Cledwyn Arthur, the village policeman.
Leading Aircraftman D.W.Bannister.
Gunner Reginald Eaton, RA.
Leading Aircraftman Leslie A.Ford.
Coastguard Officer Evan Jones.
Battery Sgt Major Alfred W.Moger, RA.
Arthur John Owen, Second Mate, Mercantile Marine.
Gunner R.K.Simons, RA.
Gunner Clarence H.Thornton, RA.
Second Lieutenant Peter T.Whysall, RA.
Gunner S.Wilkins RA.

And the crew of the Botha who died were:
Leading Aircraftman T.A.Dixon
Leading Aircraftman F.C.Glockler
Sergeant K.S.Rosiewicz (Polish)

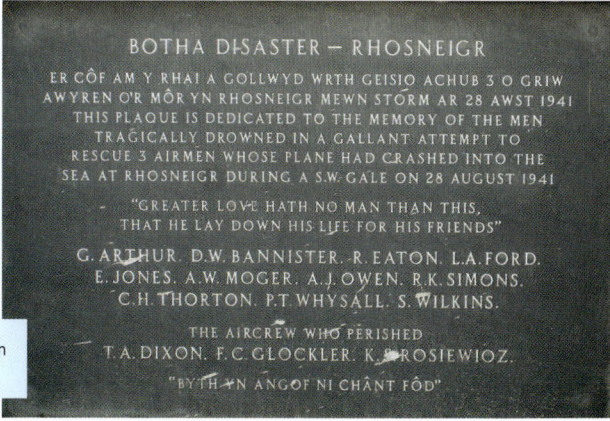

This Slate Tablet, was erected on the lawn of the Rhosneigr Fire Station in 1991.

5. Stewart Wood & the crash of a Blackburn Botha  53

The London Gazette carried the official record of the rescue and awards and this is shown in panel 5a on page 60. Brief Obituaries of Stewart Wood and Derrick Baynham are included in panel 5b on page 61.

The six Army casualties were all from the 226th Light Anti-Aircraft Training Regiment, stationed at Rhosneigr and with the exception of Gunner Simons, all five are buried at St Maelog's Church, Llanfaelog.

In addition, Sergeant John James Plunkett, who was also attached for duty at Valley with No.456 Squadron of the Royal Australian Air Force, was also nominated for gallantry and was awarded the British Empire Medal.

A plaque commemorating the disaster was erected on the lawn of Rhosneigr Fire Station on its 50th anniversary in August 1991 and was marked again by a ceremony of remembrance on its 75th, in 2016.

## Stewart Wood's Story
## August 28, 1941

This is an answer to your repeated requests of three years ago, to set out in my own words an account of the accident that occurred at Rhosneigr. It might also be called a confession of faith and of my implicit belief in God, for without doubt the circumstances of the whole affair were nothing short of miraculous — at least as far as we were concerned — and were to me a much-needed proof of the existence of a Supreme Being who can and does answer prayers.

It was rather a pleasant day when we went out that morning; true it was very windy — in fact it was blowing a full gale — but it was a fine clear day in spite of the wind. The sun bathed everything in that peculiarly penetrating and startling radiance which it has on such a day in August, darting forth its rays from between the gaps in the flying clouds like the spotlight at a ballet.

Lower High Street showing the old "Tea Caddy" cafe. c1950s.

5. Stewart Wood & the crash of a Blackburn Botha

At about 10.15 our little party was sitting round a table in the 'Tea Caddy' drinking coffee or fizzy lemonade and discussing the chances of a game of hockey before too many people had left. I left the café after about a quarter of an hour and outside met Mary[1] who was running to meet me to perform our morning pilgrimage to Auntie Hilda at the 'Work Box'. We sauntered down the road together and went into the tiny shop, bidding Mrs Hughes Butcher good morning as we passed. We stopped there a little while trying to help in one way or another, when suddenly I looked up to see people running down the village for all they were worth and Mother popped her head round the door and said 'there's a 'plane down in the bay!' We, of course, joined the flying crowd and then we saw the 'plane lying well out in the bay "just over half way to the Starvation Rocks" I thought. She looked beautiful lying there amid a shining patch of sunlit sea, with glorious, sweeping rollers, white-capped and blue-frocked careering shore-wards, and the same patch of sunlight illuminating the Starvation Rocks in the background and the Outer Harbour rocks on the left of the picture. It was a lovely scene but it obviously spelt death to the men in the 'plane unless something was done, and done quickly.

A typical tripper – clad in a neat and tidy flannel suit with an open-necked shirt and, to crown the messy vision, an A.R.P. warden's beret, complete with badge – stood beside me and said in a silly, childish, know-all manner, "Oh, they'll be all right, the 'plane won't sink, it's a flying boat!" I am afraid that I so far forgot myself as to turn on him in a fury, saying with a good deal of feeling: "Is it hell you damn fool, it's a Botha and if something isn't done she will sink in twenty minutes".

Therein lay the key to the whole thing, that wretched little man had made me so angry and being in a full blown rage I suppose I was capable of anything. What actually happened was this: I left the gaping crowd and ran back to the 'Tea Caddy' as hard as I could go. I burst in through the flimsy rattling door rather like a wild animal and shouted to Derrick Baynham – who was still sitting over his coffee with John Webb – that there was a plane down in the bay and that we had better do something about it. The rest of the people in there took one more resentful look at me and turned back to their coffee in disgust, thinking, no doubt that I was both rude and, most likely, a little mad. Derrick and John both jumped up at once and we tore out of the place followed by mild protests from Evans the proprietor, they were of little avail and anyway mostly unheard!

Once out of the café we ran straight down to the beach via Harrison Drive, past Peter Jung's house and onto the shore. We could barely see the 'plane now, as we were much lower down than when I had first seen it, though every now and then we could catch a glimpse of the dark top part of the aircraft as some wave, a little bigger than the others, lifted it up in the water. What was far more important was the sight of the crew of the aircraft hanging on as best they could to the smooth streamlined top of the fuselage, vanishing as each wave raked the derelict from bow to tail.

We wasted but little time in staring at the stormy scene I can assure you. One brief embracing look was enough for Derrick, as it had been for me, and with one accord we raced for Peter Jung's house to get oars and rowlocks for their boat which was on its homemade trolley on the shore all ready to launch.

We were given oars and rowlocks and told to take anything else we wanted, but there was nothing else to take except ourselves. So we fled back to the boat and quickly shipped the rowlocks and laid the oars inside.

John gave us a hand to push off and begged to be allowed to come with us, but being only twelve years old and we having no real use for him and a wish to travel as light as possible, we refused.

We waded out with the boat for a few yards until there was plenty of water under the keel and then we leapt in and the adventure began. At first the boat was flung up and down

**1.** Stewart's sister

with vicious jerks by the smaller frothy rollers breaking on the beach. Looking back we saw people running to the spot where we had just left from and they were shouting to us to come back saying that there was another boat already putting out, but when they saw that we were not going to return they began to call us all sorts of names.

To tell the truth, once started we could not have easily or safely turned round at all as it would have meant exposing the broadside of the boat to the waves and we should have been overturned in an instant. We were subjected to this rough tossing up and down for about ten minutes or a quarter of an hour, by which time we were out of the area in which the waves were breaking; during the passage of this broken water I got a shower of icy-cold water down my back each time the bows cut into a wave, so, anxious to take good care of my jacket, I took it off and wedged it into the bows under the anchor and rope. I was afraid that with a good soaking of salt water it would shrink and thought it would keep nicely dry where I had put it! Alas, my good intentions were destined to have a rude awakening.

At last the violent jerking stopped and we reached calmer water – calmer but infinitely more terrifying. Great rolling seas which towered over our heads and threatened to engulf us at every moment; but though they must have been twenty to twenty-five foot from the bottom of the trough to the crest, we rode up and down them in grand style, rather like a cyclist on a piece of hilly road, we pulled with all our strength up the on-coming wave and when the top was reached the boat seemed to hang poised for a second while the wind whistled round us and flecks of flung spray and foam wetted us, then suddenly she seemed to make her mind up and would put her nose down with a resounding smack and we would row as if we were in a boat-race while we had the shelter of the trough and the downhill side of the wave.

We had little time, in spite of the awe-inspiring scenes, to be frightened, as we were rowing like fiends and keeping the bows heading into the seas, and all the time we cursed and swore at each other to row yet harder. At each stroke my ash oar would bend into a dangerous-looking arc and I remember wondering what would happen if it broke – thank Heaven it stayed whole! If either of us had broken an oar we should have been in a very dirty mess.

Each time we crested another wave I turned to see that we were still on our proper course, and to look for the other boat. When I first saw it I recognised it as an old whaler belonging to one of the locals[2]. She was heading out to sea through the harbour rocks, apparently with the idea of turning when well out beyond the rocks and bearing back on a course at an acute angle to the one they followed at first, thus coming down wind and with a following sea on to the wrecked aeroplane. When we had covered about two-thirds of our trip out to the 'plane I looked in vain for the big white whaler on the crest of a wave and though I turned round again and again to look, I never saw her again until a few days after the accident; she was lying above the high tide mark with her mast gone and a great hole stove in at the bows. The sea has claimed some more victims – the whaler had been caught in the act of turning by the seventh wave of a cycle and completely overturned, all her crew were lost as but one could swim and the seas were too great for him.

As we crept out from the shore, slowly and laboriously, we watched the 'plane as closely as possible. When we set out there had been three black dots on the top of the fuselage – each with some precarious hand and foot hold; halfway out there were only two men visible; at long last we were within hailing distance of the 'plane and there was only one man left, clinging to the tail fin of the wreck and waving to us and shouting apparently, but his words were swept away by the wind and we did not hear what he was saying.

We arrived and stupidly slackened our efforts and our vigilance all at once, the bows drifted off a little from heading into the seas at right angles, and the peculiar effect the wreck had upon the waves combined to bring about our downfall.

2. It is believed that the whaler was owned by Raymond Goldsmith. [Boatpool magazine, 1983-84].

Quite suddenly a large roller swept across the starboard wing, seemed to break more than the others and buried us in a welter of foaming, seething salt water, having shaken the water from our eyes we saw that we were waterlogged. 'Get out' shouted Derrick. I was slow to obey and said 'we must try bailing', but we might have been trying to stop the tide from flowing for all the success we had; the next wave was too quick for us and we lost both oars and realised that like it or not we must jump out.

Having evacuated the inside of the boat we were determined to hold on to the outside at all costs, then, when we had carried out this manoeuvre according to plan we shouted to the airman to join us; though he looked very doubtfully at our tiny cockleshell he clambered onto the elevator and as soon as a wave had passed by he made a mighty leap and landed beside us. He was a foreigner and obviously scared stiff, as well he might be, for I am sure that to land an aircraft in such a sea must have been a nerve-racking task. Afterwards we learnt that he was a Pole. He kept on asking us when help was coming, which annoyed me greatly at the time. Each time he asked when we were going to be picked up I pointed out to sea and said 'there's another boat coming, it's bigger than this one', for I didn't realise then that the whaler had foundered.

Then began the worst part of our trip. We were absolutely powerless to do a thing to help ourselves. I shouted to Derrick to strike out with his feet and to paddle with his free hand to try and keep warm and to get us a little further away from the 'plane. These efforts didn't last long, however, as each wave that came along swept clean over us and we were momentarily blinded and choked, - but we did manage to increase the distance between ourselves and the 'plane. That wretched aeroplane was a constant nightmare to me for the greater part of the time we were drifting ashore. You see, we were at the tail end and a little behind and to one side of it, but each wave struck it at the nose and raised the whole thing up, and for a moment the 'plane was poised on top of the wave with the tail clear of the water and hanging many feet above our heads; each time this happened I was sure the tail

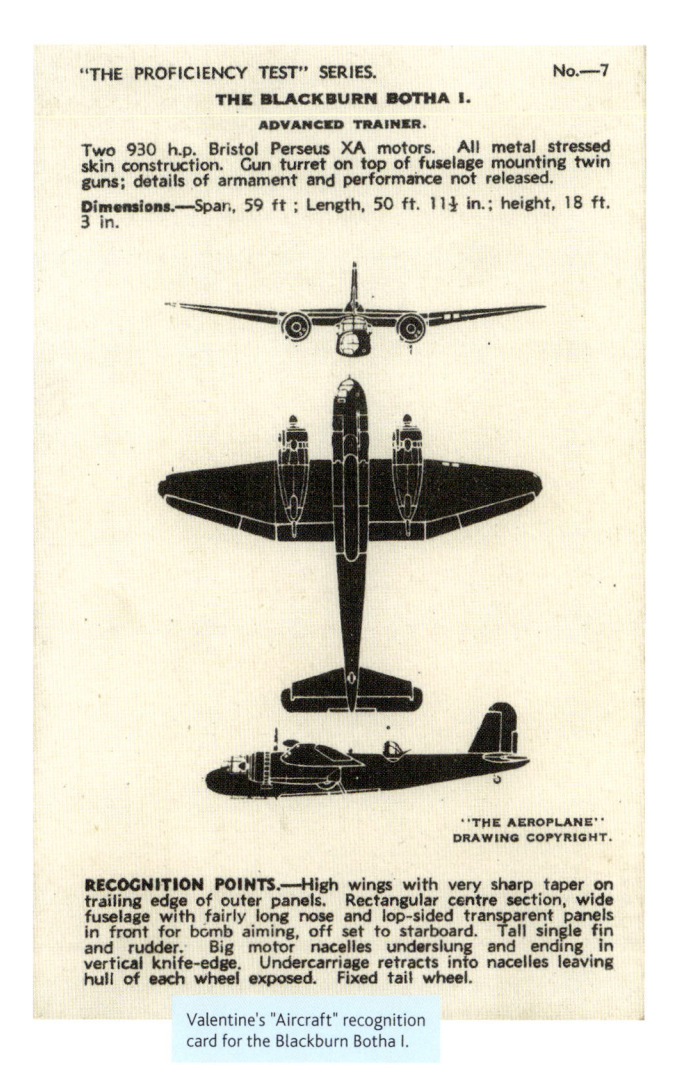

Valentine's "Aircraft" recognition card for the Blackburn Botha I.

would come crashing down on our heads and annihilate us all at one fell stroke. It still strikes me as funny that we should have had more fear for the tail of an aeroplane than for the raging sea in which we were being tossed about like feathers.

All this time I was clinging to my coat, which was still inside the waterlogged boat, as if my life depended on it. I had one arm over the side of the boat and tucked under one of the seats with the precious coat held in my hand and wedged between my arm and the underside of the seat.

Suddenly a wave caught us broadside on and overturned the whole applecart, I found myself underwater, staring up into the upturned boat. This was a most extraordinary feeling – I felt quite detached somehow – I remember quite clearly thinking – 'Well, my coat's still there, I suppose I had better get my head out of the water', which I proceeded to do in my own time, as if it was the most natural thing in the world for me to stay underwater for hours!

Holding on was more difficult now as there was only the keel which was about one and a half inches high and merely a finger-hold; but it was surprising to find that such a small grip was quite sufficient.

It was about this time that I remember looking shore-wards and thinking 'I wonder if I shall ever walk past that water tower again? Funny thing that - it looks quite close, must be the weather, it's at least a thousand yards away'.

I was feeling rather down in the mouth at that time so I said my prayers and felt much better. I also had a great piece of luck at this time, I felt something banging against and wrapping round my legs – had I been less tired and apathetic I think I would have panicked under the mistaken impression that what was in reality the anchor-rope dangling out of the upturned boat, was a sea snake or some foul monster of the deep. I didn't panic and realised, in a dull sort of way, what it was and proceeded to twine my legs thoroughly round it and loop it as many times as possible round my ankles, this I think was a very decided help, as I could draw myself up like someone standing in the stirrups when riding, which eased the boredom and my cramped limbs.

Again I looked hopefully towards the shore and saw a great crowd of people and another thing, which struck me as most important at the time – I could see the marram grass on the sand dunes waving and rippling in the wind. This I rightly took to be a sure sign that we weren't far from being saved. I shouted my good news to Derrick and the airman, who both looked pretty done, and only Derrick made some sort of reply which I didn't catch.

About this time we began to get among the forest of tall posts set up on the beach, and then a great many things happened in a hurry. I felt a sharp jar on the anchor rope and cursed out loud that the anchor had fouled, but a few minutes later I hit the sand with a long rasping bump when in the trough of a wave.

In all the broken water and breaking rollers there was but little time for coherent thought; but two or more things did manage to seep into my brain and make their import felt – one, that the airman had vanished, I looked around but couldn't see him anywhere.

Wooden posts set into the sand in order to prevent enemy landing craft from reaching the shore. Remnants are still visible in places.

Then came several roaring, ranting seas, one atop of the next and when the boat and I had stopped spinning like one great top, the second thought came soaking through – Derrick has gone – then – my feet are on the sand – the water is only up to my waist – there are people all round me – I don't want to leave the boat – airmen, half carrying, half walking me – I told them I could walk, I did for a few yards and then slowly – slowly ---- slowly------ going------------ down.

Next thing I knew of was someone bending over me and making me drink some very hot coffee and there was a terrible bumping and amazing warmth – inside and out – the noise of a car engine being driven very hard in bottom or second gear. Once more these hazy feelings and thoughts faded into total darkness.

At last I drifted back to consciousness and became aware of a great many people gathered round me again, someone was giving me a cigarette – a Star – and offered a lighter, but I was shivering so hard that I couldn't make the end of the cigarette maintain contact with the proffered light for long enough to get even one little puff in; finally after several fruitless attempts I took the lighter from him, and bracing my head against the top of the bed to stop it shaking, and doing the same with my hands, I managed to light my cigarette. From that time until we left we were hardly ever short of cigarettes[4].

People kept coming and going and I got warmer and the awful shivering finally abated to a mere sporadic twitching. Wing Commander Oliver came in to tell us we must stay where we were until the Station Medical Officer had seen us and that we couldn't have anything to eat until then. He stayed a little while chatting and asking questions about the 'plane, how many men were on it and so on. We answered these queries and asked him about the chap we had picked up, he said he didn't know for certain but thought he had revived and would find out definitely and let us know. He came back later to tell us that the poor chap had died on the beach before they could get him to hospital.

All the time that we were in the RAF hospital we plagued the two Medical Orderlies for food, but all they could find was a box of Oxo cubes which we disposed of in pint mugs of boiling water – very good!

At long last at about 5pm the M.O. arrived, had a look at us and said we could have some food and that we could send for our parents to come and take us home. He sent us ham and eggs in good quantity and biscuits and about ¾ lb of cheese each!

All this time I was making anxious enquiries about my clothes and especially my coat, but to my horror no one knew anything about any of my garments let alone my precious coat! Finally my shirt, shorts, stockings and shoes reappeared, but I was told that nobody had seen my coat.

At about 6.30pm the car turned up and we said goodbye to the two Medical Orderlies who had been so good to us and we went back to Rhosneigr in high spirits.

Later, after we had returned to Chester having finished our holiday I received a telegram ordering me to attend an R.A.F. Court of Enquiry at Valley. This was marvellous news as it provided an excellent excuse to have a few more days holiday. While I was in Rhosneigr the local Bobby asked me to pay him a visit. I duly presented myself at the police station and was confronted with a draggled and dirty piece of cloth which had obviously been at one time a good sports jacket. My coat! Now weighing about 20 lbs with sand in the pockets and lining, covered with seaweed and splashed with tar and oil. I was going to keep it dry!

**J.L.S. Wood
9.3.44**

---

[4]. Back then, before its dangers were understood, smoking was very popular and commonplace, even among teenagers.

Stewart Wood (L) and Derrick Baynham (R) at the gates of Buckingham Palace in April 1942, after receiving their medals for Gallantry from King George VI. [Photo: Wood Family Collection].

Stewart Wood, wife Betty and Grand-daughter Anna. [Photo: Wood Family Collection].

# Awarded the George Medal.— Derrick Baynham, Schoolboy, Walton-on-Thames. John Leslie Stewart Wood, Schoolboy, Chester.

An aircraft crashed into the sea three-quarters of a mile off the Welsh coast, Baynham and Wood, both aged 17, at once set forth in a small dinghy. Undeterred by the heavy sea and the high wind, they rowed hard, avoiding the reefs and keeping head-on to the waves, After forty-five minutes they came close to the aircraft but, as they were turning to come alongside, a big wave caught them broadside on and they were swamped. They then swam to the wreckage where they found the solitary survivor of the air crew in an exhausted condition. They managed to get him to their boat which had capsized and was drifting to the shore. With great difficulty the three clung to it as it reared and plunged in the waves. Eventually they got the airman to a post projecting above the water. Unfortunately, he was too weak to hold on and he was drowned before help could reach him. Baynham and Wood, by now utterly exhausted, were washed in towards the shore where they were pulled out. They had been in the water two hours. Meanwhile, other attempts at rescue had been made in the course of which eleven people lost their lives.

The two boys showed great courage and initiative in attempting the rescue.

COMMENDATIONS.
The individuals named below have been brought to notice for their brave conduct.

For services when attempting to rescue an airman from the sea: —

George Cledwyn Arthur (deceased), Police Constable, Rhosneigr, Anglesey.

Evan Jones (deceased), Coastguard Officer, Anglesey.

Arthur John Owen, Esq. (deceased), First Officer, Merchant Navy.

[From the second supplement to The London Gazette of Tuesday the 27th of January 1942.]

[Panel 5a]

5. Stewart Wood & the crash of a Blackburn Botha

# Brief obituaries Wood & Baynham.

## John Leslie Stewart Wood F.R.I.C.S.

Born 7th July 1924 at Kinnerton, Nr Chester, Cheshire.
Son of Geoffrey & Kathleen Wood.
Educated at The King's Schoool, Chester.
Married Elizabeth (Betty) Bookless in 1950.

They had 3 children: Sarah, Rachel, Judith (Bun).

Stewart led an extraordinarily full life, becoming a respected Chartered land agent with the Westminster Estate. He worked for the Estate in Durham, Scotland, Surrey and Cheshire before moving to North Wales as a partner with Cooke and Arkwright, and then founding Cooke, Wood and Caird. He led an active life: hill-walking, shooting, birdwatching, and boating!

As a founder member of the Rhosneigr Boatowners' Association, he was never happier than when messing about in boats but he also knew and understood all too well how unforgiving the sea could be, and was a great supporter of the RNLI.

He became president of the RBA in 2001
Lived in Rhosneigr at Bronant Bach.
Died 5th April 2014
(Source: Family records)

[Panel 5b]

## Derrick Hubert Baynham

Born April 13th 1924 at Walton on Thames, Surrey
Son of Major Hubert Baynham
Educated St George's College, Weybrdge
Joined the Army in 1942 aged 18.
Married Ann Park in 1949, but they later separated.
They had three sons and a daughter.
Remained in the Army after the war, rising to the rank of Brigadier.
Retired in 1979 to Dorset (and Normandy).

Derrick maintained a lifelong passion for sailing and in retirement enjoyed shooting and fishing. He had captained the British Underwater Skin Diving Team at four World championships, and was also a keen amateur radio ham.

Derrick was on holiday in Rhosneigr because at the time, his father was the Commandant of an Italian Prisoner of war camp in the area. They stayed at a boarding house on the High Street run by two women - Fanny and Lizzie, (surnames and house name not known.) That was Derrick's first and last visit to Rhosneigr as the following year he joined the army. Relatives of the family are now believed to holiday in Trearddur Bay.

Died May 16th 2006
(Source: Family records and the Daily Telegraph 6th Dec 2006)

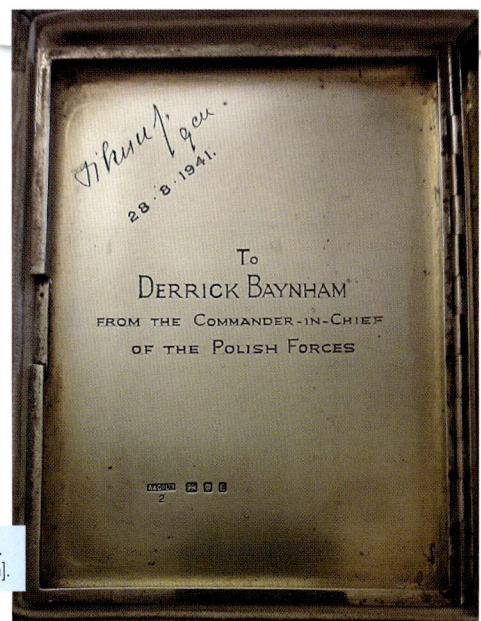

Engraved cigarette case.
[Photo: Simon Baynham].

# Chapter 6
# George Cockram, Artist & Gentleman.

George Cockram, (on left hand end of centre row, looking to the right), together with other members of the Royal Cambrian Academy. Henry Cole, R.A. (with large grey beard and no hat) is situated top right. [RCA collection].

6. *George Cockram, Artist & Gentleman.*

# 6. George Cockram, Artist & Gentleman.

The following Chapter was written in the early 1990s by Winifred Uttley (nee Ormerod), an old friend of the Rhosneigr artist George Cockram, who produced many wonderful paintings of Anglesey and North Wales.

As explained by Winifred in her Foreword, it is written more as a series of anecdotes than a biography, and has been sub-edited by Winifred's son-in-law, Martin Butler.

## Sub-Editor's Note:
Winifred Ormerod died as her draft script was being typed. So many of her friends asked what would happen to her research that I felt that I must try and complete the project for her. She had discussed sections of it with me, and I had grown to love many of the paintings she owned.

This article is a tribute to two indomitable characters who first met when one was a mature landscape artist and the other a small girl, and who stayed in touch for over 30 years – George Cockram (1861-1950) and Winifred Ormerod (1912 - 1990).

**Martin Butler**

Winifred Uttley. [Butler collection].

## Foreword by Winifred Ormerod

I hope that everyone who has a chance to read 'George Cockram: Facts & Personal Memories' will read this Foreword. It explains a lot in what follows and how it was I came to write this tribute to George Cockram so that, in the future, he will not be just a name and a few lines in a Reference Book.

In the Spring of 1916, my Father, Mother and I went to stay at The Bay Hotel, Rhosneigr, owned and run by Mr Hal Cole and his wife. The object of our visit was to see if we would like to have our summer holidays at Rhosneigr and stay at The Bay Hotel. I was 4 years old and my previous summer holidays had been at a furnished cottage at Dinas Dinlle at Caernarvon Bay, or Carnarvon as it was spelled in those days.

I presume that, having attained the age of four, I was deemed civilised enough to stay at an hotel! Mr Cole was a very good Hotel Host; he would tell his guests the best walks and, over the years, he told us of many special spots we would not have found on our own.

One day, when chatting with Mr Cole, my Father admired some pictures hanging in the hotel; Mr Cole said, "They were painted by my father (Henry Cole R.A.). My brother-in-law is also an artist and in Rhosneigr at present so, if you are interested in pictures and would like to see his paintings, I will arrange it for you'.

The artist was George Cockram and he had married the elder daughter of Henry Cole R.A.

My parents went to see the pictures but I didn't go so I expect someone looked after me. A day or two later we all went again. I have no real memories of seeing any pictures that day and I expect we had gone for my Father to confirm about the picture he had decided to buy and to arrange about framing and delivery. The picture he bought is of Tryfan, the shoulder that comes right down to the A5, which runs there between two stone walls. It is a beautiful picture but not one, I think, to appeal to a four-year-old.

Before we went home, my Father booked at The Bay Hotel for our holiday in August, three weeks or a month - I don't know now which it was.

In August, I, with my Father, Mother and Sister, went to see Mr Cockram's pictures. We lived in Rochdale, a very poor climate, and my sister who was never very strong went away to school at Llandudno, on our doctor's recommendation. She had therefore not been with us during our Spring visit.

We did not go where Father, Mother and I had gone on our second visit in the Spring. I know where that is, but I have no recollection at all of the place where he showed his pictures before his studio was built. George Cockram had sold 'The Dunes' and kept a piece of land for a studio; he bought 'The Dunes', I understand, soon after he married and from 1916 or before he rented somewhere for the Summer to show his pictures. Small children, I think, either follow the grown-up or are led by the hand, not really noticing where they are being taken. To have such a blank in my memory amazes me as I can remember incidents on our visits to Mr Cockram when I was still small enough to sit on a buffet![1]

I can't remember the order in which my Father bought his pictures but I do know 'when and why' from the age of about thirteen, and I know which he bought 'early on'. In August 1916, I can't remember any individual picture - seascapes, mountains, gorse — but I do remember the pictures of Venice: the lagoon with the fishing boats, turquoise-blue water and

1. An early 20th century word for a narrow sideboard or china cabinet.

boats with orange-brown sails, burnt-sienna sails and some multi-coloured and striped sails. Those colours came into my mind's eye 72½ years later when I saw George Cockram's picture on the Antiques Road Show on 29th January 1989. I knew the picture was a Cockram before the expert said 'George Cockram'.

## George Cockram was still only a few lines in a Reference Book and hard facts were difficult to come by.

I know colour means a great deal to me and, as I have thought about those paintings of Venice during the past year, I have realised that this love of colour must have started when I was very young though I did not realise it then. After my marriage, we went to the Studio and, in the corner on a very dark wooden corner fitment (mentioned elsewhere), we saw a picture of waves at sunset, the tips of the waves catching the sunset colours, almost like a deep-coloured opal. I walked straight to it, the beauty was such that it nearly took my breath away. Some of our wedding present money found a home that day!

I think my Mother had the same feeling for colour; in the Winter of 1922—3, she and my Father went to India (business and pleasure) and brought home Indian silk embroideries in gorgeous colours and not those which Europeans would put together. Mother would say, "Look at these colours together" and I think that also made me more aware of what can be done with colour.

From 1916 I went to Rhosneigr every year, sometimes twice a year, and we saw the Cockram pictures. In 1916 pictures of the lagoon and fishing boats and again in 1917, although there were fewer of them. After 1917 there was nothing of Venice so, if he had sold all the Venetian pictures before 1918, painting from May 1913 for I don't know how many months - say till Autumn (this is guess work), he must have worked very hard. If, as stated on the Antiques Road Show on 22nd January 1989, the picture shown was probably painted between 1900 and 1910. Knowing George Cockram's output in later years and how quickly he seemed to sell his pictures, I knew these dates were wrong because if they had been painted as late as 1910, six years later there would have been very few left, if any. I had always understood that George Cockram went to paint in Venice shortly before the 1914-18 War and Mr Cole's younger daughter Pauline (George's niece) has confirmed that he was in Venice in 1913. I think that all the pictures he had painted in 1913 would have gone by 1918; I have written more fully about this elsewhere in my 'Memories'.

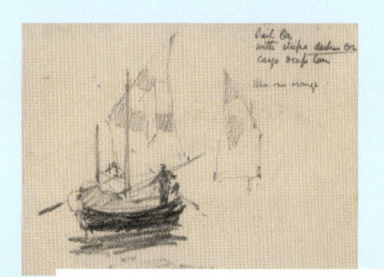

Several pencil sketches from George's sketchbooks have also been found [private collection].

6. George Cockram, Artist & Gentleman.

George Cockram was 55 when I first met him but he did not seem an elderly man, probably because of his wide interests and very active mind. I said recently to his niece, that the last time my Father, Sister and I went to the Studio his mind was as active as ever and he was then 89 . He died the following September, leaving a lot of unfinished work; by the next May this had all been sorted and those paintings which were reasonably near—finished were for sale. We each bought a picture different from any in our possession.

I seem to keep harking back to the Antiques Road Show but I have an excuse: it had seemed obvious to me as I watched the programme that George Cockram was still only a few lines in a Reference Book and hard facts were difficult to come by. I felt therefore, by the end of the evening, that it was incumbent upon me to get what I could written down. If the expert had been fortunate enough to have known more of George Cockram, this would never have been written.

On the last Antiques Road Show, Mr Nahum said, "This man was a good artist but nothing is known about him". I hope I have saved George Cockram from that fate. If more people, family friends perhaps, would write about artists they have known - where they painted at different seasons of the year, amusing stories about them, where they studied &c - and would ask Galleries who have their man's pictures if they would like a copy of the article, much more would be known. I knew of four Art Galleries who owned Cockram's so I wrote asking size and subject and, with the replies, came more information and the names of other galleries owning Cockram's. The writers of all these letters were interested and I think every letter provided a new snippet of information.

I was amazed at the interest everyone took in my project. Friends would say something about 'All the research' but, in fact, I did very little research and the information seemed to accrue from the correspondence. I had known George Cockram from 1916 when I was four - and he was fifty- five — until he died in 1950. I knew his family and, as the years went by, I learnt where he painted at various times of the year so, with knowledge of his background, I found all I learned seemed to just fit into place.

I found the work very interesting and, from time to time, there would be a real thrill: for example, Oldham Art Gallery sent me a photocopy of a letter written by George Cockram on 20th December 1905 in reply to a letter from its Curator and answering a list of questions. I recognised the handwriting before the letter was out of the envelope; it seemed a modern miracle and provided a lot of information.

Unfortunately, since I started this Foreword, I have been ill so all has been delayed. Now I am very much better and feel equal to finishing my 'effort'.

**Winifred Ormerod.**

Venice. [C. Nugent collection].

# George Cockram 1861 - 1950
## Introduction

On Sunday 22nd January 1989 I was watching The Antiques Road Show on television when a picture came on screen. The camera showed the left hand side of a painting and travelled slowly along its width. What emerged was a very large watercolour, far wider than it was high. I looked and thought, "Is it a Cockram?" It was mistier than the work I knew: but then I saw a boat with multi-coloured striped sails and, in a flash, I was four years old looking at Mr Cockram's pictures of Venice in 1916 – boats with light brown and orangey sails, some multi-coloured, others striped, and the pale blue water of the lagoon. I looked at the frame and then at the frames of my Cockram's in the drawing room – it must be! Then, Mr Nahum's voice said "George Cockram", and the well-known signature came into view. I felt thrilled beyond words – I was right!

6. George Cockram, Artist & Gentleman.

Mr Nahum said that George Cockram lived a long life and painted a lot of pictures, but when he said that this picture was painted between 1900 and 1910, I burst out aloud "Wrong! Wrong! Wrong!" I had always understood that his Venice work was painted not long before World War 1. Before the end of the programme I decided to write to Hugh Scully at the BBC.

I had known since the mid-1960's that very little information was available about George Cockram, and that evening I had much food for thought. My own 77th birthday was a week away, and I doubted if there were many people left who had known him for so many years – from 1916 – 1950 – even though I only saw him once or twice a year. I decided there and then that I must try to write something down before it was too late.

I knew of four galleries who owned Cockram's and wrote to them asking for details. With their replies came more information and the names of other galleries owning his work. Each reply contained a new snippet, and the interest the writers expressed encouraged me to continue my task. I knew his family, and as years went by I learned where he painted at various times of the year, and the information that came in response to my enquiries fell into place; the pieces started to come together.

The eighteen months I have spent on my contribution to George Cockram's memory have been exciting for me. I was amazed at the interest by friends and galleries, and I thank them all for their encouragement. I am particularly grateful to members of his family who have added considerably to my own memories.

In all the years I visited Mr Cockram's studio, I never thought in my wildest dreams that it would be incumbent upon me to get something written so that there would be some record of the man and his character, something more than a few stark lines in a reference book – he was worth far more than that.

## The Bay Hotel

In the Spring of 1916 my parents and I stayed at the Bay Hotel, Rhosneigr, then owned by Mr Hal Cole. When my father admired some of the pictures hanging in the hall, Mr Cole explained that they were painted by his father, Henry Cole R.A., and that his brother-in-law was also an artist, currently in Rhosneigr. If my father was interested, he would arrange a meeting.

I was four at the time, and have no memories of seeing pictures on that first visit to George Cockram's studio – but I do know which picture my father bought on that occasion – Tryfan, the shoulder that comes right down to the A5, which runs there between two stone walls. The mountain sides have big boulders, and the other wall is not far from the waters of Llyn Ogwen. The mountain shoulder and the lake are on the picture, and the water looks very wet. A friend once said, "The first time I saw that picture, I felt I could throw a stone in the water, it looked so wet and real". The upper part of the mountain has misty clouds, looking as if they are slipping down the slope of dark grey rocks, the sky is grey, the grass grey-green, and there are brown rushes in the lake. It is a beautiful picture, but not one, I think, to appeal to a four year old.

We returned to The Bay in August, and while I cannot remember seeing any paintings of seascapes, mountains or gorse, I do remember the pictures of Venice; the Lagoon with fishing boats, turquoise blue water and boats with orange-brown sails, burnt sienna sails, multi-coloured and striped sails. These colours came into my mind's eye seventy two years later when the painting of an Island in the Lagoon with, in the foreground, a boat with furled, multi-coloured and striped sails, was shown on "The Antiques Roadshow". The suggested dating of the painting of 1900-1910 seemed all wrong, as I had always believed that he went to paint in Venice shortly before the 1914-1918 war. In 1916 there were pictures of the Lagoon and fishing boats in the studio, and I remember others, though not so many, in 1917. After 1917 I cannot remember seeing any Venice paintings – presumably they had all been sold. Knowing of his output in later years, and how quickly he seemed to sell his pictures, I was sure that the Venice paintings were only just pre-war, and a sketchbook owned by George's niece, with a Venice sketch dated 1913, confirms this.

Tryfan [Butler collection].

6. George Cockram, Artist & Gentleman.

## His Early Life

George Cockram was born on March 9th, 1861 at Birkenhead. His father, William Cockram, a coachbuilder, had moved from Leicester to Liverpool in about 1847. George was one of twelve children. The only other boy to survive was Stephen, born 1866 and died 1938, who was a fairly well-to-do fruit merchant. (After an illness Stephen stayed at Rhosneigr with the Cockrams where my family and I met him). His grandson, the only male Cockram surviving lives in Johannesburg. The Cockram family bible is in the possession of Mr William Leece, George's great-nephew.

He was educated at Liverpool Institute School, and in 1884 studied under John Furnis at Liverpool School of Art. After leaving, he was employed as a catalogue illustrator for Turner Dunette, Printers, of St James Street, Liverpool.

He exhibited his first picture at the Royal Academy when he was twenty-two, and from 1883 to 1924 he was a regular exhibitor at the Royal Institute of Painters in Watercolours and at the Royal Academy of Art, Conway. He was a member of Liverpool Academy of Arts and the Royal Cambrian Society before 1895.[2] He was commissioned to paint a postage-sized picture for Queen Mary's dolls house, and his painting 'Solitude' is in the Tate Gallery, having been purchased by the Chantrey Bequest.

2. Cockram was elected to the Royal Cambrian Academy (RCA) in 1890.

"Solitude" was purchased by 'The Chantrey Bequest' and is now in 'The Tate Gallery', London. [Tate Gallery Collection].

6. George Cockram, Artist & Gentleman.

On May 8th, 1890 he married Lucy Mary Bolongaro Cole, elder daughter of John Henry Cole R.A., at the Chapel of our Lady, Llandudno. They had two daughters Mary Doris (Kit) who married Frederick Bancroft Turner, Stipendiary Magistrate for Salford and, later Manchester (three of his Cockram's were bequeathed to the Whitworth Art Gallery, Manchester); and the second daughter, Winifred Edna, who served in the Ambulance Service during World War 1 and as a Health Officer in Kensington in World War II.

George Cockram was not a big man physically. My father, who was five feet ten inches tall, was definitely taller, and I would estimate that he was about five feet eight inches. He and my father were alike in that neither of them carried any spare flesh. They also both wore fine tweed suits, my father's usually greyish herringbone, and Mr Cockram's brown, with no definite pattern. He wore a brown trilby hat well down over his eyes, so that the sun did not stop him seeing the true colours of everything. When he was in his studio and took off his hat, his high and slightly sloping forehead was pink, while from halfway down his nose his face was tanned and weathered. His nose was pointed from his chin firm, and he always had a moustache.[3] His hair had receded a little with the years, but he had no bald spot. He had some grey hairs, but there were far more dark ones.

George Cockram section enlarged from the Plas Mawr photo on p85. [RCA collection].

As a young man he went to stay many times, with other young men, to paint pictures in the Conway Valley. I think near Llanwrst. On one of our visits to the studio he told us that the Welsh farmers in that area spoke very little English, and their lack of fluency could lead to misunderstandings. They also invented their own idioms, which stuck, as it was well-nigh impossible to break the habit. The young painters were staying with a Welsh lady in the 1880's who always spoke of "ahn egg", and would ask if they wanted "one ahn egg or two ahn eggs. One day expecting a friend to join them for tea, they instructed the lady that she should ask him if he would like one egg or two eggs, and not refer to "ahn egg". The friend arrived before their return from a day's painting, and they were agog to hear what she had said to him. Needless to say, she had asked, "would you like one ahn egg or two ahn eggs?"

On another occasion they were up a hillside, where they met a distressed farmer. They enquired what was wrong, and were told, "I have lost four ships". As the Conway in that area was only really suitable for rowing boats, they were very puzzled. Later they realised that the farmer had lost four sheep – much more likely!

George Cockram was a self-effacing man, and never held forth on his achievements, but he knew his worth, and was content to go on painting to give himself and others pleasure. Had he been more flamboyant, he might have been better known. Following a request for personal information, he wrote in 1905 to the curator of Oldham Art Gallery, "Exhibited my first picture at the R.A. when seventeen years of age"[4] Commissioned to contribute a postage-size painting of Queen Mary's Doll House, exhibited at the Wembley Exhibition in 1923/4, he told us that the letter sent to him had asked for a typical Cockram. He used a brush with about 3 hairs in it to paint so small a picture. I never knew what was the subject, but when he went to see it, he found it stored with many others in a set of drawers.

[3]. Photos of him at a younger age do not show an obvious moustache.
[4]. The Royal Academy records note that his first exhibition entry was in 1883, when Cockram would have been 22.

6. George Cockram, Artist & Gentleman.

After his death, his younger daughter went to Australia and New Zealand to see her father's pictures in the galleries out there. She had the same sense of humour as her father, and she told us of the concern at one gallery when they could not find "The Cockram!" She found it amusing that, after the attack on Pearl Harbour, when the contents of Australian art galleries were hastily dispersed to private houses, "The Cockram" had missed being booked out! I wonder if they have found it yet? George was 55 when I first met him, but he did not seem an elderly man, probably because of his wide interests and very active mind. Typically, the family would be walking along the road towards the station, and we would meet him with his little easel, his three legged stool with a leather seat, and his canvas shoulder bag with paints, water and other impedimenta, all very safe and looking comfortable to carry. We would all stop and chat for a few minutes, then he would say "I have something in the studio that I would like you to see". There would follow a pause while he considered which afternoon was free. Then – "would Monday about 4pm be all right?" After saying goodbye, he was off to the spot where he was painting the unfinished picture often wrapped in brown paper.

In the main George Cockram painted seascapes, beaches, mountains and landscapes. His home for many years was in Rhosneigr, where he stayed from the time gorse came into bloom until the end of September. Then, I think, he went to Ogwen Cottage, now a youth hostel, by the path up to Llyn Idwal, where he painted Tryfan, Llyn Ogwen, Idwal and the Devil's Kitchen. As he showed us one of these pictures he would say where it was – he knew that the district was well known to us, as we travelled along the A5. One day he told us that in a boulder under a bridge, where *[detailed location not included to preserve its mystery – Ed.]* there was a beautiful, perfect fossil. He didn't tell anyone, so that nobody would arrive with a little hammer and remove it. I suppose it is now long gone.

Beach at Evening Sunset, (Queen's dolls' house painting). Actual size 1.5" x 1", 37 x 25mm [Royal collection].

"In a boulder under a bridge."

When the Autumn tints started to appear, he moved to Betws-y-coed, and painted there until the end of November when the leaves fell. My mother said she would like a picture of autumn leaves and was very surprised when he said he would paint them in November. In Rochdale, the leaves on our trees started to go dry and brittle during August, and all had gone just after the middle of September – so no autumn tints. It had always struck us that trees in North Wales possessed a variety of colours unfamiliar to us – our industrial pollution was such that, if you touched a tree, your hands were black.

I don't know what he did after Betws in his younger days, but from, I think, the 1920's he spent the winter in Cookham, on the Thames. He did that for three or four years, but we didn't like the Cookham pictures as much as the others. I couldn't work out why, until I saw Cookham from the air during a Treasure Hunt programme, but then I knew the reason at once. It was far too well manicured; the trees even looked as if they dare not have a leaf out of place. Having lived 51 years with a fairly close view of the Lancashire Pennines, Cookham seemed too soft and lush to me.

Bluebells at Kew.

After Cookham, Mr & Mrs Cockram spent the winter in Hale, south of Manchester, near where their elder daughter, Mrs Frederick Bancroft Turner lived. Mr Bancroft Turner gave three Cockram's to the Whitworth Art Gallery after his wife's death. It was at Hale that he worked on completing pictures started during the summer, and framing them.

"Within the Sound of the Sea" [Butler colllection].

## My Twenty First Birthday Present

My sister's twenty first birthday was early in 1924 – before the slump started. Apart from presents she received a useful sum of money. When next we went to Rhosneigr and saw Mr Cockram and his pictures, she fell for a middle-sized one of a cornfield with stooks, a glimpse of the sea in the distance and, nearer, a little piece of the Maelog Lake.

When I became twenty one, nine years later, the slump, which hit everyone, was at its height. I had presents and gifts of money, but these only totalled about six pounds, and I kept wondering what to do with it. I wanted something which I would keep and value. I wondered if Mr Cockram would let me buy a corner of one of his pictures, and my mother suggested that I ask him on my next visit.

At last we went to Rhosneigr and met him on the road, with his easel, folding stool and canvas shoulder bag. After a chat he said as usual, "I have something at the studio which I would like you to see". Then a pause, while he decided which day would be convenient, "Wednesday, four o'clock; is that all right for you?"

So in due course we arrived and sat on the settle while Mr Cockram displayed his pictures as usual. His output was prolific and, except for the big pictures on the two very solid easels, his sales kept pace with his output. He chatted away as he showed his pictures, talking about their surroundings, telling comic stories. When he had shown us what he had intended us to see, I said, "Mr Cockram, I was twenty one in January, and I had some money given to me. It's not very much about six guineas. Could I buy a corner of one of your pictures?" I had seen one or two very small, framed sketches, about 5 inches square, and that was what I had I thought of.

76    6. George Cockram, Artist & Gentleman.

He smiled and said "I'll have to see what I can find," and he went round the studio. It was obvious that he knew every picture and where it was, and so, in a very short time, he had found four small ones. He put each on the easel, as if it were an important picture, and let me have time to have a really good look. When I had seen all four, he said "Which do you like best?" Mr reply was prompt; "The sunset, how much is it?" He gave me a lovely smile and said, "can you spring another guinea?" I looked at my mother, and she nodded, so I turned back to Mr Cockram and said, "yes, please can I buy the sunset?"

At the time I was working the family business, a forty eight hour week for under two pounds, I gave my mother my wage packet and she gave me my pocket money, keeping account of the rest in a little book. She had a better idea of my finances than I did – so I had to look for her approval before I could say "yes".

A couple of days later, Mother said to me "Winifred, I think that the picture you have bought from Mr Cockram should have been more than seven guineas. It is Mr Cockram's way of giving you a present; it is only a very nice man who does something like that".

If that were so, I could never thank him personally for his kindness, but I have never forgotten it. The remembrance of buying that picture is still very clear fifty six years later. Wanting to buy something I would keep and value was true; 'The Sunset' is on the wall opposite my bed, and it is what I see every morning when I wake.

One day having been invited to the studio, we arrived to find that Mr Cockram had either not been watching the time, or, for once had forgotten that we were coming. He had a large watercolour out of its frame, and was holding it upright on a table which was covered with newspaper. He had a wash brush and a container of phenol solution. He said "Please excuse me, I can't stop in the middle of doing this.

The picture is mildewed and I must paint it all over with this solution rapidly – it must not dry".

So we sat and watched him. He dipped the wash brush in the solution, painted straight across the whole picture, and then repeated the process, the edge of the brush just covering the edge of the previous wash. When he was about half way down, he started to laugh. The picture looked terrible; the paper had turned yellowy-brown and the colours of the paint were practically unrecognisable. Then he said "It's a good thing the owner can't see this now – she'd have a fit!" Still laughing, he proceeded to paint over the rest of the picture. As he worked he said "I am doing this for an artist who passed on. I hope that someone will do the same for my pictures when I have gone".

When he had finished painting the phenol solution all over the picture, he explained that the solution would kill the mildew fungi and that, once they had dried out, the paper and the paint would regain their former colours. He would then put the picture on a flat table, get a thin knife with a very sharp edge on the blade, lay the knife flat and slide the blade over the surface. That would remove the mildew which had grown on the paper without doing any damage.

"The Evening Tide" (the correct title of Winifred's 'Sunset' painting) [Butler collection].

## The Big Pebble

Near the mooring rocks at Rhosneigr, there is a large boulder, known locally as 'The Big Pebble' or 'The Crab'. It has a flat top and is wedged firmly in the indigenous rocks so that, when there are extra high tides, it is possible to dive off it. In the last Ice Age it travelled a great distance with the ice and was finally deposited where it now lies. There are no other rocks of that sort near.

"The Big Pebble" Postcard by Wickens, postmarked 1913. Unfortunately, the artist at the easel is too indistinct to be able to identify as George.

George Cockram told us its history when he showed us a painting of it. Some time ago I received a photograph of a picture featuring the big pebble. I knew the owner as a small boy, when his family were on holiday at the same time as us. Maybe it was that picture we saw when Mr Cockram told us the story of the ice-borne boulder. One of the Cockram's owned by the Walker Art Gallery in Liverpool – 'The Lonely Shore' – also features the big pebble.

On one occasion, while showing us a picture of the Welsh mountains, he said "when I was young I saw pictures with blue mountains, but I did not really believe they could look so blue – until the first time I went to North Wales. I got off the train, and there, from the platform, I saw the mountains for the first time – they were blue!"

I think it was one morning when we met George near Noddfa (his home after he had sold The Dunes), and he said, "Do come here and look at this". He showed us a small watercolour of an old man with a round, red face. Inside the frame, between the picture and the glass, was a dead furniture beetle, "look" he said. "It chose the wrong direction in getting out of the wooden backing. There is the hole; because it could not get through the glass, it died". He was very amused at the idea of a beetle getting lost.

One day, while showing us a painting of a sunset, Mr Cockram said that some years before, he and his wife were taking an evening stroll in front of The Dunes. They had met an elderly neighbour and were admiring the sunset together, when the old lady said "It is very funny; sometimes the sun sets over there and sometimes over here!" He was very amused that she had never realised that where the sun sets depends on the time of year.

Once, in the late 1940's so far as I can remember, we had gone to the studio a few days after his customary roadside invitation – "There is something I want to show you." (He never said which picture it was he wanted us to see when he showed them to us – I think it was his way of giving an apparent purpose to a visit).

On this occasion as he put the pictures on the easel one at a time, chatting away all the time, I noticed that he kept talking about Jim. I couldn't think of anyone of that name whom we and Mr Cockram knew so I was puzzled. Then I suddenly realised that 'Jim' was Mrs Cockram! The Mrs Cockram I knew was a dignified lady and inclined to be portly. It was very hard to imagine her as a young and agile Jim, as she was described to us. As I thought about the incident recently, I remembered something my husband had once said to me out of the blue – "Winifred, you still look the same to me as when we first met. You haven't changed". My very dark brown hair had by then become white and our first meeting had been well over thirty years before. So, perhaps, when George Cockram looked at 'Jim', he still saw the Jim of over fifty years before. It is a nice thought!

Undated postcard circa late 1940s by Valentine's showing the lower High Street and Russian-born Carl Balkin & his wife, Annie's Antique and fishing tackle shop.

Large stock of genuine Antiques of every description

Expert advice given

A. BALKIN
ANTIQUE DEALER
RHOSNEIGR

Also every kind of Fresh or Sea Water fishing tackle kept in stock

## You Can Tell its old by The Hinges

There was a family run shop in Rhosneigr which sold antiques and fishing tackle, the antiques were unpolished, the shop unattractive, the fishing tackle not much more than hooks and reels. On fine days, the contents of the shop edged onto the footpath, and a wooden chair with arms was occupied by the father of the family. He was very well upholstered and nearly all the chair disappeared from view when he sat there, practically immobile. There were few customers, and we often wondered how they made a living. Sometimes the sons went on an expedition in a rickety vehicle and returned with a couple of antiques from a sale or some farmer or cottager.

One afternoon when we turned up at Mr Cockram's studio at his invitation; he was in high spirits, and led us to a cupboard which stood between the settle and the storeroom. "Now, look at these hinges. The old hinges were completely worn out, but I found a craftsman blacksmith who has made exact replicas of them. This afternoon the younger son from the antique shop delivered an order for me, and he passed this cupboard on his way to the storeroom, he stopped and admired it, drawing attention to different parts. As he was leaving, the young expert added: 'You can tell it's very old by the hinges'.

George continued laughing and chuckling as he told us "They've only been on a few weeks!" It had made his day.

This postcard dates from the late 1920's and shows (from left to right) The Dunes, Tan-y-Fron and Tre-Iago in the foreground, with the imposing Frongogh and Frondeg in the background.

The Dunes was built in 1895 on a plot of land purchased from Sir George Meyrick on 3rd February 1893 for £100. Cockram lived there until 1925 when The Dunes was sold to Henry Palethorpe and the Cockrams moved to Noddfa further along the road. (Noddfa is now the home of another resident Rhosneigr artist, Brian Entwistle.)

## The Studio

The Dunes, which George had bought when he had married, and where he had his studio, had been sold before we first met him, and from 1916-1919 he worked in various rented buildings in Rhosneigr.

In 1919 or 1920 he built a wooden framed asbestos-sheeted building on the piece of land he had kept when he sold the Dunes, his niece, Pauline and I visited the site shortly after work started. The workmen were digging trenches for the walls, and were told in no uncertain terms that we were not welcome! We did not go again until it was finished.

At last it was completed. It was rectangular in shape, with a fireplace, behind which was a small narrow room in which he kept his materials. The shorter sides of the building faced east and west, with the door on the south side, and the window, under which was a settle, on the north. Between the settle and the storeroom there was an antique cupboard, very dark oak, with a lot of carving. At the far end was a corner fitment, taller than the table height and also heavily carved and black, on which sometimes stood a painting.

Along the west wall was a dresser on which, for many years, stood a small picture with a hedgebank, hedge and a gnarled tree. It may have been a study for larger work. The south and west walls were stacked with pictures, two or three or more deep, mostly on their stretchers.

On the carpet – greyish blue with a small all over pattern, stood two large, heavy wooden easels on castors, usually each of these carried a big picture shrouded in green woollen material. Often these pictures remained for several years, and then they went. There was one magnificent one that stayed longer than most; it was of rain deluging down – very grey. Not, I think, a view most people would want to live with, but eventually that too was sold.

There was also a smaller, lighter easel on which he showed his pictures, with a couple of chairs and a buffet or two. We would sit in a row on the settle to view pictures. Mr Cockram would put one on the easel and, if it was of Rhosneigr, he would describe it. "That is round by............. you know, where the.......... is and the path goes...........".

As we studied the pictures, he chatted away. He told us how the Old Masters ground lapis for their paints. He showed us paint he had just bought, viridian green and others. He felt that Turner had been born too soon, before the development of fast watercolours. It was not easy, he said, to make sand look wet, and on another occasion he explained how difficult it was to keep sand looking flat. Sometime we were shown pictures in the course of completion – a Coal Boat at the Mooring rocks. The Old Man leaning, once, he had just received some large sheets of special painting paper, and unrolled one end. He said they were of a quality he had not seen for some time, but he had only been able to get four or five sheets. He was pleased as punch to have them.

After his death, his second daughter, Edna had the studio demolished and built a small bungalow on the site for her own use. The walls of the sitting room were painted gloss white with a beautiful, large seascape on the wall, and other of her father's pictures round the room.

Cockram's studio (on the extreme right here) was built at the back of The Dunes. Sometime in the mid 1950s, a couple of years after George's tragic death, a house named 'Studio Gate', was built there for George Cockram's youngest daughter Edna. Postcard published by D.C.Evans, Bon Marche, Rhosneigr.

## Flower Paintings in the Winter

George Cockram started to paint flower pictures sometime in the 1930's, after he was seventy, when he found he couldn't keep warm outside in the colder weather. His fingers became so cold and stiff that they could not control his brushes to his satisfaction – and he was a perfectionist.

It is not as strange as it might seem that a painter of the sea, shores, mountains and landscapes should turn to flowers. He painted pictures of gorse every year, and I have a small picture called 'The Warren', with ragwort and rabbits, and, in the foreground a foxglove. Also in the early years of our visits to the studio there was a painting of oriental poppies. Somebody's gardener had put a root on a rubbish tip, where it flourished exceedingly. Behind the rubbish heap was a whitewashed wall, and the painting of the red flowers with bright green leaves against the whitewash was breathtaking. Several years later my mother remarked after a visit that she wished he would paint some more poppies, but, so far as I know, he never did. *[Editor's note – yes, there is one in my collection.]*

His 'Anemones' is a beautiful picture and the Medici Society bought the copyright and produced postcards and a small framed print. We were in Rhosneigr when the original was returned, and visited the studio just after it had been unpacked. He remarked that he was not allowed to sell it for eighteen months. My sister had a good look at it and asked the price, and told him that she would like to buy it as soon as he could sell it.

A few years after 'Anemones' was published, he wanted to give a friend a small present and decided on one of the Medici framed prints. In the Medici shop in London he asked if he might have a copy of 'Anemones' by George Cockram. The assistant said "that is the best anemone picture we have". Mr Cockram replied "Thank you very much – I painted it". He told us the story, but not the assistant's reaction.

George Cockram knew a lot about wild flowers. One day. When showing us a picture, he asked "Do you know the sea bindweed? It grows just round there (pointing at the picture); it is pink and very pretty, and it grows right across the path to the shore by the Coastguards". On another occasion he said "There is a lovely patch of Bloody Cranesbill on the path around the corner from the Post Office". I had been watching it come out every day as I passed. The flowers were purplish-crimson and about an inch across; a very striking colour.

He grew a very unusual succulent plant on the south-facing bank outside the studio, and told us that it grew on the cliffs at Bournemouth, but hardly anywhere else. He was very pleased that it flourished at Rhosneigr.

I can only remember one other flower picture in detail – of forsythia – but I know I thought his flower studies were beautiful pictures.

## Tyn-y-Cai Pool, Betws-y-Coed

In 1923 my mother decided to give my father a Cockram for his fiftieth birthday the following year. I remember her discussing with Mr Cockram the theme – a picture of Betws-y-coed, showing the river and the trees turning colour. When we visited the studio in the Summer of 1924, there it was – the salmon pool at Betws. The water looked really wet, and the variation of the Autumn tints were amazing. We all liked the picture immensely. It cost Mother 45 guineas.

Anemones [Butler Collection].

Oriental Poppies.

Gorse Banks, Cymyran Bay.

6. *George Cockram, Artist & Gentleman.* **83**

## In The End

George Cockram died in September 1950 in Rhosneigr and is interred at Hale Cemetery, Cheshire, and so there was a considerable quantity of unfinished work. After these had been sorted out, those which were near completion were put on sale, and we each bought a picture different from any in our possession. Father bought one of the Maelog Lake (rushes in lovely shades of brown), my sister one of rough seas and rocks, and I bought one which I think he painted a considerable time before. It is of the Conway Valley in Spring, with a willow coming into leaf, a good spring breeze, fresh grass and mountains in the distance.

The Gathering Dusk. [Private collection].

Waves [Butler Collection].

84   6. George Cockram, Artist & Gentleman.

George Cockram seated in the centre of this group, also taken at the Royal Cambrian Academy c. late 1890s. [RCA collection].

Royal Cambrian Academy at Plas Mawr, Conway, c1897. George Cockram is standing in the centre of the front row (no beard). Clarence Whaite is standing on his left (long white beard), George Harrison on his right (short grey beard) and Lester Sutcliffe immediately behind him (in the hat). [RCA collection].

# Artist Dies of Burns

Mr George Cockram. R.A., aged 89, landscape painter, of Rhosneigr, Anglesey, died yesterday without regaining consciousness as a result of burns. He had been found enveloped in flames from a paraffin heater in his locked studio by a taxi driver.

Mr William Hughes, aged 49, Hillside, Rhosneigr, the taxi driver, knocked at the studio door where Mr Cockram was presumably painting, but receiving no answer looked through the letter-box and saw flames. He burst open the door, found Cockram enveloped in flames and dragged him away. After putting out the flames Hughes ran for assistance.

Dr Wilson was called and he examined Cockram who is stated to have said, "I must have fainted".

# Coachbuilder's Son

Mr Cockram was lodging at Bodawen, about 150 yards from the studio and he shared his time between Hale, Cheshire and Rhosneigr.

The son of a Leicester coachbuilder, Mr Cockram was born in Birkenhead. He exhibited his first picture at the Royal Academy when he was eighteen. He adopted watercolour as his medium, and was a frequent exhibitor of drawings at the Royal Academy, the Royal Institute of Painters in Water Colours and leading provincial galleries. Liverpool Art Gallery bought his work "The Lonely Shore". Other works are to be found in the Corporation permanent collections of Hull, Oldham, Birkenhead, Dudley, Stretford and Bournemouth.

Mr Cockram was married in 1890 to Lucy Mary, daughter of Mr J H Cole. R.C.A. and had two daughters.

Liverpool Daily Post (Welsh Edition)
Thursday September 28th 1950

# Chapter 7
# The Owens &
# Florence Nightingale

Paran is described as a Calvinistic Methodist Chapel but is also now part of the Presbyterian Church of Wales. Welsh Presbyterian Churches were religiously a lot 'stronger' than the English Presbyterian Churches.

Paran was first built in 1827 and renovated in 1850, 1857 and 1867. It was rebuilt again in 1887. Though active and thriving during most of the 20th Century, congregations have gradually dwindled away. Paran now only has a small congregation and is struggling to make ends meet.

When the Chapel House was sold off in 2015 (for around £200,000) all the receipts had to be passed down to 'head office' in Cardiff, despite the fact that refurbishment costs continue to mount. Any donations would be gratefully received.

[Photos: enlarged section from 1893 photo on page 166 showing Paran from the beach (top), more recent images below].

# 7. The Owens & Florence Nightingale

Owen was an intriguing man. Born in 1874, his childhood was spent in the Bryngwran area close to Lake Traffwll, and he stayed on at school to become a Pupil Teacher. His training continued in Bangor and in 1895, at the age of 21, he qualified as a science teacher, taking up his first posting in the rural hamlet of Joy's Green in the Forest of Dean, Gloucestershire. In 1898, after working there for a couple of years, he took up a more senior post in Clay Cross, Derbyshire, where he spent the next decade of his life.

It was there where he met his future wife, Gwen, and gradually moved from teaching, into school administration and then into the Law. He joined the Middle Temple, trained as a barrister, and was called to the bar in 1909. He and Gwen, moved to Muswell Hill, north of London, where she took up a career in publishing and he continued to practice law.

At around the time of the first World War and partly for health reasons, Owen and his wife moved back up to Anglesey and settled in Rhosneigr – by this time a thriving and popular holiday village. Owen changed career again, training and practising as a solicitor and throwing himself into village life. He played golf, became a freemason and went to chapel.

Owen and his wife, Gwen, lived for a time at 'Seaforth' on Warren Road, before moving to 'Ashton' at No.5 Station Road.

Owen wrote two romantic novels and possibly others under a pseudonym that have not yet come to light. Both were originally serialised just before the start of the first World War in the Welsh Language newspaper, 'Y Genedl Gymreig' *[The Welsh Nation]*

William David Owen, 1874-1925, Author of 'Madam Wen' [photo: Sara Richards collection].

There was a great deal of religious prejudice in the 19th Century against fiction, as it was thought to pollute the minds of young people. However, there were those who aimed to reverse this prejudice by creating novels of the highest moral standards. One person taking advantage of the new demand for this style of fiction, was Rhosneigr's William David Owen.

'Ashton' at No.5 Station Rd. Morristown, Rhosneigr. Valentine's postcard postmarked August 1924.

## Elin Cadwaladr

Owen's first, but little known, romance is entitled 'Elin Cadwaladr'. It is principally set around Rhosneigr and the Anglesey parish of Llanfaelog, which Owen parodies as 'Bryn Siriol' *[Pleasant Hill]*. Contrasting the traditional way of life, with the growing popularity of the new holiday village, he weaves a tale amongst petty parochialism, national politics and the relentlessness of tuberculosis, from which Owen himself eventually died.

The following extract is from chapter one:

*Bryn Siriol is a village, and also a parish, in the hundred of Hirfon, on the island of Anglesey. Although the parish boundaries are more than five miles from the sea, there are places in the district from which its shores can be clearly seen on fine days. But Bryn Siriol is an agricultural district. Until recently its inhabitants took little interest in the splendid sands of the Big Beach. But after it became a Mecca for strangers from the towns of England, in search of health, and after a trim little townlet was built on the sandbanks, some enthusiasm was kindled in Bryn Siriol. The price of butter went up. The price of eggs rose too.*

*The people of the parish are people who work hard, and live hard. They laugh when they see the Englishmen of the Big Beach walking miles in all weathers through the heather and ferns after a small white ball. They laugh just as heartily when they hear the English talking about health rules and the relationship between sick cattle and consumption. But let no-one jump to the conclusion that the people of Bryn Siriol lack sense. They are astute and thoughtful people; men of mental abilities stronger than the usual amidst country folk and wise, skillful women...*

"To the south side of the lake and half encircling it, are the fields of Traffwll. Here, years ago, the gorse grew tall and thick, forming a dense forest, and, in the shadows of that dark forest lurked Madam Wen's cave at the edge of the water".

## Madam Wen

Owen's best known story, however, is 'Madam Wen'. It is based on the Anglesey legend of the same name and tells the story of Morys Williams, an honest country squire, and his love for Einir Wyn, a beautiful and intelligent woman of society who, unbeknown to him, leads a double life as Madam Wen, the leader of a band of robbers and smugglers.

Early edition of 'Madam Wen'.

An extract from the foreword to his novel gives some insight into the adventure to follow:

*Tradition had little to say about the career of Madam Wen and what it did say was misleading. Were it not for a discovery that was made some time ago it would not have been possible to write the chapters which follow.*

*To search for the home of Madam Wen one must go to the south-west of Anglesey, to an area which could be called the District of the Lakes. There are three lakes of substantial size, the biggest of the three being Traffwll Lake. To the south side of the lake and half encircling it, are the fields of Traffwll. Here, years ago, the gorse grew tall and thick, forming a dense forest, and, in the shadows of that dark forest lurked Madam Wen's cave at the edge of the water.*

7. The Owens & Florence Nightingale

*Late one summer's day, a man from the area was sitting on a tree trunk near the cave gazing at the silvery face of the lake. His meditations may have strayed back to childhood, when any mention of Madam Wen endowed the cave and its surroundings with a kind of magic. Whatever the reason, he was overcome by an urge to go and explore the cave.*

*It was somewhat stealthily, and fearing that someone would see him, that he took a mattock and a spade, went to the cave, and started to dig at the far end. It did not surprise him in the least when the tip of the mattock went straight through, revealing the true entrance to Madam Wen's underground hiding place...*

By 1925, Owen had made up his mind that 'Madam Wen' should be published as a book. During that year, he continued to work as a solicitor whilst adapting the previously serialised story for publication. Unfortunately, his own health deteriorated at the same time, and barely 2 weeks after receiving the first copies of his newly-published novel, Owen sadly died from tuberculosis. He was just 51 years old.

'Madam Wen' received enormous critical acclaim after his death and the legacy of the romance still lives on today. In 1982, S4C, the newly set up Welsh language version of Channel Four, decided to make 'Madam Wen' their first Christmas film. As a result, the making of the film on Anglesey during 1982 and subsequent press coverage in 1983 revived the legend and the author.

The film became controversial for being significantly over-budget and for its largely unsuccessful attempts to depict an (obviously model) ship at sea in a storm.

Of course, all of this has been virtually invisible to those of us who are non Welsh speaking residents of, or visitors to, Rhosneigr, as both the 'Madam Wen' and 'Elin Cadwaladr' stories were written entirely in Welsh and had never before been translated into English.

Knowing that both novels had interesting Rhosneigr references, I wanted to read them, and so an (abridged) English translation of 'Madam Wen' was commissioned followed up by a similar translation of 'Elin Cadwaladr'.

The translations turned into a book, and "The Rhosneigr Romanticist"[1] was published in 2009. It includes both these stories, together with a detailed biography of William David Owen himself.

Owen was clearly a man of principle with an appreciation of religion and politics – and the humour within them both - at a period when great changes in society were taking place. He drew inspiration in his writing from his early years as a schoolteacher, from the community he later served as a solicitor and of course, from his many family influences – including links through his sister to Florence Nightingale.

---

[1]. The Rhosneigr Romanticist, ISBN 978-0956296207.

## Working for Florence Nightingale

Owen's elder sister Ellen, who in later life lived at Bronant on Rhosneigr High Street, was born in 1867 and left school in her middle teens.

Her recently widowed mother was trying to make a living as a dressmaker and her brother William and younger sister Sarah, were still at school. Ellen would have had little choice but to try to find work and went into domestic service at an early age. At some point she encountered, and went to work for, the Verney family.

The Verney family were major landowners with a number of properties on Anglesey at that time, and had a sizeable complement of staff. Margaret Verney (née Hay Williams) was related to Florence Nightingale through marriage and lived at Plas Rhianfa, on the banks of the Menai Straits (now converted into the 'Chateau Rhianfa' hotel). The family also had a holiday house at Rhoscolyn, known as 'Plas Rhoscolyn'.

So it was that sometime around 1885, at the age of eighteen, Ellen, who became known as Nelly, began to work for the Verneys as a housemaid at Rhoscolyn, and later at Rhianfa.

Margaret Verney must have thought quite highly of Nelly, for it is clear that she had recommended her to Florence Nightingale, who on April 12th 1886 writes:

"do you know, I shall be so pleased to try that girl you mentioned - the little housemaid at Rhoscolyn".

Florence wanted her to be a "half housemaid and half kitchen maid" at her South Street home in London and was "very glad...of the prospect of having Nelly Owen".

Nelly worked for Florence Nightingale for around seven years in total, and from the correspondence between them we can see that they mostly had a good relationship.[2]

Nelly Owen, sister Sarah & their mother, Jane on the steps of 'Bronant' c1910. [photo: Bryngwran School collection].

Her responsibilities grew over the years, and Nelly gradually took on more duties in the kitchen, later becoming Florence's cook. However, Florence was fastidious about her food and it is not altogether clear that Nelly always lived up to Florence's expectations.

**2.** Correspondence in the Verney Collection, part of Claydon House Trust Archives.

On Lady Day[3] 1890 Florence gave Nelly a small book by Lady Barker entitled "First Lessons in the Principles of Cooking". (A short extract of which is shown in panel 7a).

Florence also wrote a personal inscription in the book as follows:

"The Modern Giant Killer tames the three giants who used to do mischief - Water, Fire, Steam: instead of killing them: & cooks good & wholesome meals every day of the year."

This book, though physically small in size could best be described as a fairly technical manual. Though Florence's inscription was clearly intended to motivate Nelly Owen, it may have had the opposite effect, as barely a week later, on April 1st 1890, Margaret Verney wrote to Florence:

"If you have not found any suitable place for Nelly Owen by the time we return to London about the 15th, I am sure I could find her a situation by talking it over with Mrs Hunt, she has a registry office in Duke St, where so many of our friends inquire (sic) for servants. How good you have been to Nelly Owen, she will never be so much considered again".

"If I can hear of another Nelly Owen, I will let you know, alas cooks are most difficult, I do not know of one, Maude recommends Miss Paget, who interests herself in getting servants places, I believe she is Sir James' daughter, if I can see her for you, pray let me know."

Nelly left Florence Nightingale's employment and the 1891 census shows her working for James D. Hill of Onslow Gardens, Kensington – an Australian Merchant and Shipowner. This was a bigger household than Florence Nightingale's with twice as many servants and whilst it is possible that Nelly has seized an opportunity – it is perhaps more likely that the Hills were well acquainted with the Verneys, and the opportunity was by word of mouth and only a temporary arrangement.

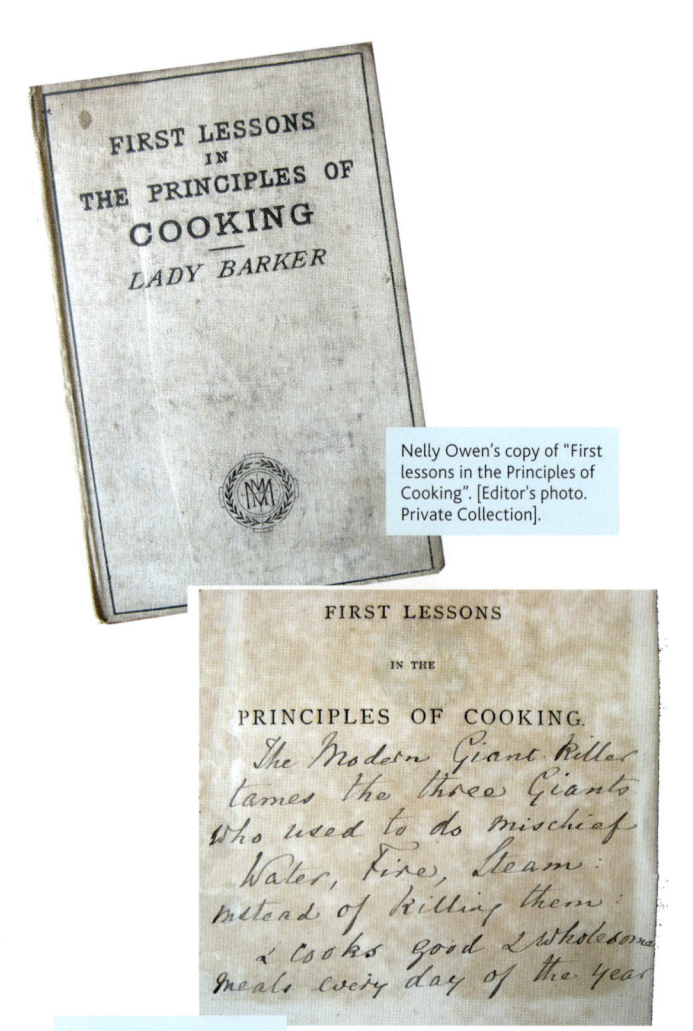

Nelly Owen's copy of "First lessons in the Principles of Cooking". [Editor's photo. Private Collection].

Inscription to Nelly Owen by Florence Nightingale. [Editor's photo. Private Collection].

3. Lady Day is March 25th.
4. Lady Barker became the Superintendant of the National Training School of Cooking in South Kensington.

One of the last photos of Nelly Owen with her pet tortoise in the lane behind 'Bronant' c1950.

**BRONANT**

Apartments:
2 SITTING, 4 BEDROOMS.

Sea View.

Misses OWEN.

Advertisement from the 1926 'Guide to Rhosneigr'.

Some time afterwards, Nelly returned to the Verney family, and a year later, in January 1892, Florence wrote to Nelly asking her to return to South Street as her cook "as soon as Mrs Verney can spare you".

Florence took Nelly back on as her cook in January 1892, but clearly all does not go well and by August of the same year, Nelly and Florence had parted company for good. Nelly returned to work for the Verney family, and later for other employers, before returning to Rhosneigr in 1904 to look after her sister Sarah, who was ill with pneumonia, and their elderly mother.

Nelly Owen was interviewed in 1951 about her time with Florence Nightingale, and remembered her fondly:

"She was a kind and gentle lady who loved everyone. No one was too humble to Miss Nightingale. She had a kind word for everyone - the wicked as well as the good."

Nelly & Sarah Owen took in summer visitors at Bronant until Nelly's death in 1954 and Sarah's in 1960 and they are both remembered with affection.

The following text is from chapter one of 'The Principles of Cooking'.

> The day has come in English social history when it is absolutely the bounden duty of every person at the head of a household - whether that household be large or small, rich or poor - to see that no waste is permitted in the preparation of food for the use of the family under his or her care. I am quite aware that such waste cannot be cured by theories, and that nothing except a practical acquaintance with the details of household management, supplemented by a conviction of the necessity of economy, can be expected to remedy the evil. At the same time, it is possible that ignorance of the fundamental principles of the chemical composition and of the relative nutritive value of the various sorts of food within our reach, added to the widespread ignorance of the most simple and wholesome modes of preparing such food, may be at the root of much of that waste.

[Panel 7a]

### Editor's Note:

*A longer and more comprehensive exploration of Nelly Owen & Florence Nightingale's relationship, together with her 1951 interview, is set out in 'The Rhosneigr Romanticist', pages 48-59.*

# Chapter 8
# Ken Rees & The Sandymount

The Sandy Mount Cafe, c1920. "High Class Luncheon & Tea Rooms".

The Sandymount Club 1989.

The Sandymount 2016. [Photo: Lisa Hale].

# 8. The Sandymount

Built in around 1902, The Sandymount and its other half, Craigside, were originally built as a Café and a Guest House. The original owners have unfortunately not been traced, but an advert from 1913 indicates F. Fleming at the helm.

**Sandy Mount Cafe.**

HIGH-CLASS LUNCHEON & TEA ROOMS

Apartments and Board. Bath (h. and c). Modern Conveniences.

Facing Sea. Central for Golf. Schools, Parties, &c., catered for.

Terms Moderate. Tariff on Application.
F. FLEMING

*Advert for the Sandy Mount Cafe from the 1913 "Guide to Rhosneigr".*

Frank Fleming and his wife Emmeline were listed in the electoral register for 1919 as occupying both properties. They ran the "Sandy Mount" as a Boarding House whilst its neighbour became a Branch of the National Provincial Bank of England.

In March 1945, Mrs Fleming died as a result of an accident and Frank died the following year. In April 1950 the Sandymount was advertised for sale as a going concern as an AA-Approved residential private hotel.

It was purchased by Bob & Betty Heaps who changed the boarding house/hotel into a private members club. An advantageous state as private clubs were allowed to open and serve alcohol on Sundays, at a time when public houses were not permitted to do so.

On their retirement in 1972 it was taken over by Ken & Mary Rees, about whom we shall learn more later.

Ken ran the club for about 10 years, after which his son Martyn ran it for a while in partnership with Charlie Parsons and his wife, Heather.

Larry & Jane Hughes bought the club in July 2002 and in the face of significant changes to the licensing regulations, changed the club into a straightforward Free House. At the time of writing, Larry and Jane too are planning on retiring, and the Sandymount club is once again on the market.

|  |  |
|---|---|
| 1902 | Built. |
| 1911 | census - no entry. |
| 1913 | Frank & Emmeline Fleming |
| 1950 | Bob & Betty Heaps |
| 1972 | Ken & Mary Rees |
| 1974 | Ken & Mary Rees + Martyn Rees |
| 1982 | Martyn Rees & Charlie Parsons |
| 1986 | Charlie & Heather Parsons |
| 2002 | Larry & Jane Hughes |

Ken was born in 1921 and brought up on his family's farm at Ruabon, Clwyd. He played a lot of rugby at school, winning Victor Ludorum[1] at junior, middle and senior level. He spent a 'dull and dreary' couple of years as apprentice in the drapery trade at Gorringe's in London, before six months at Agricultural college and then signing up with the RAF in the late 1930's, just before the outbreak of the Second World War.

Ken's autobiography[2] gives a good indication of the pressure that the RAF were under to get pilots up and running quickly.

Lectures on Maths, the Theory of Flight, Meteorology - and much more of the same were mandatory but:

"It didn't seem to matter that most of the lecturers were themselves only Volunteer Reserve Officers and barely knew any more than we did - they just kept one page ahead of us in the text books !"

Ken Rees on Broad Beach. One of several photographs taken to publicise his autobiography. [photo: Christopher Jones].

Ken Rees, who ran the Sandymount from 1972 to 1982 was the last surviving member of the team that tried to tunnel their way out of Stalag Luft III, during the Second World War - an event which led to the Steve McQueen 1963 blockbuster film 'The Great Escape'.

Ken was fortunate to survive the breakout - he was the last man to emerge from the tunnel while German shots rang out around him after they discovered the escape attempt. Ken rushed back to the camp along the tunnel on all fours after the Germans opened fire.

Only three of the eighty-one who escaped reached Britain - twenty-eight of the remainder were recaptured and sent back to POW camps, but tragically fifty were killed by the Nazis.

Postcard of Menai Bridge by Valentine's. Undated, c1920. From a painting by Brian Gerald.

However he passed successfully and became a fully qualified flying officer in 1941.

**1.** Literally 'the winner of the games'. The all-round champion.
**2.** "Lie in the Dark and Listen" by Ken Rees, published by Grub Street, London. Isbn 1-904010-77-6.

100    *8. Ken Rees & The Sandymount*

Ken married Mary Sinfield in 1942 and went on to have a distinguished career in the RAF, flying bombers such as the Whitley, the Wellington and the Lancaster.

As he comments in the introduction to his book:

> "When I was twenty-one I had already flown fifty-six missions, got married, been shot down into a remote Norwegian Lake, questioned by the Gestapo and sent to Stalag Luft III where I took part in what became known as The Great Escape."

After the war, he was demobbed from the RAF, only to rejoin again shortly afterwards and train as a Flying Instructor. He played more rugby, and raised a family - Martyn and Suzanne.

In fact, Ken Rees also enjoyed a top level rugby union career, playing for the likes of Birkenhead Park and Cheshire County as a flanker.

His playing style is said to have embodied the defiance and aggression that made him a thorn in the side of the Germans. He became the first North Walian to captain London Welsh and had a trial for Wales but failed to make the breakthrough, due to a previously dislocated thumb!

Ken retired from the RAF in 1968 at the age of forty-nine and ran a Post Office in Bangor on Dee for five years.

Ken knew Frank Wingett from school and it was Frank, in his capacity as an Anglesey and North Wales Estate Agent, who drew Ken's attention to The Sandymount, which had been put on the market by its current owners, Bob and Betty Heaps. Ken and Mary bought the club in 1972.

At the time it was a private members' club, with the special status of being a semi-official and quasi-approved Officer's club with the RAF at Valley. As an ex-RAF man, this was a perfect opportunity for Ken and Mary, who were joined a couple of years later by son Martyn, when he also left the RAF.

No.10 From the Gallaher Cigarette Card 'Aeroplanes' series. "The Whitley heavy bomber is one of Britain's principal weapons of attack. It is capable of 245mph and can carry a crew of five.

WHITLEY

No.23 From the Gallaher Cigarette Card 'Aeroplanes' series. "The Wellington has a wingspan of 86ft and is powered by two Bristol Pegasus engines of 900hp. A crew consists of four or seven.

WELLINGTON

Charlie & Heather Parsons joined the team in 1976, Ken & Mary retired in 1978 and Martyn moved on to other ventures in 1986.

Mary Rees died in 2012 and Ken himself died in August 2014, aged 93. A touching eulogy was given by longstanding family friend Nigel Bruce - see panel 8a, overleaf.

Ken Rees in R.A.F. uniform c1945.

"At the age of 17, I craved danger and excitement I liked fast planes and cars, rugby and women – not necessarily in that order."

One of the amazing attributes of Ken Rees was his ability to find something amusing in even the most unpleasant of situations. As a very active member of the Stalag Luft 3 awkward squad he often spent time in the solitary confinement cell and, of course, being gregarious by nature, found the deprivation of human company very hard to bear. He recounted the incident of the German guard's bicycle where the guard had brought his bike into the prisoners compound and lent it against the wall of the guard hut. This, Ken decided, was too good an opportunity to miss. He was busy letting the tyres of the bike down when the guard emerged from the hut. "Vat are you doing?" enquired the German. "the tyres on your bike looked a bit flat so I was just pumping them up for you" explained Ken. There was, of course, a fatal flaw in this explanation in that there was no bicycle pump. Two weeks in solitary confinement was the inevitable outcome. One of many such visits.

In his book (Lie in the Dark and Listen) Ken reports that "At the age of 17, I craved danger and excitement I liked fast planes and cars, rugby and women – not necessarily in that order." Hardly surprising, therefore that he was eager, at that age in 1939, to volunteer to join the Royal Air Force. However, he came to realise how deadly serious the war was when, on a home visit, he was told by his mum that his hero, Harold Star, had been shot down in his fighter plane over the English Channel and then strafed and killed whilst parachuting to ground. Harold Star was married to his oldest sister, Betsy.

Despite the enormity and seriousness of the conflict, the youthful exuberance would often break through-like the time he flew a Wellington bomber through the uprights of the Menai Bridge for a bet.

It was many years before Ken would talk about his war experiences but, gradually, bits would leak out. Typically, the amusing bits. I mentioned to Ken, after discovering that the prisoners had been told, in the early hours of a frozen February morning in 1945 that they were all to be marched away from Stalag Luft III to avoid the approaching Russians, how horrendous that must have been. His reply was typically dismissive. "Yes, it was a bit uncomfortable." But then told me the story of a group of prisoners who, along the route, had acquired a pram from a Frau in exchange for chocolate, the bitcoin of its day, and cigarettes. In this they had dumped a lot of their belongings. After a couple of days some of their German guards had asked if the prisoners could also carry their rifles in the pram as well. It was the somewhat surreal sight of a group of dishevelled men trudging through the snow pushing a pram with rifles sticking out that amused Ken. Ken and a colleague had themselves, in the hour that they were given to prepare for the evacuation, built a sled using two hockey sticks and a wooden box.

Research on the interweb reveals that the whole episode has become known as the Long March or Death March. It turned into one of the most harrowing events of the war with over 100,000 prisoners of war intermingled with all sorts of refugees traversing Poland and Germany largely living off the land. Many died from cold, it was the coldest winter of the twentieth century across Europe, dysentery and various

"Quite a lot of time was spent flying as a crew on cross country exercises. On one such flight, to win a bet, I took us on a slight detour and flew the Wellington under the central span of the Menai Straits Bridge. My home is now on Anglesey and whenever I see that bridge, I have to shudder at my earlier foolhardy self and that stupid exploit."

[panel 8a, Extracts from the eulogy given at Ken Rees's memorial service by Nigel Bruce]

8. Ken Rees & The Sandymount

other horrible ailments. Ken never spoke about that particular experience.

On his retirement from the RAF in 1968 Ken and Mary moved to Bangor-on-Dee, close to other members of the Rees clan, where they bought the Post Office and village store. As Ken remarked at that time there were not many employment opportunities for retired V bomber pilots. They succeeded to turn the enterprise into a delightful home and profitable business.

The move to The Sandymount Club in circa 1972 was a huge change for Ken and Mary but the Post Office and shop life did not entirely suit them, despite the undoubted success that they enjoyed. The prospect of running a pub had a much greater appeal. And so it was that they entered into village life in Rhosneigr. This turned out to be just the challenge that suited their individual abilities. Ken as the amiable host and Mary good at organising the back of house workings and a formidable collector of subscriptions.

It is very fitting that Ken's last working years should be spent at the Sandymount Club. He was well suited to the hospitality industry having spent much time in catering for large numbers of friends over the years. Ken always joined the entertainments committee at every RAF station at which he was stationed, and there were quite a number throughout the world.

One could not help noticing that Ken had, at one time, played rugby. I mentioned during one of our many conversations that I knew he had played for three clubs at the same time when he corrected me and said that it was four. I reeled off the names of the three that I knew about Birkenhead Park, Cheshire County and the RAF what I enquired was the fourth. The Combined Services. He said that it was a bit embarrassing having to write to his station commander saying that if there is to be a war then unfortunately he

[panel 8a continued]

Mary & Ken Rees behind the bar at the Sandymount in 1974. Leonie Callister (Martyn's partner at the time) in the centre.

would be unable to take part this week as he is playing rugby in Paris. At a later date he captained the London Welsh team for three years.

Martyn persuaded his father to write down his war time experiences because, at that time there was little history around pertaining to the individuals who had been engaged in such a huge upheaval. Much history of the Second World War was about the big events and we were interested about what the ordinary soldier, sailor, airman thought or felt about the situation in which they found themselves.
Ken allowed me to read the manuscript of his book before it was published. When I returned it to him he asked me – you don't think that there were too many parties do you? I suspect that there were actually a lot more than the book admitted.

Not long ago he told me that he was not afraid of dying. "When you have flown 56 operations and lost so many friends the idea that it might be me on this mission was always there."

He also remarked, quite recently, that if he had only known he was going to live so long he would have taken better care of himself.

Adieu old friend.

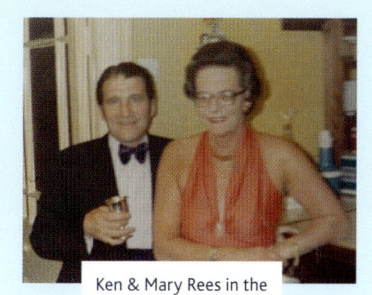

Ken & Mary Rees in the Sandymount c1975.

We shall resist the temptation to list all the well-known visitors to the Sandymount club over the years, but there have been several quiet visits by Prince William whilst he was training at RAF Valley nearby. One incident in 2010 made the tabloid press though and is recorded here almost verbatim.

*[The following article was printed in the Sunday People, on 17th October 2010. Subsequent checking of the 'facts' appertaining to the story, reveal many discrepancies. These are annotated in the text below. Although an amusing story, I will leave it up to my readers to decide which parts of this story they believe.]*

# Embarrassed Prince William was turned away by three bars on a boozy night out with pals.

## Wills suffered the triple snub as he celebrated qualifying as a search and rescue helicopter pilot with 30 fellow RAF men.

The pals had already drunk one bar dry before they left at closing time.

But they were left high and dry after three other bars refused to sell them a late drink.

Wills, 28, and his mates began their pub crawl at Sullivan's in Rhosneigr, Anglesey, near the RAF base where he trained.

They emptied the place of Taittinger champagne, wine and beer before leaving at about 11.30pm.

One of the group was picked as a spokesman to talk to staff at the nearby Sandymount club into serving them.
But no amount of charm – or name-dropping – could persuade barmaid Lizzie Owen, 39, to let them into the members-only bar for a late tipple.
When the royal friend told Lizzie his party included William, she replied: "Yeah, yeah. Pull the other one."

The pal persisted, insisting Wills really was outside hoping to enjoy "a cheeky pint or two".

But the barmaid stood her ground and said: "I don't care who you've got with you, you're not coming in."

*[Lizzie Owen has confirmed that whilst the exact words are an exaggeration for effect, this is broadly the gist of what was said.]*

*[Sullivan's owner, Stephen Crompton, confirmed that the Prince had dined at the restaurant that evening with RAF friends, but they had left without incident. Sullivans has never stocked Taittinger champagne, but by sheer chance, when the reporter arrived a few days later, they had two bottles in the display fridge which had been specially purchased for a gift. The reporter was turned away without comment, to protect the Prince's privacy, and the short creative sentence above was the result.]*

Jane Hughes, who owns the club with hubby Larry, said: "They were evidently celebrating passing their course.

"But Lizzie had already shut the tills for the night and she was worn out – she wanted to get to her bed and I don't blame her in the slightest.

**"Any earlier and they'd all have been very welcome."**

Jane added: "William can come back anytime – during opening hours."

The Prince's group then spotted the owner of another pub in the village, Sandy's Bar and Bistro, and one of them was despatched to ask her if she'd open up.

*[Larry & Jane Hughes had been out that evening, and had given strict instructions to Lizzie to close on time.]*

*[The bar however remained closed. Bar owner, Sandy Bingham, has pointed out that in fact her Bar & Bistro had been closed for the entire evening and all the staff were out for a staff party. Had they been open, the Prince and his friends would have been most welcome.]*

*[Claire, (correct spelling) now married and living away from Rhosneigr, was astonished at the sheer fiction of this report. She did see the Prince among the group of friends quietly sitting on the wall opposite Y Morfa, but the quotations she is supposed to have said, are "completely made up".]*

But Wills and his drinking buddies -refused to give up – and set off to another bar called Y Morfa.

This time the prince's chum was confronted at the main door by barmaid Clare Edwards, who told them: "I'm shutting for the night and I'm not serving you."

Clare said: "At first, I spoke to his friend and told him I was closing and he couldn't have a drink. I shooed him outside where I could see he had a group of four or five friends, including Prince William, who I instantly recognised.

"A minute or so later I went outside and the guy again asked if they could have a drink and I said No again.

"Then he said, 'Can you see who's here behind me?'

"I said, 'Yes – but you're still not having a drink.'

"William didn't say anything – he just looked extremely embarrassed, to be honest."

Clare added: "They'd run out of booze and were trying to get a drink somewhere else.

"They'd drunk everything in the bar they were in earlier.

"They had literally drunk the place dry."

[Original Source: The Sunday People, 17th October 2010. Reproduced by permission, Mirrorpix, London.]

*[Panel 8b]*

# Chapter 9
# Tea Clippers &
# The 'Norman Court'

'Days of Adventure - Norman Court racing Thermopylae', Oil painting by Barry Mason. [Courtesy the Artist & his agent www.richardjoslin.com'.]

# 9.1. Tea Clippers & the 'Norman Court'

## Introduction

The coastline of Anglesey is surrounded by some of the roughest and rockiest seas imaginable. Yet before the advent of diesel or even steam engines, there were many hundreds of sailing vessels operating around these coastlines. Whether fishing or ferrying, delivering supplies or collecting produce such as grain or copper ore, all of them - small and large - had to run the gauntlet of rocky shorelines and swift-flowing currents (and be wary of wreckers and pirates) to carry out their trades.

For the larger vessels passing by the Island on their way to bigger ports, their dependence on the wind often led them into danger off the Anglesey coastline. Magnificent sailing ships such as *The Nimrod*[1], *The John O'Gaunt*[2] and most famously, *The Royal Charter*[3] were wrecked off Anglesey, and Rhosneigr rocks can lay claim to many more. One ship in particular has an interesting story to tell.

In the bay, on the far side of Ynys Feirig ("Meyrick's Island", previously Ynys Wellt (Wild Island) and known colloquially as "Starvation Island") lies the remains of the Tea Clipper, *'Norman Court'*. The account of her sinking and the heroic efforts of the Rhosneigr Lifeboat to try to save her crew, are included in this chapter and have been well reported in many publications over the years, but little has been said about the context of the disaster. What was a Tea-Clipper? Why did they race? Where did the *'Norman Court'* fit in all this? And what happened after she ran aground on Cymyran rocks?

Two distinguished 19th century Sea Captains have documented the history of the Tea Clippers in great detail - Basil Lubbock and Andrew Shewan.

Basil Lubbock on the deck of the Cutty Sark. [photo: Brown, Son & Ferguson collection].

## Captain Basil Lubbock

Alfred Basil Lubbock was born in England in Sept 1876 of parents Alfred Lubbock and Louisa (nee Wallroth). He was educated at Eton and instead of going on to Cambridge as expected, he left for Canada and joined the Gold Rush of 1896-7 when he went into the Klondyke over the harsh and infamous Chilkoot trail. Returning via Vancouver and San Fransisco, he signed on the four-mast barque *'Ross-shire'* as an ordinary seaman in the apprentices' half deck at £2 a month. He fought in the Boer war of 1899-1901, during which time he witnessed what was probably the largest fleet of sailing ships ever gathered together, in Table Bay (South Africa) - several hundred.

---

1. *Nimrod* sank off Holyhead in 1827.
2. *John O'Gaunt* sank off Trearddur Bay in 1854.
3. *Royal Charter* sank off Moelfre in 1859.

In 1912 he married Dorothy Warner but they had no children. Basil served during WWI with the 1/3 Wessex Brigade Royal Field Artillery and was awarded the Military Cross. He devoted the remainder of his life to recording the history of the sailing ships and those who manned them, writing around two dozen books on the subject. He was founder and first Commodore (1919-1931) of Hamble River Sailing Club and was a member of the Royal Yacht Squadron 1923-1943. He died in September 1944.[4]

His book "The China Clippers" was first published in 1914, and revised in 1916. It has been reprinted several times, and is still available today (along with many of Lubbock's other books) from the original publishers, Brown, Son & Ferguson Ltd of Glasgow. Its 387 pages, plus 34 pages of Appendices, contain a fascinating and detailed account of the 1850-1870 period of Tea Clipper activity, until their decline around 1881, when the Racing Tea trade ceased.

## Captain Andrew Shewan

Andrew Shewan was born in Peterhead in 1850, the son of Andrew Shewan (Snr), Master Mariner, and his wife Jane (nee Thomson). Born into an old seafaring family it was quite natural that he should want to go to sea from an early age. According to the foreword of his book, by fellow maritime author Rex Clements:

*"His grandfather was a whaling captain who died as far back as 1830, through exposure on an ice floe, his ship being nipped in the Greenland ice. His father becoming master of a schooner in the St John's fish trade at the age of twenty-one, rose to the command of that early "crack" the 'Lammermuir' and afterwards of the 'Norman Court'."*

Shewan's childhood was spent in Stepney, just a short distance away from London Docklands and he was massively influenced by the comings and goings of the sailing ships, as he details in the first chapter of his book 'The Great Days of Sail':

*"Most of my schoolmates and associates were sons of seafaring men, and our outlook was to the sea."... "Stepney in those days was a grand place for a boy who wanted to be a sailor".*

'The Great Days of Sail' was first published in September 1927 and republished in December of the same year, following the author's death. Published by Heath Cranton Ltd of London, its 240 pages are a fascinating collection of reminiscences and stories about the many ships he both served on and captained, including almost 20 years on the *'Norman Court'*.

From reading these first hand accounts of manning and Captaining Tea Clippers, it becomes abundantly clear just how difficult and perilous it was to handle such a craft. Even in good seas, one had to keep alert at all times for potential trouble, and - as the reader will see in the sections which follow - dealing with perilous waters, gale force winds and hidden rocks could quickly bring a good ship to disaster, despite the best efforts of Captain and crew.

**4.** The Times obituary 5 September 1944.

Andrew Shewan [photo: Marion Shewan, Conway Maritime Press, an imprint of Bloomsbury Publishing plc].

## Tea

The history of Tea is a subject deserving of a book all to itself and indeed very many have been written. Apart from the 885 million entries on Google for the word, (at the time of writing) there are hundreds of well researched articles on the subject ranging from detailed university theses to briefer histories by almost all the major tea producing companies. For the purposes of this book and its relationship to the sinking of the 'Norman Court' in Rhosneigr bay, our interest is in understanding the importance of tea during the 1800s and what happened afterwards.

Tea, as a commodity, first came to the attention of the British population in the 1650s although it had been "discovered" in China several thousand years earlier. It became popular among the English aristocracy and subsequently spread to the coffee houses, which were popular places of sobriety and moderation at the time.

Until the 1700s, tea was only a small part of Europe's trade with Asia, but this changed after 1720 when the English parliament banned the import of finished Asian textiles, with a view to encouraging local textile manufacture. As a result, tea began to replace silk as the primary Chinese export.

Over the next few decades, tea continued growing in popularity, despite the fact that the government, who were losing taxation revenue from the reducing sales of alcohol as tea grew more popular, imposed high taxes on tea, to compensate. This of course also had the effect of encouraging tea smuggling and the dangerous adulteration of tea with many bulking agents, including (it is claimed[5]) sawdust and sheep dung.

In 1784, the Government realised that high taxation was creating more problems than it was worth and slashed the tax on tea. Its price stabilised and tea's popularity continued to grow.

In 1834, the East India company's monopoly on trade with China ended. While a monopoly was in place, there was no particular rush to bring the tea from China to Britain, but after 1834, the market opened up completely.

As new treaty ports became available, tea became more plentiful and the tea ships began to increase both in size and numbers. The first dedicated clipper ships to visit the China Seas were Americans. They began to load tea in Canton in the early 1840s, and made racing passages back to New York and Boston. They were running between China and the United States for some seven years before the first British Tea Clipper appeared on the scene.

5. www.tea.co.uk

Individual merchants and sea captains with their own ships, raced to bring the tea back home first, secure the highest prices for it and thereby make the most money. This ushered in the era of the British Tea Clipper and in particular there was competition between British and American merchants, leading to the famous Clipper races of the 1860s and '70s. The *'Norman Court'* proved to be among the fastest of these ships, typically making the passage back from China in about three and a half months, which was fast for the period.

> "We have noticed the competition between the owners of fast-sailing vessels employed in the China tea trade for the honour of bringing to the port of London the first cargo that arrives here of the freshly gathered crop of tea, which is always plucked in the spring season. The market in Mincing-lane is very busy in this month of October with the "New Season Teas," both those of China and those of the Himalayan provinces of India, which have latterly found favour. The unloading of the tea-ships and warehousing of their cargoes on the wharves of the East India Docks is also a scene of great activity, as shown in one of our Illustrations." [Illustrated London News, October 26, 1867].

UNLOADING TEA-SHIPS IN THE EAST INDIA DOCKS.

*9.1. Tea Clippers & the 'Norman Court'*

## The Tea Clipper

Surprisingly, a simple definition of a tea clipper ("A very fast three-masted sailing ship designed to carry Tea back to market in the shortest time") is not given in either Lubbock's or Shewan's books; nor indeed in Ansted's 1920 'Dictionary of Sea Terms' and therefore we have to look to other authors of the time for a contemporary definition.

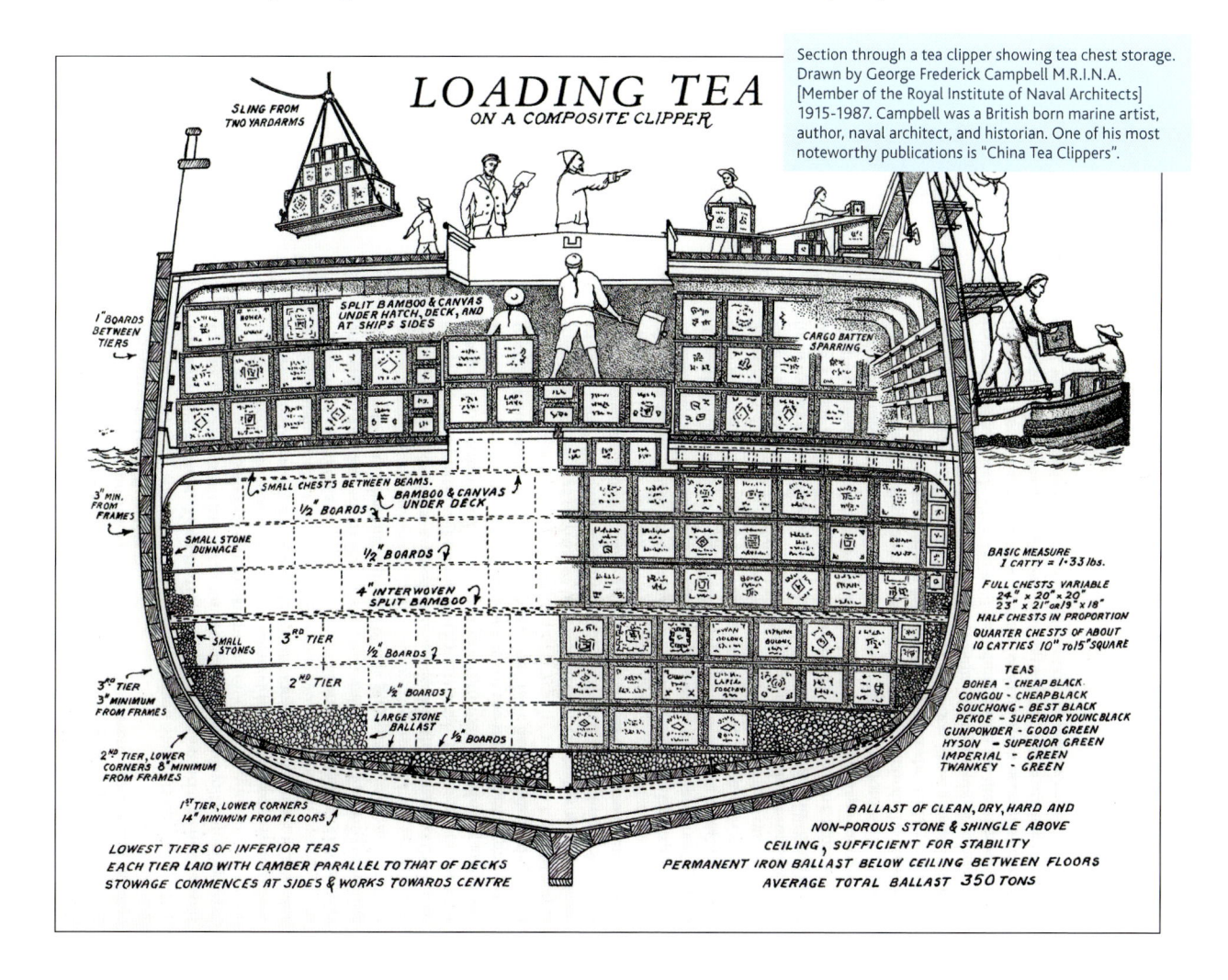

Section through a tea clipper showing tea chest storage. Drawn by George Frederick Campbell M.R.I.N.A. [Member of the Royal Institute of Naval Architects] 1915-1987. Campbell was a British born marine artist, author, naval architect, and historian. One of his most noteworthy publications is "China Tea Clippers".

9.1. Tea Clippers & the 'Norman Court'

Arthur H. Clark writing in his 1911 book "The Clipper Ship Era" states:

*"The first ships that were ever built with speed instead of carrying capacity as the chief desideratum were the long, low, flush-decked Baltimore brigs and schooners, which by reason of their unusual sailing powers became celebrated the world over under the name of the 'Baltimore Clippers.'*

*Its chief features were great beam, placed far forward, giving a very fine run from a high bow with plenty of sheer to a low stern. Both stem, sternpost and masts were unusually raked, and it was this feature in the masts of a ship, together with a low freeboard, which, in the eyes of a stranger, gave immediate cause for anxiety and alarm, for any vessel described by the lookout as" a rakish looking craft" was at once suspected of being an ocean freelance."*[6]

*"For some time the word clipper was only applied to Baltimore ships, but gradually as fast ships began to be built in other ports for trades in which speed was of great importance these also were called clippers, though none of these later clippers in the least resembled the Baltimore schooners"*

As the market became more specialised, the designers of these ships began to refine their designs so that they would hold as many chests of tea as possible, with protective ballast being accommodated around the principal cargo, where it was needed.

## The Norman Court

Designed by the respected Naval Architect William Rennie and built by A.J. Inglis Ltd of Glasgow, there is no doubt that the Norman Court was a very handsome ship.

Her measurements are shown in panel 9a opposite.

According to Lubbock: "The ship was named after the Hampshire seat of her owner, Thomas Baring (see page 127), and her figurehead was a splendidly carved likeness of one of the family beauties."

The *Norman Court* was launched from Inglis' yard at Pointhouse on the Clyde in the Summer of 1869 and Captain Andrew Shewan (Snr) took command.

**6.** ie a pirate or privateer

### Overall Dimensions of "Norman Court".

| | |
|---|---|
| Length | 197 feet 60m |
| Breadth | 33 feet 10.1m |
| Depth | 20 feet 6.1m |
| Tonnage | 850 tons |

### Spar Measurements of "Norman Court".
**Bowsprit:**

| | |
|---|---|
| Jibboom (extreme length) | 68 feet 4½ inch |
| Boom end | 2 feet 4½ inch |
| Flying Boom | 12 feet |
| Outer boom | 15 feet |
| Inner boom | 17 feet |
| Heel | 22 feet |

**Foremast**

| | |
|---|---|
| Topmast | 43 feet |
| (masthead 7 feet 6 inches) | |
| Topgallant mast | 25 feet |
| Royal Mast | 15 feet |
| Lower mast | 58 feet deck to cap |

[Panel 9a]

| | |
|---|---|
| (masthead, 13 feet 3 inches) | |
| Extreme length (deck to truck) | 120 feet |
| Foreyard (extreme) | 71 feet |
| Lower topsail yard | 61 feet |
| Upper topsail yard | 56 feet |
| Topgallant yard | 41 feet |
| Royal yard | 32 feet |

**Mainmast**

| | |
|---|---|
| Top mast | 46 feet 6 inches |
| (masthead 7 feet 6 inches) | |
| Topgallant mast | 26 feet |
| Royal mast | 16 feet |
| Skysail mast | 10 feet |
| Lower mast | 61 feet 6 inches, |
| deck to cap | |
| (masthead, 13 feet 6 inches) | |
| Extreme length (deck to truck) | 139 feet |
| Main yard | 74 feet |
| Lower topsail yard | 65 feet |
| Upper topsail yard | 60 feet |

| | |
|---|---|
| Topgallant yard | 44 feet |
| Royal yard | 32 feet |
| Skysail yard | 24 feet |

**Mizen Mast**

| | |
|---|---|
| Top mast | 33 feet |
| Topgallant mast | 18 feet |
| Royal mast | 12 feet |
| Lower mast | 50 feet 6 inches, |
| deck to cap | |
| (masthead, 10 feet) | |
| Extreme length (deck to truck) | 98 feet |
| Crossjack yard | 60 feet 6 inches |
| Lower topsail yard | 50 feet |
| Upper topsail yard | 44 feet |
| Topgallant yard | 32 feet 4 inches |
| Royal yard | 24 feet |
| Spanker gaff (extreme) | 31 feet |
| Gaff end | 5 feet |
| Span | 21 feet |
| Spanker boom | 48 feet |

---

LAUNCH.—On Thursday last Messrs A. & J. Inglis launched from their shipbuilding yard at Pointhouse a very handsome composite clipper ship, for Messrs Baring Brothers & Co., London. Her principal dimensions are—Length, 195 feet; breadth, 33 feet; depth, 20 feet; tonnage, 850 tons. The ceremony of naming the ship "Norman Court" was performed by Miss Walkinshaw, daughter of W. Walkinshaw, Esq., merchant of London and China, one of the owners. The Norman Court will be employed in the China trade, under the command of Captain Andrew Shewan.

Launch of the Norman Court. [Greenock Telegraph and Clyde Shipping Gazette, 31st July 1869].

## Outward Cargo

Of course the tea races could only begin once the Tea Clippers had reached the Chinese ports, and their outward cargoes were far less exotic. Shewan describes *'Norman Court'* on one occasion:

"As deep as a sand-barge, down to her marks and a little over. We were bound to Shanghai with a cargo of lead, pig and scrap-iron with chalk flints below; the fine goods consisting chiefly of Manchester bales[7], a cargo of such weight that the ship's 'tween decks were practically empty."

7. Manchester bales - compressed bales of raw cotton or cotton yarn.

## The Tea Clipper Races

Having reached China, there was some waiting time before the races could begin. In practical terms, it allowed a Captain and crew to recover from the long journey out and - as beautifully described by Lubbock (see chapter 9.3)- enabled the ships to smarten themselves up ready for the race back home.

The race itself typically began when, after loading the tea, the ships would race down the China Sea, across the Indian Ocean, around the Cape of Good Hope, up the Atlantic and into the English Channel. The Clippers raced to get to the docksides first and the winner would claim their rewards of securing the best prices for their cargo and large prizes for the crew of the winning ship[8].

The Tea Clippers all carried slightly different cargo weights, but the premium for arriving first at the dockside with the new season's teas was typically £1 per ton in the 1850s and 1860s, dropping to 10 shillings a ton in the 1870s, before it ceased entirely. This would be worth around £500 - £1000 (with a current value estimated between £40,000 - £80,000). This of course was on top of the general freight rate. For example *Norman Court* carried 1180 tons of tea in 1873 at £3 per ton so any premium could add 15%-30% to the total received, and was certainly worth racing for.

In 1869 the Suez Canal opened, allowing the steam ships access to much shorter routes to China and providing competition to the Tea Clippers that ultimately they could not beat. This led to the end of the Tea Clipper races, and within a decade, to the end of an era.

As Basil Lubbock put it *"In 1881 Thermopylae made her last passage in the tea trade – leaving Foochow on 30th October she arrived in the Downs 107 days out. The same year Hallowe'en made a passage of 103 days from Shanghai. And these are the last records worth noting, for by this date all the tea ships which were still afloat had had their wings clipped and crews reduced, with economy as their guiding star and not speed."*

*'Norman Court'* continued in the tea trade until 1880, though her rigging had been reduced in 1877 following the depression in freights, and she was converted into a Barque[9] in 1878. After many years of service, Captain Shewan decided to take a rest, partly due to ill health, and her new master was Captain James Lawrence 'Dandy' Dunn about whom little is known. (His wife, Susan Dunn was a niece of the captain of the *Black Prince* and he is believed to have gone on to captain the Barque *'John Thompson'* of Sunderland after the *'Norman Court'* was sold).

During her last few years *'Norman Court'* had carried other cargo, and visited other places including South Africa and the Coromandel coast of South East India, but her best days were over and she carried her last Tea cargo in 1880.

## After Tea – Sugar

In 1882 *'Norman Court'* was sold by Barings to a Glasgow shipowner – James Grieve Junior - for the Java Sugar Trade. Grieve had four vessels at the time, of which *'Norman Court'* was the biggest at 834 tons. The others being: *Corisande* (187 tons), *Octavia* (226 tons), and *Aline* (718 tons).

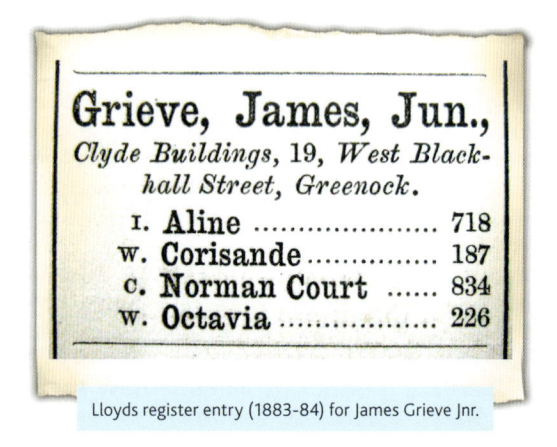

Lloyds register entry (1883-84) for James Grieve Jnr.

8. More details of clipper racing is detailed in both Lubbock and Shewan's books.
9. Barque - a sailing ship with less rigging than a full rigged ship.

Java Sugar Factory showing split bamboo baskets, lined with palm leaves, used for holding the raw sugar for shipping away. [photo: Philadelphia Museums].

Her new captain was Charles McBride[10], previously master of the Barque *'Aline'*. In the previous year (1881) whilst in command of the *'Aline'*, Captain McBride had:

*"been sent to the Greenock Jail for sixty days for cruelly ill-treating one of his seamen, on the voyage from Sourabaya to Greenock, by keeping him six weeks in irons in a most constrained position, and refusing to supply him with sufficient food and water".*

The 60 day sentence was the maximum penalty which could be imposed and the full story of the event[11] reveals McBride to be a strong-willed man, clearly capable of running a tightly disciplined ship.

The island of Java – now part of Indonesia, but then part of the Dutch East Indies – had a number of principal exports including Coffee and Indigo, but Java sugar was to be the final cargo of the *'Norman Court'*.

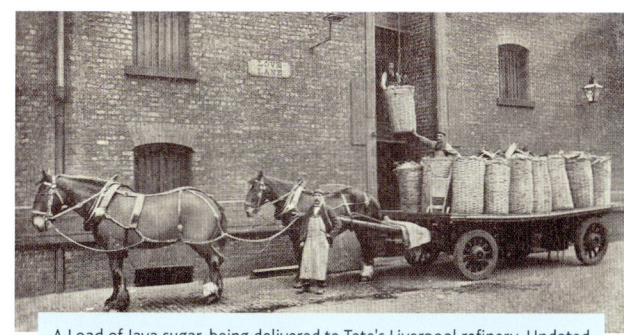

A Load of Java sugar, being delivered to Tate's Liverpool refinery. Undated postcard (c1910) published by Sir Joseph Causton & Sons of London.

**10.** By a strange quirk of Scottish printing convention of the time, the name McBride (and other names beginning 'Mc') were often shown in print as M'Bride.
**11.** A Captain Imprisoned for Cruelty - Liverpool Mercury 25th April 1881.

9.1. Tea Clippers & the 'Norman Court' 117

## The last voyage of the Norman Court

By the time of her fateful last voyage in early 1883, her racing days were over, her rigging had been reduced to save manpower and she was on the last leg of a winter journey from Surabaya in Java, bound for Greenock[12] on the Firth of Clyde. She was laden with 1,100 tons of sugar for the Glen Sugar Refining Co. in Greenock , and had been at sea for over three months - A long and tiring voyage.

Although reports differ on the exact reason (and the court could not reconcile the courses steered with the position reached), the ship somehow found its way into Cymyran Bay[13]. There was a severe gale blowing, and despite the frantic attempts of Captain McBride to turn the ship around, it grounded with such force that the mainmast, mizzen topmast and foretopgallant yard came down and her own lifeboats were rendered useless. It was about 7 pm on the evening of 29th March 1883.

The wreck of the Norman Court in Cymyran Bay, Rhosneigr [Photo: E.D.Mee collection].

12. Shields Daily Gazette, 2nd April 1883.
13. Cymyran - The bay between Ynys Feirig ("Starvation Island") and Rhoscolyn.

The Rhosneigr Lifeboat, *Thomas Lingham*, could not be launched that evening due to the very heavy seas and the time was spent in manhandling the lifeboat across the expanse of sand from the lifeboat house to a position nearer the stricken ship. This was achieved by about 11 pm and the volunteer crew stood by all night.

At first light of the following day a rescue was attempted. The rocket apparatus[14] was fired several times without reaching the ship and so the lifeboat *Thomas Lingham*, was launched. Luck was not with them however and the treacherous seas filled the lifeboat with water causing one of her crew to be washed overboard.

Fortunately he was still attached to the lifeboat by his safety cord and was able to be pulled back onto the boat.

This event, coupled with the breakage of several rowlocks, forced the lifeboat to return to shore.

It was now about 11 am and by this time the Holyhead Lifeboat, *Thomas Fielden*, had arrived offshore (towed first by the steamer *George Eliott* and after by the steam tug *Challenger*) and made several fruitless attempts to reach the *'Norman Court'* before being forced to return to Holyhead.

After several more, gallant but unsuccessful, rescue attempts by the Rhosneigr crew[15], which took up most of the remaining daylight hours, the Coxswain, Owen Morris of 'Tyn Cerrig', ordered his cold, wet and exhausted men home for a change of clothing and some sustenance, after more than 20 hours on the shore. It was now about 8 pm and the crew of the *Norman Court* were still clinging to the rigging.

Whilst the Rhosneigr crew were away, the Holyhead crew, having summoned a special train for the purpose, arrived to render further assistance. The Rhosneigr Coxswain preferred to wait for the return of his own men, so the Holyhead Coxswain, Thomas Roberts (who was 66 years old), took over the *Thomas Lingham* with his own crew and despite the darkness bravely set out again. This time the *'Norman Court'* was reached and her crew were all brought back alive, except for two who had perished from exposure. In all, twenty were saved.

## The Crew of the Norman Court.

Captain Charles M'Bride, Greenock; A. Stevenson, chief mate, Dundee; John Nason, second mate; A. Malcolm, carpenter, Arbroath ; William Marshall, steward, London; Thomas Moses, cook; John Gough; Frank Penkey; Joseph Ambrose; Alick Wyllie; Alexander Robinson; Henry Fitz; F. Jenson; P. Nelsen; James M'Fadden; A. M. Carter - all A-B's ; W. B. Cottell, O.S.; William Hallett, O.S.; E. Goodard, London; and W. Farquhar, Greenock - apprentices ; and W. Fraser and R. Neville, - apprentices from the Cumberland Training Ship.

In total 20 men were saved. William Marshall (Steward) and Archibald Carter (Seaman) were lost.

[Source: Dundee Evening Telegraph - Saturday 31 March 1883, and others]

refs
1. A.B. = Able Bodied Seaman
2. O.S = Ordinary Seaman (subordinate to an A.B.)

The ship was a total loss and what remained of the wreckage was stripped of all salvageable materials and sold from the beach where they lay, on April 18th 1883. It perhaps goes without saying that none of her sugar cargo was saved!

**14.** Captain G. W. Manby, (1765 - 1854), is credited with inventing the 'rocket apparatus' which used a small mortar shell to project an attached rope from the shore over a stricken ship. If successfully caught, the rope could then be used to provide a lifeline to the shore from the wrecked vessel. See p130.
**15.** See crew list on p127.

> **Sales by Mr. W. Riva.**
>
> SALE OF WRECK AT CYMYRAU, ANGLESEY.
>
> IMPORTANT to SHIP OWNERS, FARMERS, MARINE STORE DEALERS, and others.
>
> MR. W. RIVA has been instructed by R. COOPER RUNDELL, Esq., Secretary, Underwriters' Rooms, GLASGOW, to SELL BY AUCTION, for the benefit of whom it may concern, at CYMYRAU (distance of three miles from the Valley Station), on WEDNESDAY, 18th day of APRIL, 1883, at TWO o'clock in the afternoon, the Wreck of the Composite Barque,
>
> **"NORMAN COURT,"**
>
> 834 Tons Register, Coppered and Copper Fastened, Built at Glasgow, by Messrs J. and R. INGLIS in 1869, as she now lies stranded on GYMYRAU Beach. Also, Materials saved from the Wreck, consisting of a large quantity of Sails, Warps, Ropes, Hawsers, Anchors and Chains, and about Two Tons of Pure Copper, Spars, Timber, &c., all in lots to suit purchasers.
>
> For further particulars apply to R. COOPER RUNDELL, Esq., Underwriters' Rooms, Glasgow, or to the AUCTIONEER, Holyhead. 572

Sale of wreckage of the Norman Court [North Wales Chronicle, 14th April 1883].

'Norman Court' had been insured for £9,000 and her cargo for £25,000. Today those value equivalents would be around £810,000 and £2.3m[16].

The Holyhead Coxswain Thomas Roberts received the RNLI Silver Medal for his bravery, and the story of the event was fully recorded in the Lifeboat records, and appeared in press articles across the country. One of the best contemporary reports is entitled "A Thrilling Lifeboat Story" and is shown in panel 9b.

The loss of the Norman Court was the subject of an official inquiry, and the Judgement of that inquiry is shown in panel 9c on page 124. A fund-raising concert for the Holyhead lifeboat was later held, and this is shown in panel 9e on page 128.

16. www.measuringworth.com
17. The Tuskar is a prominent small rocky island, some 11km off the South East coast of Co. Wexford in Ireland. It bears a lighthouse which was completed in 1815.

# A THRILLING LIFEBOAT STORY.

A Board of Trade Inquiry Into the circumstances attending the stranding and loss of the barque "Norman Court," which occurred on the Carnarvonshire coast, on the 29th of March, was opened on Tuesday, at St. George's Hall, Liverpool, before Mr Raffles, stipendiary magistrate, and Captain Hight, Admiral Grant, and Captain Beazley, assessors. Mr Paxton represented the Board of Trade, and Mr Warr (Messrs Bateson and Co.) appeared for the owner and captain of the vessel.

It appeared from the statement of Mr Paxton that the "Norman Court," the registered tonnage of which was 854, was built on the Clyde in 1869, and was owned by Mr James Green, of Greenock. She left Sourabaya on the 16th December last, commanded by Mr Charles M'Bryde, and with a crew of twenty-three hands all told. She carried 1100 tons of cargo, and her draft on leaving was 19ft. 6in. forward and aft, but on Getting to sea the ship was trimmed two or three inches to the stern. On the morning of the 29th of March she arrived off Queenstown and there received orders to proceed to Greenock, which she did. Later in the day Ballycotton Light was seen bearing W. by N. about five miles distant, and that was the last landmark they made until they sighted the shore of the bay, in which the vessel stranded. The wind at the time was blowing a fresh gale from the south and a course was set which, according to the captain, would take them about twelve miles outside the Tuskar[17]. At noon the master calculated that the Tuskar bore N. by W. about twelve miles distant, and a sounding then made gave them sixty-five fathoms of water. A course was then set N.E. E. and, the wind freshening, sail was shortened and as they proceeded up the Channel, according to the master, soundings were taken. About seven p.m. the master was consulting the chart, when a light was reported on the port bow which it was thought was that of the South Stack, six miles distant, and bearing N.N E. An effort was made to get the vessel round, but without success, and shortly afterwards land was made out on the port bow, distant about five miles. The Captain then saw they were in a bay, and an attempt was made to get out, but without success, and the vessel went ashore about seven p.m. Signals were shown and rockets were sent up which were answered from the coastguard station in the neighbourhood, and a number of efforts were made to get the crew off the vessel. The Rhosneiger Lifeboat crew made the first attempt to save life, but the crew were ultimately saved by the Holyhead Lifeboat crew. Mr Paxton then said that the main points for the court to inquire into were as to the navigation of the vessel and how the stranding came about; also as to the efforts made to save life—whether the Rhosneiger boat was properly manned and managed. The crew were twenty-four hours exposed on the rigging, and with the exception of two they were all saved.

Charles M'Bryde, master of the vessel said he attributed the stranding to an indraft which had taken him on the port bow stronger than he had made allowance for. The first order he gave after the ship struck was to clear away the boats. It was impossible to launch them, as the sea was too rough. As they were lowering the lifeboat, the mainmast went by the board, carrying with it the mizzen topmast and the fore topgallant yard, and at the same time smashing their three boats. They continued to make signals of distress until the vessel was covered by water, and they all took refuge in the mizzen rigging. Rockets were fired on shore in response to the distress signals, but none were fired that night towards the ship, nor was any effort made to reach them by the lifeboat from shore. The vessel struck about one thousand yards from the shore, but drifted in afterwards, bumping over the rocks to a distance of about 600 yards. The witness thought it would have been impossible for the lifeboat to have reached them that night in consequence of the heavy sea. They had to pass the whole of that night in the rigging. During the night the chief officer, who was below him in the rigging, called out that the steward was dead. The steward and witness were the only members of the crew in the rigging who had not their oilskins on, and they were, therefore, exposed to the severity of the weather. The steward died about three o'clock in the morning.

Next morning the rocket apparatus was brought down to the rocks, and they fired four or five times, but each time the line fell short of the ship. He did not think that blame attached to anyone on account of that, because the vessel was about 600 yards from the land. About nine or ten o'clock the same morning the life boat was brought down to the water on a car, and the crew got into it, and brought it right under the jibboom of the vessel, and a heavy sea broke over the lifeboat, and carried away one of the men, who was afterwards picked up. The lifeboat then returned to the rocks. Some time afterwards a lifeboat, in tow of a tugboat, endeavoured for nearly two hours to reach the vessel but without success. Shortly after this last attempt to reach the unfortunate men one of the latter, an A.B. named Carter, died from exposure. Subsequently another attempt was made by a lifeboat from the shore to reach them, but it got no further than half-way from the shore, and then turned back. Evening coming on, it then began to get dark, and the twenty-one men, left clinging to the rigging gave up all hope of life. At ten o'clock that night witness heard the chief officer calling out that the lifeboat was alongside. He was then, as he had said, more dead than alive, and hanging onto the rigging, but he replied that he did not think that this could be so because if they could not reach them in the daylight it was not likely they would try at night. He soon discovered however that it was the Rhosneiger lifeboat, but manned by the Holyhead lifeboat crew. This boat succeeded in getting up to the stranded vessel, and got off the whole of the twenty-one men from the rigging. The men who were in a terribly exhausted condition, were afterwards conveyed to a farmhouse, where their clothes were dried, and they received every attention, remaining there until the following morning.

Evidence of a similar nature was then given by the first mate, after which the inquiry was adjourned.

[North Wales Chronicle, Saturday April 28th 1883]

*[Panel 9b]*

## Today

The wreck site is listed under the Royal Commission on the Ancient and Historical Monuments of Wales as site 272304. The wreck is no longer visible above water, but can be seen under water where parts of the hull, timbers and Iron frame are visible.

The wreck has been the site of many diving expeditions over the years and souvenirs from the wreck are not uncommon. There is still enough to see to make a dive (or snorkelling visit) worthwhile as the following recently-taken photos show.
For a time, her beautiful figurehead was preserved in a garden near Holyhead, but this is no longer the case.

Norman Court wreck artefacts.

A selection of underwater images of the wreck, [Taken from videos by Ian Gardner and Kevin Phillips].

122   9.1. Tea Clippers & the 'Norman Court'

The ship's Bell however, was safely recovered and is on display at the Baring Archive in London.

The bell of the *Norman Court*. [photo: Baring Archive Collection].

After the wreck of the *Norman Court*, Captain Charles McBride was taken to Llanfair Bach, Holyhead, the home of Richard Pritchard (head of a family of seafaring men) and his wife Elizabeth, to recuperate.

There he met their daughter, also named Elizabeth.

However, despite the fact that Captain McBride was already married and living with his wife at West Blackhall Street, in Greenock, the couple are said to have kindled a relationship, such that when Captain McBride's wife, Catherine, died later the same year, Elizabeth and Charles are said to have married and set up home together back in Greenock[18].

McBride later went on to captain other ships, the final one being *The Atalanta*, which sank in November 1898 off the coast of Oregon, North America, and in which Charles McBride also lost his life.

Captain McBride (centre in bowler hat) with Mrs McBride and some of the Crew, on the deck of The Atalanta. [photo: Derek Bartley collection].

**18.** Some of the corroboration of the Llanfair Bach /McBride story comes from the history of the Bartley family. See panel 9d.

9.1. Tea Clippers & the 'Norman Court'  123

# THE LOSS OF THE NORMAN COURT
## JUDGMENT

Yesterday, Mr. Raffles gave judgment in reference to the stranding and subsequent loss of the sailing ship Norman Court, in Cymryan Bay (sic), on the Carnarvon coast, on the 29th March, an inquiry into the circumstances attending which was opened on Tuesday. The vessel was going from Queenstown to Greenock for orders when she stranded. The crew, numbering 23 hands all told, including the master (Captain Charles M'Bride), took refuge in the rigging, and all but two, who succumbed to the terrible exposure of the weather, were rescued in the Rhosneigr Lifeboat by the Holyhead lifeboat crew, after having clung to the wreck for twenty-four hours.

The Board of Trade desired the opinion of the court as to whether a safe and proper course was set and steered after passing Ballycotton, and whether due and proper allowance was made for tides and currents;[19] whether proper measures were taken on the morning of the day she stranded to shape a course up channel: whether a safe and proper alteration was made for tides and currents; whether proper measures were thereafter taken to ascertain and verify the position of the vessel from time to time; whether the lead was used with sufficient frequency, and, whether reasonable care was taken to obtain correct soundings; was a good and proper lookout kept; whether when the light was seen on the port bow about six p.m. on the 29th of March proper measures were taken to prevent the ship going ashore; whether the vessel was navigated with proper and seamanlike care; what was the cause of the stranding; what were the circumstances in which no assistance was rendered to the vessel for upwards of 24 hours after the stranding, and whether every possible effort was made by the coastguard officer in charge of the rocket operations and by coxswains of the lifeboats to render assistance with all possible despatch; and whether the master or mate were in default.

The court found that the course set and steered after passing Ballycotton was a safe and proper course up to the Tuskar, but they did not consider that at eleven o'clock on the morning of the stranding proper measures were taken by the master to ascertain and verify his position before

[Panel 9c]

shaping a course up channel. In point of fact, the assessors, having laid down upon the chart the course and distance run from Ballycotton according to the master's evidence, found that he was considerably more to the eastward of Tuskar than he supposed himself to be. Still, even taking him to have been so much more to the eastward than he thought, a N.E. half N. course would have been a safe and proper course up channel had that course been steered and made good. But as to the course steered, the evidence of the witnesses was anything but satisfactory, there being singular differences in their several statements at different times, and the court could not arrive at the conclusion that a N.E half N course had really been set and steered, for on that course the court considered that the current or indraught would not have affected the ship to such an extent as to have stranded her when she struck. Soundings were stated to have been taken three times in the course of the afternoon, but the statements in regard to them were not satisfactory or reliable. Had the soundings been more carefully taken, the lead was used with sufficient frequency. A good and sufficient look-out seemed to have been kept. When the light was seen on the port bow about six p.m. or later, there was little probability that anything could have saved the ship, as she was then embayed and close to the rocks. The master seemed to have acted according to the best of his judgment. The court could not say that the vessel was navigated with proper and seamanlike care, as already indicated by the opinions already expressed. The court were satisfied that every effort was made by the Rhosneigr lifeboat to reach the wrecked vessel after daylight on the 30th, but the sea was so heavy that their efforts were frustrated. The coastguard did their best with the life-saving apparatus; but the distance from the wreck to the shore rendered their exertions also useless. The Holyhead lifeboat was towed down in the afternoon by a tug but could not succeed in getting alongside, and had to return to Holyhead. But her coxswain and crew did not abandon their efforts to get at the wreck, for they returned by train to the nearest railway station, walked to the beach, manned the Rhosneiger lifeboat, and, about ten p.m. succeeded in rescuing the unfortunate crew of the ship.

The coxswain of the Holyhead boat, Mr. Thomas Roberts, aged 66 years, gave his evidence before the court in a manner which greatly impressed them with the skill, energy, and determination which he showed. The court wished to add that in giving so much praise to the crew of the Holyhead Lifeboat they had no desire to detract from the credit due to the coxswain and crew of the Rhosneigr lifeboat, which was not manned to any extent by seafaring men. The court were compelled to say that the master was in default in the navigation of his ship, and they would have dealt with his certificate had it not been for the hardships he had undergone, which had made them hesitate to do so. Neither, under the circumstances, did they deal with the mate's certificate.

[Liverpool Mercury, 27th April 1883]

*[Panel 9c continued]*

**The Bartley & McBride connection by Derek Bartley.**
*[The connection between Captain Charles McBride and his 'wife' Elizabeth Pritchard is not entirely clear. This source material is extracted from 'The Bartley's of North Wales', used by kind permission of Derek Bartley. Published online at www.walesearch.com/Articles.html.]*

The link came in this way: Samuel and Elizabeth Bartley, of Pant y Gloch, Llandrillo, had a daughter, Elizabeth. She married a John Hughes of Llanddulas. They had a daughter, Elizabeth born 1833, who married Richard Prichard of Llanfair Bach, Holyhead. They had a daughter, also Elizabeth, born 1864. When she was probably only about 19 she met Captain Charles McBride.

In about 1884 +/- she is said to have married him. This may well be the case – on a later Census, (1901), she says she is his widow – but no record of the marriage can be found. Charles McBride, had been, and possibly still was, married, to a Catherine, and had two daughters.

Many years earlier Charles McBride had command of the Norman Court and this ship foundered in Cymyran Bay, Rhosneigr. To recuperate, Charles McBride went to Llanfair Bach, Holyhead, the home of the Prichard family. Here, he met, and eventually 'married', Elizabeth Prichard, daughter of Richard and Elizabeth Prichard of Llanfair Bach.

John Richard Prichard, born 1862, had married a Matilda Seed and had four children, all of whom had pre-deceased him. Richard had not married, having the services of his housekeeper and when he died he left everything to her.

Several years ago, on visiting Holyhead graveyard looking for the grave of Rev. John Bartley, we came across some Prichard graves, noted the name Llanfair Bach, and decided to visit the farm for photographic/family history purposes.

*[Panel 9d]*

Invited in, we met a man[20] who was now living with the real owner of Llanfair Bach, an old lady who had been housekeeper for Richard Prichard – one of a family of seafarers.

To an extent the house was like a museum for it had many seafaring artefacts, maritime objects and pictures belonging to Richard Prichard. There were portraits, sea chests, a cupboard full of his meticulous housekeeping notes – and a very large painting of the Atalanta. One other small photograph showed a ship's crew with Charles McBride in the centre.

Whether Elizabeth Prichard went through a legal marriage is uncertain – could it have been on board a vessel at sea, or somewhere outside the UK, or was she simply his 'partner', in modern day parlance?

**Editor's note:** Although an interesting source, this still leaves several elements unexplained. For example, exactly why was Llanfair Bach at Penrhos, near Holyhead chosen as a place to recuperate?

There is no Marriage certificate in the names of McBride and Pritchard on record for the period 1883 (when the Norman Court sank) to 1898 (when Charles McBride died on the Atalanta). Furthermore, some newspaper reports from the 1880s state that Charles McBride was married but had no family, other records state that he had two children. (One daughter, Catherine, married Adam Brown at St Luke's Chelsea on 21st March 1878.)

However, to add further to the McBride confusion, there were two Captain Charles McBrides! The 'other' one also lived in Greenock in the 1870s-80s but was Master of steam ships.

In fact, Lloyd's register of Captains for the period 1816 to 1911 lists no less than nineteen 'Captain McBrides' on their register. It makes for a very confusing story!

[Photo: undated postcard, no publisher named]

As a footnote to the loss of the ship, the *'Norman Court'* estate in Hampshire was advertised for sale in June 1883. [Devizes and Wiltshire Gazette].

> **HAMPSHIRE.**
> *IMPORTANT ANNOUNCEMENT.*
> **THE NORMAN COURT ESTATE,**
> A HIGH-CLASS FREEHOLD & SPORTING PROPERTY, situate adjacent to the picturesque village of *Clatford*, within a mile of the improving market town of Andover, with its extended railway accommodation, and comprising 517a. 3r. 33p. of highly productive Arable, Pasture and fertile Water Meadow Land, with a superior FAMILY RESIDENCE, ample Homestead Accommodation, and 8 first-class Labourers' Cottages with good Gardens. The noted River Anton flows through the Estate, and affords nearly two miles of *first-class Trout Fishing*. The Property also carries a good head of Game.

The Norman Court estate at West Tytherley (near Salisbury) in Hampshire can be traced back to the 14th Century when Roger Norman, after whom it is named, bought the land on which it sits and became Lord of the Manor. Norman Court itself was rebuilt in 1753 and the entire estate - by now a sizeable acreage - sold to Charles Wall at the beginning of the 19th Century. His son Charles Baring Wall later inheriting. Thomas Baring, a relative, inherited the estate in 1853 and in 1873 it passed to his cousin, William Henry Baring.

The National Archives list almost 30 properties as part of the estate in 1945,

The 1883 advert above relates to just 500 acres on the North-Eastern fringe of the entire estate, which in 1906 was recorded at 20,000 acres.

Norman Court is now a nursery and private school.

## Thomas Lingham - Rhosneigr Crew:

Coxswain William Morris, Ty 'n Cerrig
William Owen, Storws
Thomas Robert, Maelog Villa
William Robert, Glandwr
John Robert, Ty Gwyn
John Owen, Belan
John Hughes, Ty Main
Hugh Hughes
Thomas Williams, Cefn Dref Bach
Hugh Jones, Trewyn Bach
Richard Jones, Pentowyn
Harry Owen, Cefn Dref

Source: RNLI archives. Unfortunately, the names of the Holyhead crew, apart from the Coxswain, Thomas Roberts, have not been retained in the RNLI archives.

19. It was well known that magnetic deviation to a ship's compass could occur, particularly with Iron Framed ships heading north or south in line with the magnetic field of the earth. However, as reported, this does not seem to have been considered by the Inquiry and Judgement of the case.
20. Derek Bartley met Richard Pritchard's old housekeeper.

In response to the Holyhead Lifeboat's heroic efforts in saving most of the crew of the *Norman Court*, some 3 weeks after the rescue, on April 20th 1883, a "Grand Fund-Raising Concert" took place for the Holyhead lifeboat.

# HOLYHEAD LIFEBOAT CONCERT.

Yesterday, Mr. Raffles gave judgment in A grand concert, having for its object the raising of funds towards the Holyhead Lifeboat Testimonial, was given at the Town Hall on Friday evening.

Rarely, if ever, has a subscription list come before a town and met with such a hearty and spontaneous support at the one just mentioned. Commencing with the owners of the vessel " Norman Court," who subscribed £50, we find the names of the Hon. W. O. Stanley, Admiral Dert, Admiral Mackenzie, Mr Thomas Fanning Evans, High Sheriff; Mr H. Edwards, J.P., Mr Eyre, Bryngolen, &co. Among those who subscribed very handsomely, an opportunity was given the general public of adding their mite in the shape of the concert mentioned.

Long before the appointed time on Friday evening, the hall was filled with a most respectable audience, amongst whom were many of the elite of the town and neighbourhood. Just before the time of commencing the proceedings, the Lifeboat crew marched in. Headed by their coxswain. It is needless to remark that this was the signal for an oration - such as is seldom accorded to individuals.

Mr Thomas Fanning Evans, High Sheriff of Anglesey, was voted to the chair. On his assuming the chair, Mr Evans met with a most cordial reception. He said: "Ladies and Gentlemen - I thank you for the honour conferred upon me. There is no honour I would court more—associated as I am with the National Lifeboat Institution—than

[Panel 9e]

that of presiding over a meeting where we are met together to recognise the bravery exhibited by the crew of the Holyhead Lifeboat (hear, hear).

Had it not been for these men, what would have become of the crew of the ill-fated "Norman Court?" Driven as she was upon the rocks at Cymyran - many ineffectual attempts had been made to save the perishing ones - courage and gallantry were not wanting - these noble hearted men, urged on by two gentlemen (Mr Eyre and Mr Elliott), resolved to try again, or die in the attempt. Right nobly under Divine protection did they effect their purpose (applause).

Now. my men (addressing the Holyhead Lifeboat crew, I feel proud of you for having accomplished such noble work ; Anglesey feels proud of you; and, doubtless, her Majesty the Queen feels proud of you. No amount of money that can be given you will compensate you for the work done. Whatever has been the past history of the Holyhead Lifeboat crew, and we have no reason to think that heroism has been wanting in the past, you will have the satisfaction to know tin I so long as the present generation exists, your bravery will be green in the minds of the community, and when your grey hairs are laid in the tomb doubtless some will remain who will relate with pardonable pride the story of "The Norman Court" (hurrah).

[There followed a full programme of songs and musical pieces by many individuals and musicians.]

Captain Cayin, in proposing a vote of thanks to the chairman, complimented the crew of the lifeboat upon their gallant conduct, and mentioned the names of Mr Guest, station master, and Mr Riddiford, chief officer of coastguards, as having assisted very materially in effecting the rescue. Before terminating the concert, rosettes were pinned on the coats of the lifeboat crew by Mrs Fanning Evans and daughters, and Mrs Edwards, Rosemount.

A letter was read from the secretary of the National Lifeboat Institution, intimating that the medals, vellum, and telescopes would not be ready for presentation for some days. We understand that the local subscription list amounts to nearly £150,

Subsequently, on Tuesday May 1st 1883, the Hon. William O. Stanley, Lord Lieutenant of Anglesea, presented the Holyhead Lifeboat crew with the rewards given by the National Lifeboat Institution, and their portions of the public subscriptions made for them. In consideration of their services in rescuing 20 of the crew of the Norman Court in Cymyran Bay on March 30th.

The presentation took place at the Market Hall, at a public meeting. The Coxswain was invested by Miss Adeane with the second-class silver medal of the institution. And each of the crew was presented with a scroll of vellum with a suitable inscription. And Mr W.P. Elliott with a binocular glass and a scroll of vellum.

[Manchester Courier,
Saturday 5th May 1883]

[Panel 9e continued]

*Rocket Line carried over Wreck.*

*Landing the Crew in the Breeches Buoy.*

The Life Boat & Apparatus For Saving Life In Case Of Shipwreck from The Popular Encyclopedia or Conversations Lexicon Being A Dictionary Of Science And Arts, Literature, Biography, History, And General Information Edited By Charles Annandale, M.A. Published by Blackie & Son 1884.

*'Norman Court'* by J.Spurling. [Undated postcard by Blue Peter Publications of London].

*Norman Court* navigating the Min river and drifting with a Kedge [a small anchor carried by large vessels for use in shallow water]. Drawn by George F. Campbell, 1915-1987, author of "China Tea Clippers".

## 9.2 The Great Days of Sail

Selected excerpts from *'The Great Days of Sail'*[1] by Andrew Shewan, Master of the *'Norman Court'*. Shewan's book is full of interesting stories and amusing anecdotes about events which happened on the *'Norman Court'* and other ships.

### FOREWORD (p9) by Rex Clements, editor of 'The Great Days of Sail' and author of 'A Gipsy of The Horn'

Captain Shewan himself made his first voyage to sea in the ChA-sze in 1860 and followed his father in command of the *'Norman Court'*. He is to-day *[1927]* probably the last survivor of the tea-clipper captains who, in the sixties and seventies of the last century, added one of the most striking and picturesque chapters to British maritime history.

His memories have an interest and his opinions a weight to which few seaman-authors can lay claim. What those of us whose seafaring began with the century, know about the tea-clippers of the halcyon age of sail, we know almost entirely from the written or the printed word. At best our information is from the yarns of old shipmates who loved to remember the feats of their youth.

But Captain Shewan knew the ships whose names are now almost household words as one can only know the intimate associates of a lifetime. Brought up in Blackwall of the old days, his knowledge of the clippers is from first-hand experience, his judgements from professional estimates formed at the time. He has been on board almost every one of the British Clippers he mentions and raced with many of them on the high seas. It is Caesar who tells the story of his own wars.

### London River
### Chapter iv - p32

After a boyhood spent in Stepney, with occasional trips to Peterhead and Aberdeen, it was from Blackwall I sailed on my first long voyage southward in the *ChA-sze*, a ship of about six hundred tons register, bound to Sydney, N.S.W.

It was to Blackwall we returned at the end of that voyage, and it was at Blackwall a few years later that, as mate of the *Norman Court*, I had the satisfaction, as we dropped alongside the famous pier, of being told by one of the dock officials who had known me from childhood that we had made the best passage of the season from China with teas.

It was at Blackwall again, in 1874, as master of the same clipper, when we docked on a dark autumn night, that I enjoyed one of the supreme moments of my career—that of being hailed by Captain Stevens, the dockmaster, with the news that we had beaten our great antagonist on that passage, the celebrated *Sir Lancelot*, from whom we had parted company in the China seas. "A feather in your cap, my boy," he shouted cheerily, and so, in truth, I felt it.

---

1. "The Great Days of Sail" originally published by Heath Cranton Ltd. The 1927 edition is now out of copyright. Later edition published by Conway Maritime Press (now an imprint of Bloomsbury Publishing Plc), but also currently out of print.

## Chinese Pirates
## Chapter vii - p68-69 -

Many a ship mysteriously disappeared from the face of the waters in those days, but though nothing was ever heard of them, there was little doubt in the minds of sailors as to their fate, supposing they had not got clear of the Malay islands.

All vessels that could do so reported at Anjer Point;[2] and there a sort of record was kept of all ships entering and leaving the Malay and China waters. "Pirates got her" was the verdict on a missing ship.

Sometimes the Chinese or Malay pirate craft, coming along under their long sweeps, would surprise a vessel in a calm at the dead of night; sometimes a ship would run aground in these shallow waters, and then from the creeks and coves of the nearby land flocks of swift proas[3], crowded with murderous gangs, would dash down upon her. The fights put up by the white crews would be brave and desperate; but the numbers of their ferocious opponents would prevail. The end was always the same, once the pirates took the ship. "Dead men tell no tales" and every soul, passengers as well as sailors, would be murdered, the ship looted of all valuables and then burned, scuttled and sunk.

Bowling *[an old friend and fellow seaman]* asserts that pirates were an ever present and real danger during the time of his service in the *Wynaud*, especially in narrow waters.

*"All these waters, reef dotted and shoal-infested, and the coasts of the great islands that hemmed in the narrow seas, wooded from the water's edge to their cloudy summits, swarmed with pirates of the Malay and China breeds. Borneo Sumatra, Java, Banca, Billiton, Lombok and a hundred smaller islands harboured their ruffians of the seas; and when the wind came ahead in restricted waters, and the ship had to anchor to save herself from being swept back or shorewards by the strong currents, a close and anxious watch was kept for the silently—stealing proas".*

A Chinese Pirate Junk. Undated Tuck Oilette postcard from their 'Life in China' series.

2. Anjer point – a Java town in the straights of Sunda, between Java and Sumatra.
3. Proas - colloquial name for Malaysian boats propelled by sails or oars.

## Tea at Pagoda Anchorage
### Chapter xiii - P127-130

There are few scenes that linger in my memory more vividly than the Pagoda Anchorage in Foochow River a day or two after the "new teas" market had opened, when the first flight of clippers was getting ready for sea.

The "opening of the market" was a feature peculiar to the Foochow tea trade. In the city of Foochow stocks of the first pickings from the tea-gardens in the interior had accumulated since early in May, but the Chinese merchants were slow in making up their minds to sell at prices acceptable to foreign buyers.

"Chops"[4] bearing a well-known name were bought year after year by the same foreign merchants, yet, even so, weeks were often spent in haggling. The price was slowly and reluctantly lowered by the Chinese merchant, the foreign buyer sitting tight. When it had been reduced sufficiently, some one of the more important firms was tempted to close, and "opened the market". Then the hurry began.

Speed was the order of the day. Forty-eight hours or so were required to weigh and label the tea-chests then each "hong"[5] made all haste to load the same into the lighters[6] which waited to convey the fragrant leaf from Foochow to the Pagoda Anchorage, a distance of about twelve miles.

Generally some three or four of the clippers with good records were chosen as "going ships," and combinations of shippers would concentrate on filling these, each clique endeavouring to have their ship first away. It was a keen contest; yet it was not always the ship which was considered the fastest which got away first. Much depended on the tonnage of the vessel and the status and influence of the agents concerned.

Pagoda Anchorage at Fou-Chow-Foo. "One of five ports opened for commerce and situated on the Min river, about 25 miles from its mouth." [Illustrated News of the World, 21st August 1858].

As a rule, each clipper in the running had already shipped "ground chop," that is, a sufficient number of chests of tea of an inferior quality, carried at a slightly lower rate of freight than the new teas, and just sufficient to cover over the shingle ballast and so add protection to the aroma of the new crop.

4. Chops - a number of boxes of the same make and quality of leaf, variable as to weight, but usually the product of one particular garden.
5. Hong - Mercantile Houses.
6. Lighter - a powerful flat-bottomed barge for transporting heavy goods ashore or up-river.

## The Finest Display
### Chapter xiii - P130-132

The finest display of clippers that I ever remember seeing, waiting for the market to open was in 1869. In that year no less than fifteen of these beauties, more like yachts than merchantmen, lay moored off the Pagoda, with holds ready, ballast levelled, ground chop stowed, waiting for the new teas. I do not suppose that in any other port in the world one could have seen such a fleet of beautiful craft as were assembled in the River Min on that occasion.

Among them were the *Thermopylae, Leander, Windhover*, and *Kaisow*, all on their first trip; the *Spindrift* and *Lahloo* on their second; the proved and noted flyers *Sir Lancelot, Ariel, Taeping,* and *Serica* as well as the somewhat older but still handsome vessels, *Black Prince, Falcon, Min, Flying Spur* and the little *Ziba*.

At this time, when the tea-clippers were at the height of their glory, we were often complimented on the appearance of the *Norman Court* as she lay at anchor in the River Min, and the finishing touch to her good looks was the size of her ensign[7] and the angle of the staff from which it flew. I happened once to be on board a steamer when the merits of the various clippers in the Reach were discussed. One man, an American, having no idea who I was, remarked to me: "Ah ! but that's the pride of the river, the ship at the lower end of the tier with the big flag over her stern." He alluded to the *Norman Court* and, considering the splendid clippers with which she was compared, I felt no small pride that such was the generally accepted opinion.

> **7.** ENSIGN, a large standard, or banner, hoisted on a long pole erected over the poop, and called the ensign-staff. The ensign is used to distinguish the ships of different nations from each other, as also to characterise the different squadrons of the navy. The British ensign in ships of war is known by a double cross, viz. that of St. George and St. Andrew, formed into an union, upon a field which is either red, white, or blue. 'Falconer's Dictionary of the Marine, 1780'.
> **8.** Sprue - a tropical disease characterised by a sore throat, raw tongue and digestive disturbances.

## Master of the "NORMAN COURT"
### Chapter xiv - p140-151

The honour of command came to me at an early age, and unexpectedly. I had served as chief mate for fifteen months under my father's command of the tea clipper *Norman Court*, owned by Baring Brothers & Company of London. During that time my father had had several illnesses of short duration, the precise nature of which puzzled the doctors. At length his malady was diagnosed as "sprue"[8], a complaint frequently met with in the East. In less than a year I am sorry to say it had proved fatal to him.

While we were in London, prior to sailing, father had enjoyed fairly good health, though there had been some question as to the propriety of his making another voyage. But finally he decided to do so, while I continued to act as mate. Fortunately I had been able to obtain my master's certificate during the last occasion we were at home. So we sailed; and, encountering wretched weather running down Channel, father had a sudden attack of his strange complaint.

It came upon him suddenly one night during a blinding snowstorm, with a hard south easterly gale blowing. The ship was making about ten knots, and canvas had been reduced to afford some degree of safety should we come unexpectedly upon another craft during the thick drift. Father felt so ill he was compelled to leave the deck and go below-an absolutely unprecedented thing for him to do in heavy weather in the Channel. As a consequence I had my first taste of supreme control of a clipper under somewhat trying circumstances and was not sorry when daylight appeared and my vigil became easier.

"So pleased were Baring Bros, with their vessel that they commissioned Dutton to execute a picture of her at a cost of £100. He chose the moment at which she picked up her pilot off the Ness, and the illustration given is from a litho of this picture." [from 'The China Clippers' by Basil Lubbock].

"NORMAN COURT" - NAUTICAL

During the night the captain had called for me and giving me evidence of the serious nature of the trouble, asked my advice. What course should he take? Should he continue the voyage, or put into port in order that he might consult the owners and come to some arrangement? He gave me to understand he was considering my welfare. I might not like to sail under another master; and he had hoped, as he was part owner of the *Norman Court*, that after another successful voyage Baring Brothers might be content to hand over the command to me. I was so alarmed at the change I saw in his appearance that

9.2. The Great Days of Sail 137

I begged him not to think of me, but to make up his mind at once to stay at home, and I would take my chance under whatever master might be appointed. He agreed to my advice, and as the wind had shifted into the southward and we were then standing in under the Start with Dartmouth under the Lee, it was then decided to put in there.

Luckily we picked up a pilot almost at once, and as he boarded us he said we could not have arrived at a more opportune moment. The tide was making and the shift of wind would enable us to negotiate the somewhat difficult entrance to Dartmouth Harbour without difficulty. We should soon be as snug, he said, as in "London Dock itself".

So it was: and before noon we were safely moored in the lovely landlocked basin. Father's paroxysm, meanwhile, had subsided and he felt a little embarrassed at the action we had taken. He said he felt ashamed to go up to London on such an errand. He was worried also at who might be found to take his place at a moment's notice, and uncertain what would be the best thing for me to do. Seeing this, a sudden idea struck me and I spoke up what was on my mind. "Look here" said I, "if the owners are willing, why shouldn't I take the ship to Hong Kong? I have my captain's ticket". Father brightened at the suggestion. "Would you now" he asked "I never thought of that". "Rather" said I, "I'm sure I could do it" and so, after a little more talk, the matter was settled.

The upshot of it was that father went to London and proposed that I should be given the post of master. Barings raised no objection. They merely said, "Well captain, if you have confidence in your son's ability to command the *Norman Court* let it be so; we are satisfied".

So father returned to Dartmouth the next day with my appointment to the command in his pocket. He also brought with him a new mate, in the person of an old friend of his who had been master in Dunbar's service, but had fallen on evil days. Mr. Brummell was his name, and he was a most worthy gentleman, though rather old for chief mate of a clipper. Father had selected him because he thought, as a man of much experience, he might be trusted to advise me if necessary: But he put the matter diplomatically "Don't give my son any advice unless he asks for it", he said. Thus as a youth of twenty three years, my name was put on the *Norman Court*'s register, and I became a master of a full blooded tea-clipper.

I accepted the responsibility with a light heart, but soon realized that though a shipmaster has certain privileges, he has also many responsibilities. The safety of the ship and the lives of her company are in his keeping. He can leave the deck and come and go as he pleases, but he cannot relieve himself of responsibility. As an officer he may have sole charge of the deck, but at eight bells[9] he can hand this ship over to his relief and to retire below to sleep the sleep of the just, free of all care.

Not so as master. He is still "in charge" and cannot escape from his anxieties. Especially is this the case, outward bound in Channel, facing westerly gales, with a multiplicity of craft about and with a tea-clipper more heavily sparred than heavily manned, under his feet.

---

9. Eight bells signifies the end of the watch.

## Factors in Passage Making.
### chapter xvii - p170

Speed was everything in the tea-clippers, and the factors which made for fast passages were in consequence of prime importance. Superiority of model and equipment were, without doubt, the two most essential points. Yet it was only rarely that a clipper was produced of undeniably better sailing qualities than her rivals, so that this factor was not so prominent as it would otherwise have been.

In the first place came the question of equipment. There would not be much difference in quality between the gear of any two cracks of the tea fleet, but so keenly were they handled that the difference between the unworn canvas of a new ship and that of one on her second or third voyage would be a matter of consequence.

The trim[10] again was by no means a negligible factor. Here the advantage would be in favour of the ship not on her first voyage, for in such cases the captain and officers would have better knowledge of the precise trim which suited the ship and be able to act in accordance.

To trim a ship to get the last fathom of speed out of her was not such a easy matter as might be imagined. It was a difficult thing to estimate in a new ship, and had to be judged by her model or by comparison with other vessels similarly constructed. Most clippers would sail better by the wind when on an even keel, but when running free were considered to do better when trimmed a bit by the stern. The Chinese stevedores were past masters in the art of judging trim by the eye. Experience was the best teacher.

A third factor was the state of the ship's copper sheathing. This was usually renewed every two years. It was considered that a ship was more speedy during the first year, as when the copper was worn thin by friction it was more easily displaced. It was no uncommon thing to find, after two year's wear, that twenty or thirty sheets of the metal had been torn and wrinkled up in such a manner as to obstruct the vessel's easy passage through the water and so diminish her powers of sailing.

To a certain extent these were all minor matters in actual practice, yet taken together they had a material influence on the success of a voyage, when the fact of docking three or four hours before a rival might mean the gain of anything from £1,000 to £1,500.[11]

Of course, among the half-dozen clippers of recognized powers that would likely to be in the running from Foochow with the first batch of new teas, every attention would be given to this point. Even if one did not gain the coveted premium, which could only fall to the lot of one, it was still necessary to be close behind the winner to ensure being "laid on the berth" the following season, and so command the highest rate of freights.

---

**10.** Trim - ensuring the boat is level in the water.
**11.** Approx £80,000 – £120,000 at today's values. www.measuringworth.com

**The Cutty Sark**
**Chapter xxii - p218-221**

I know on this point I differ from an eminent modern historian of the clipper-ship era. Mr. Basil Lubbock has called the *Cutty Sark* "the fastest ship that ever left the ways." It is a difficult point to decide; the *Cutty Sark* today is a clipper whose name is known all over the world, and I venture to think that it is more from the fact that she is still with us than from any particular performance she made as a tea-clipper, that she owes her reputation as the fastest ship ever built.

When I was second mate of the *Blackadder*, a new iron ship belonging to John Willis, and said to be constructed on much the same lines as the *Cutty Sark* and *Hallowe'en*, I saw the *Cutty Sark* enter the Blackwall Dock in January,1870, on her arrival from the Clyde, a brand new ship. She was very much admired at the time and looked every inch a tea-clipper, but, as it transpired later, had serious faults of construction(not in her hull, but in her gear), owing to being hastily finished.

Her owner, John Willis the younger, had made cheap contracts for his three new tea clippers. Messrs. Maudslay, Sons and Field, who were primarily an engineering firm, started a ship building yard at Greenwich, and undertook to build the *Hallowe'en* and *Blackadder* at an unprecedentedly low rate for the Thames. Both ships were turned out very roughly, insomuch that the *Blackadder* was dismasted six weeks after leaving London; and there was a lawsuit over the acceptance of *Hallowe'en*.

A shipbuilding firm on the Clyde were given the contract to build the *Cutty Sark*. They became bankrupt before she left the stocks, and the ship was finished off hurriedly by another firm.

The consequence was that much of her ironwork was scamped, and on her first voyage, Captain Moodie complained bitterly of her weakness in this respect. In her great race with the *Thermopylae* in 1872, she lost her chance of winning through her rudder collapsing off the Cape - a queer accident which, so far as I know, never happened to any other clipper.

It has been said that John Willis had the *Cutty Sark* designed and built on purpose to lower the records of the Steele clippers, particularly the *Thermopylae*. If this were indeed so, he never achieved his object. I do not think the *Cutty Sark* ever made a record passage, though her averages in the London-Sydney trade were equal if not better than those of any other ship.

She was undoubtedly exceedingly fast in strong winds, though I think the record days' runs she was reported to have made will not bear analysis. I have an idea that she dragged a bit in light winds on account of her hollow lines forward. At least it is recorded that the tea-clipper *Wylo*, a vessel of no great pretensions and never considered a flyer, once outsailed her in the light winds of the Java Sea.

The *Cutty Sark's* westerly current simply will not stand. Yet the resultant record-breaking claim has often been reiterated and has been capped by another no less unlikely. Under the pseudonym of "Master Mariner" a writer assured the public that the *Cutty Sark* had run a distance of 2,163 miles in six consecutive days, naively adding that "she must have travelled 370 miles on one or more days".

I should imagine she did! She must have touched four hundred at times, or she had an unprecedentedly steady wind. The claim is impossible absolutely to verify or

"CUTTY SARK"

Postcard of Cutty Sark by Nautical Photo Agency. On the back is written "Cutty Sark taken from ship's boat by the late captain Woodget in 1886."

disprove, but it is a pity that it has been made. The *Cutty Sark* has titles enough to fame, without the addition of these legendary achievements.

## Conclusion: Then And Now
### Chapter xxiv - p234-235

By 1870 the Suez Canal was open, and "steam", which had already tried to deprive the tea-clipper of her being, was furnished with its final opportunity. By 1880 it had definitely triumphed; the graceful clipper was a thing of the past and the China tea trade emptied of romance. Gone past recall were the tall ships and the officers and men who manned them, and whose spirit of rivalry was as keen as their seamanship. No more would they watch their racing craft reel off the knots, with stunsails alow and aloft, and "Jamie Green"[12], ringtail, skyscrapers and moonrakers set, as they traversed the region of the steady trades, or with reefed topsails literally "hung upon the gale" while they fought the fierce squalls of the adverse monsoon of the China Sea.

Never again will a straining clipper make the Channel and race neck and neck from the Scilly to the Foreland with a foeman worthy of her steel —finally to win or lose the world-wide race by a bare twenty minutes. This is now all over and done with, though I trust not yet wholly devoured by that " great-sized monster of ingratitudes "—Oblivion.

Tea was the prime commodity in which I traded, and the great dispersal of the tea fleet came about 1880. Some of the China "cracks," notably the *Thermopylae* and the *Cutty Sark*, gained further renown in the wool trade with Australia. Others, among them the *Lothair* and *Leander*, diverged to the New York tea trade for a few further seasons. But the great majority of them were condemned to ignominious service under foreign owners, and in course of time the wrecks of them were scattered up and down the seven seas or they were dismasted to serve as hulks in foreign harbours.

The *Norman Court* herself, true to her high lineage, made a heroic end by dashing headlong on to the Welsh rocks near Holyhead. Her crew took to the rigging and hung there for twenty-four hours, until the remnant of them were rescued by the Holyhead lifeboat.

That was the end of her sailing days; but visitors to Anglesey may still see, defiant of wind and wave, the splendid iron frame of the *Norman Court*, half-buried and half-exposed, on the Welsh sands near Rhosneigr. *[No longer visible above water unfortunately - Ed]*

**12.** Jamie Green - four-sided, fore and aft sail used when the wind is very light.

Rhosneigr's largest and most noticeable island, and the one which brought the Norman Court to a watery grave, is Ynys Feirig - now known locally through years of colloquialism by the English visitors, as Starvation Island.

Its name means Meyrick's Island, after Sir George Meyrick, a substantial landowner of the district who owned it in the 19th century. However the earliest name of the island appears to be Ynys Wealt or Ynys Wellt. It is this name which appears on maps of the 17th and 18th Centuries, and may come from "Gwyllt" meaning "Wild", rather than from "Gwellt" meaning "Straw" or "Grass", hence Wild Island or Grass Island. It is still privately owned and not open to the public.

The importance of the Island as a danger-marker is highlighted by the size it is shown on the early maps of Anglesey. The Crigyll and Cymyran reefs are clearly important places to be aware of.

The sections of maps illustrated are (clockwise from top right): John Speed, 1610; J.Archer c1645; Owen 1736; G.Rollos c1770.

9.2. *The Great Days of Sail*  143

Painting of the rescue of the *Norman Court* by the Rhosneigr based Artist, Brian Entwistle. Few prints of the *Norman Court* are still available but the Artist still undertakes Commissions. [photo: Private collection].

# 9.3 The China Clippers

The following extracts are taken verbatim from the 1916 (third) edition of Captain Basil Lubbock's book, "The China Clippers".[1] These extracts, relating to the *Norman Court*, were never designed to be read as a single entity, as here presented, and should perhaps be treated as information bullet-points, to be dipped into as the mood takes you.

## The Builders and Designers of the Famous Tea Clippers – p.143

As a rule these famous clippers were designed in the drawing lofts of their builders; in fact, there were only two outside designers of any note, Bernard Waymouth, Secretary of Lloyd's Register, and William Rennie.

Waymouth was responsible for the lines of the *Leander* and *Thermopylae*, whilst Rennie designed *Fiery Cross, Black Prince, Norman Court,* and *John R. Worcester.*

## Speed of the Crack Tea Clippers Compared - p.156/157

*Norman Court* could outweather and outsail the fleet on a wind but was not so fast running. *Thermopylae* and *Cutty Sark* being larger and more powerful stood driving in heavy weather better than the graceful steele flyers and had much the best of it when running their easting down. In hard breezes *Cutty Sark* was the fastest ship of the fleet but in light weather *Thermopylae* and the Steele cracks could beat her.

Yet taking them all round there was very little difference in speed between the best known of the clippers, and in the racing one can safely say that their captains had as much or more to do with their success or failure than the ships themselves.

## The Captains – p.162/163

First class men were so scarce that I can barely scrape up a dozen worthy of remembrance....... It required dash and steadiness, daring and prudence to make a crack racing skipper, and these are not attributes or character which are often found in conjunction.

However there were a few men, who held the necessary qualities of a tea-ship commander, whose endurance equalled their energy, whose daring was tempered by good judgement, whose business capabilities were on a par with their seamanship, and whose nerves were of cast iron. These men could easily be picked out of the ruck, for their ships were invariably in the front of the battle. Amongst the best known were Robinson of *Sir Lancelot*, Keay of *Ariel*, McKinnon of *Taeping*, Kemball of *Thermopylae*, Andrew Shewan of *Norman Court*, Burgoyne of *Titania*, John Smith of *Lahloo*, and Orchard of *Lothair*.

## Tea Clipper Crews – p.168/169

The crews of the tea clippers would make a modern shipmaster's mouth water. Britishers to a man, they were prime seamen and entered into the racing with all the zest of thorough sportsmen. Many are the stories of their keenness on the homeward run. And Captain Shewan of *Norman Court* declared: "With all hands going about, we would have the ropes coiled up in ten minutes from the ready about order." The Shanghai pilot once timed the *Norman Court* getting underway and swore that her anchor was lifted and sail made in twenty minutes. She was an easy working ship and her crew were accustomed to walk her topsail yards to the masthead in smooth water.

---

[1] "The China Clippers" originally published by James Brown & Son. The 1916 edition is now out of copyright.

## Outward and Intermediate Passages – p.173/174

The voyages of the tea clippers, though barely a year in length, showed a remarkable mileage. The outward passage was either to Hong Kong, Shanghai or Melbourne. The outward cargoes were heavy ones, consisting generally of Manchester bales and lead. Between their arrival in China and the time for loading the first teas the clippers traded up and down the coast, sometimes as far north as Japan, at others round to Singapore and Rangoon, but, as a rule, carrying rice from Saigon, Bangkok, and other rice ports to Hong Kong.

## The Pilots on the Coast - Chinese and European – p175/179

The ships were further handicapped by the unreliability of the pilots. It was considered a most risky thing to take a Chinese pilot. They knew the waters well enough, but were generally in the pay of the pirates, or even coast fishermen, and thus rarely missed an opportunity of putting the ships in their charge ashore or wrecking them on some uncharted rock, which they purposely kept secret for such occasions. Such a rock was the pinnacle rock at the mouth of the Min River, where the charts gave 15 fathoms. This rock was struck by the *Norman Court* in 1878.

The European pilots declared that it must have been a sunken wreck. However when the clipper was docked in Shanghai, oysters were found sticking in her bottom. Captain Delano of the Yankee clipper *Golden State* also stated that he had a shoal cast about the same place. But it was not until two years later, when the *Benjamin Aymar* had stuck on an uncharted rock close by and remained there, that the pilots began to believe in the *Norman Court's* rock. Then H.M. gunboat *Moorhen* was sent down, and found a pinnacle rock, only 9 feet below low water springs, right on Captain Shewan's bearings. Curiously enough, just before the *Norman Court* had discovered this uncharted rock with her keel, she had successfully employed a Chinese pilot. Coming down from Shanghai for Foochow in thick N.E. monsoon weather, Captain Shewan, on hauling in for the regular channel, found himself to leeward of the White Dogs.[2] He picked up a Chinese pilot at daybreak. It would have taken a day beating up for the usual channel, and when the pilot said: "Suppose you like, I can take the ship in as we go, I savvy plenty water, can do all right". Captain Shewan agreed to risk it, knowing that the Chinaman was licensed by the consul. And the pilot took him through a short cut into the Min river without mishap.

## The Tea Ports – p.187

In the old days the tea was only loaded at Canton, Whampoa, and Macao. Then Shanghai became a favourite port, if a late loading one. But when Foochow was opened it outdid the others in popularity, owing to the early date at which its teas were ready for shipment. Later in the seventies Hankow began to attract attention, but by that time the racing was practically over.

## Preparations for the race home from Foochow – p189/191

The crack ships, which were always the first to load, began to assemble about the end of April; and until the tea came down were all engaged in painting, varnishing and smartening themselves up and in other ways, such as sheathing over their channels, preparing for the fray. Then what a sight they made when all was spick and span, with their glistening black hulls, snow-white decks, golden gingerbread work with carving at bow and stern, newly varnished teak deck fittings, glittering brass and burnished copper! Every ship, of course, had her distinctive mast and bulwark colours. The amount of brass work on these tea clippers would have put a modern steam yacht to shame. *Norman Court*, another beautifully finished ship, had a solid brass rail all round her bulwarks. When all the

[2]. White Dogs – Islands in the Formosa Straits, South China Sea.

ships had been polished up, and lay with their yards crossed and sails bent, all ready for the arrival of the tea, a day was set aside for a grand regatta, in which all the boats of the fleet took part. This was always a great occasion, a whole holiday for the crews, with liberal prizes for the best cutters, gigs and sailing yawls; and, naturally, the rivalry between the different ships was intense.

## Loading the Tea – p.191/192

The tea came down the river in sampans[3], and the loading of it at the Pagoda Anchorage was done with all the hustle of coaling a man of war against time. The first lighters[4] down distributed a ground tier to each of the first ships, after which there were two or three sampans alongside each ship until she was loaded. The tea was beautifully stowed, tier by tier, by Chinamen using big mallets.

Real photo postcard of a Chinese 'Lighter'.

Clark in his *[book]* Clipper Ship Era, gives a very good account of this scene, which I cannot do better than quote:- "Cargo junks and lorchas[5] were being warped alongside at all hours of the day and night; double gangs of good natured, chattering coolies were on board each ship ready to handle and stow the matted chests of tea as they came alongside; comfortable sampans, worked by merry, bare-footed Chinese women, sailed or rowed in haste between the ships and the shore; slender six-oared gigs, with crews of stalwart Chinamen in white duck uniforms, darted about the harbour; while dignified master mariners, dressed in white linen or straw coloured pongee silk, with pipe-clayed shoes and broad pith hats, impatiently handled the yoke lines"

## The Tea Race of 1867 – p.245

Owing partly to the dead heat finish in 1866 but perhaps more to the slump in tea, the 10s per ton premium, which amounted to about £500, was withdrawn in 1867; but for all that the racing continued as keen as ever. With the abolition of the premium it was arranged that the vessel making the best time was to be considered the winner and not the first in dock as heretofore.

## Norman Court – p.297/230

Next to *Cutty Sark*, the most important clipper launched in 1869 was the *Norman Court*. Designed by Rennie, she bore a strong family likeness to *Fiery Cross* and *Black Prince*, and was a very beautiful ship in every way. She should have been Rennie's masterpiece, but the builders made some slight deviation from his design in the moulding of the iron frames, which, though it did not interfere very much with her speed, made her more tender than she should otherwise have been. These little mistakes were no uncommon occurrence when ships were built from outside plans, and it was generally found that a builder was more successful with vessels built to his own design than with those he built from the plans of an outside architect.

3. Sampan - Chinese flat-bottomed small wooden boat.
4. Lighter - a powerful flat-bottomed barge for transporting heavy goods ashore or up-river.
5. Lorcha - light three-masted Chinese sailing vessel with European style of hull but with Chinese style rigging.

However, with the exception of this error which affected her stability, *Norman Court* had beautifully fair lines, and she was most perfectly built and finished. Unlike *Cutty Sark's*, her iron work was specially good. In fact, a London blacksmith, who was employed repairing one of her trusses some years later, was so lost in admiration of her iron work that he declared it must have been made by a watchmaker.

As to her deck fittings, her bulwarks were panelled in teak, with a solid brass rail on top all round. And even her foc's'le lockers were panelled better than those of many a ship's cabin.

*Norman Court,* indeed, rivalled the Steele clippers in looks and beauty, and was considered at one time to be the prettiest rigged vessel sailing out of London. She was very heavily sparred and extremely lofty, so lofty, indeed, that one 4th of July, when she was lying in Shanghai with several other clippers, including *Thermopylae*, the American superintendent of the Hankow Wharf came off with a star-spangled banner and asked Captain Shewan to fly it at his main truck, remarking that it would be seen further from there than from any other point within leagues of Shanghai. Captain Shewan was also asked whether he gave an apprentice a biscuit before he sent him up to furl the skysail. Indeed, if the Baring clipper had been as square as *Thermopylae* with her own loftiness she would have been very much overhatted, but luckily for her stability, she had a narrow sail plan.

Like most of the tea clippers, her masts were raked well aft, in fact, they had more rake than was usual, and this, Captain Shewan thought, rather spoilt her sailing in light winds. The chief reason for this rake was that it kept a wooden ship from diving too much into a head sea.

In her paces *Norman Court* was a bona fide tea clipper in every way - fast in light airs, at her best with fresh whole sail beam winds but not the equal of *Cutty Sark* when the royals[6] were fast, and perhaps a good half knot slower than the Willis crack when off the wind, for *Norman Court's* best point was to windward - indeed, she was one of the most Weatherly of all the tea clippers. Owing to the way in which her bilge was carried right away to her stern (though there was nothing above the water line to stop her) she went into a sea like a rubber ball, and very rarely buried herself like some of the Aberdeen ships. She required careful watching, however, and if caught by the wind freeing two or three points in a squall when going close-hauled under a press of sail she would go over till the lee bunks of the midshiphouse were under water.

With regard to trim, she sailed best, especially running, when well down by the stern. On one occasion, when she left London for Sydney with a light load-line, Captain Shewan kept her on an even keel, but found that she did not do as well as usual running the easting down. On the other hand, in 1871, when she made the fast run of 67 days to the South Cape, Tasmania, she was very deep with Manchester bales and nearly a foot by the stern. This trim gave her some splendid runs in the "roaring forties", but she also took a tremendous lot of heavy water over aft in making them. Once she left Macao in heavy weather with no chance to get her proper trim. This passage she sailed first rate on a wind, though very wet forward, and on her arrival she was found to be 6 inches by the head[7].

---

**6.** Royals - Small sails flown above the topgallant sails for use in light winds.
**7.** By the head - the boat trimmed down at the bow.

French Postcard 'Au Temps de la Marine a Voile'. No.4 - Le *"Norman Court"*, Clipper Anglais 1870, sous les huniers.' (under topsails). Publisher *'TP'* c1950's. Artist not stated.

## Tea Trade of 1873 – p.346/347

The year 1872 may be said to have been the last year in which there was any real racing amongst the clippers. Henceforward though the captains still did their best to make fast passages, they no longer had any chance of bringing the first teas to market, which were all taken by the racing steamers through the Suez Canal, there was therefore no need for daring feats of navigation or sail carrying, added to which, as freights fell before the onslaught of the steamers the clippers grew more and more scattered and only two or three of the most celebrated of them, such as *Thermopylae* and *Cutty Sark*, continued to load home in June and July.

BARING BROS.

9.3. The China Clippers

# Chapter 10
# The Paddle Steamer 'Rhos Neigr'

'Steamer Prince Leopold arriving at the Pier'. Real Photographic postcard by Horrocks & Co, Printers of Rhyl and Ashton. This card postmarked Bootle on 31st July 1906.

152    10. The Paddle Steamer 'Rhos Neigr'

# 10. The Paddle Steamer 'Rhos Neigr'

Colour postcard of the Paddle Steamer 'RHOS NEIGER' (sic) postmarked Caernarvon 18th June 1908. No printer or publisher named on the reverse.

Built in 1876 by Barclay, Curle & Co. of Glasgow, for the "Southampton, Isle of Wight & South of England Royal Mail Steam Packet Co." this 196 ton steam-driven vessel was originally named the *'Prince Leopold'* and spent most of its life ferrying passengers around the South East coast of England.

The ship was 165ft long, 20ft wide, 8ft depth and had a gross weight of 196 Tons.[1]

Whilst operating off the Isle of Wight in its first season, the *'Prince Leopold'* had an unfortunate mishap when, on August 23rd 1876, under the helm of Captain Beazley, it crashed into Yarmouth's newly opened wooden pier, damaging almost a quarter of the 685ft long structure. Despite the seriousness of the event, Captain Beazley was a well respected man, and "has won golden opinions here by his careful and seaman like management of the *'Prince Leopold'* " according to the editorial of that week's Hampshire Advertiser.

---

**1.** Gross Registered Tons is defined as "The entire internal cubical capacity in tons of 100 cu ft each". However for cargo carrying, this is usually calculated at "40 feet to the ton" due to the deductions necessary for provisions and stores for the length of the voyage. A separate deduction for passengers and crew must also be made. Net Tons is obtained by deducting crew and navigating spaces, and allowances for the propulsion machinery, from the Gross Tonnage. [Stevens on Stowage, 3rd Ed, 1863.]

### YARMOUTH, Aug. 26.

COLLISION.—On Wednesday afternoon the Southampton and Isle of Wight new steamer Prince Leopold, Captain Beazley, in coming alongside the new pier, no doubt through some error in miscalculating the strength of the tide, came into collision with the pier, and seriously damaged two or three piles on the east end. The steamer was also damaged, one of the sponsons being carried away. The steward's pantry, with a considerable stock just laid in, was smashed, entailing a heavy loss upon him. The steward was also slightly injured. The pier was crowded at the time, as was also the steamer, but we have not heard of any serious accident having been sustained by any one. The noise of the concussion, which was very great, was heard for a considerable distance. It is hoped that Captain Beazley will not suffer in consequence of the accident, as he has won golden opinions here by his careful and seamanlike management of the Prince Leopold.

Hampshire Advertiser, August 26th 1876.

## Ventnor 1887

At Ventnor on the Isle of Wight, the Esplanade Pier, which had been partly destroyed by storms five years previously, had been rebuilt and reopened in July 1887. The *'Prince Leopold'* was recorded as one of the first of the Paddle Steamers to call at the pier, bringing passengers from the mainland who spent several hours in town, helping improve Ventnor's economy.

The pier later became the Victoria Pier, after Her Majesty the Queen agreed to lend her name to it.

## Yarmouth 1878

Several column inches of the Isle of Wight Observer were taken up by yet another incident, in which the *'Prince Leopold'*, still under Captain Beazley, 'became helpless' just off Victoria Fort, some two and a half miles from Yarmouth pier. Her rudder chain had broken, and although there were approaching 400 passengers on board, the steamer managed to discharge all the passengers safely into its lifeboats and two additional steamers (the *'Vectis'* and the *'Lady of the Lake'*) which had been despatched to help. Fortunately, little damage was done to the hull, and the *'Prince Leopold'* was re-floated at the second high tide the following day.

Paddle Steamer excursion tickets from Ventnor. Issued by the Southampton & Isle of Wight Steam Packet Co. Ltd.

154   *10. The Paddle Steamer 'Rhos Neigr'*

Ventnor pier with a Paddle Steamer alongside c1925. Real photo postcard by G. Digweed.

## North Wales 1906

In 1906, The *'Prince Leopold'* (together with her sister ship, the *'Carisbrooke'*) was sold to the Colwyn Bay & Liverpool Steam Ship Co. where both ships operated for just one season before again being sold, this time in 1907 to the Mersey Trading Company, which operated a variety of excursions along the North Wales Coast. Stopping-off points included Menai Bridge on Anglesey, and a postcard from that time clearly shows *'Prince Leopold'* listed amongst the steamers on the excursion board.

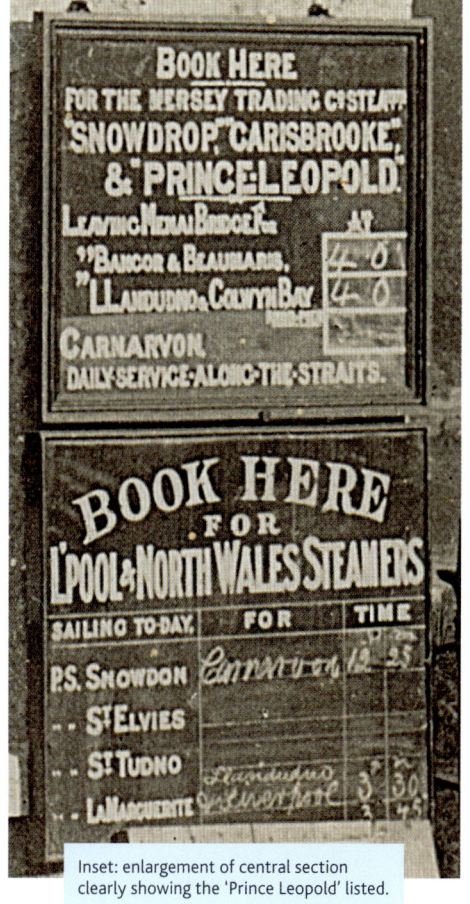

Inset: enlargement of central section clearly showing the 'Prince Leopold' listed.

10. The Paddle Steamer 'Rhos Neigr' 155

Photographic postcard by W & Co [Wright & Co of Bootle] of the Pier & Promenade entrance at Menai Bridge, showing Pleasure Steamer notices. Photograph printed with postcard back. Postmarked Menai Bridge on August 12th 1908 & sent to Mr T.G.K.Beattie of Bootle.

Entry for A.W. Watt from Lloyd's Shipping Register, 1908-9

**Watt, A. W.,**
38, South Castle Street, Liverpool.
(Mersey Trading Co., Ld.)

| | Net Tons |
|---|---|
| s. Mary Horton | 551 |
| s. Rhos Colwyn | 60 |
| s. Rhos Neigr | 88 |
| s. Rhos Trevor | 89 |

By the following season, the *'Carisbrooke'* had been renamed the *'Rhos Trevor'* and the *'Prince Leopold'* was renamed the *'Rhos Neigr'*.

The *'Rhos Neigr'* continued to operate up and down the North Wales coast as normal, but then, on 20th July 1908, disaster struck and the ship sunk.

A detailed report from the following day's Lancashire Evening Post reveals what happened. (see panel 10a).

156    10. The Paddle Steamer 'Rhos Neigr'

'Sinking of the Rhos Neigr July 20th 1908' (with an additional steamer in the distance). Caption reads 'This is the boat on which we were Shipwrecked'. Postcard published by W. Booth & Co. Photographers. Card posted to Borcaston, Nr. Tetbury but with undecipherable postmark.

Following this disaster, at the end of the 1908 season, the Mersey Trading Company went out of business.

The remains of the wreck have been visible near to Rhos Point at Rhos on Sea ever since, although nowadays only at the lowest tides.

Photographic postcard showing the Wreck of the Rhosneigr off Rhos Pier. Photograph printed with postcard back. Otherwise unmarked.

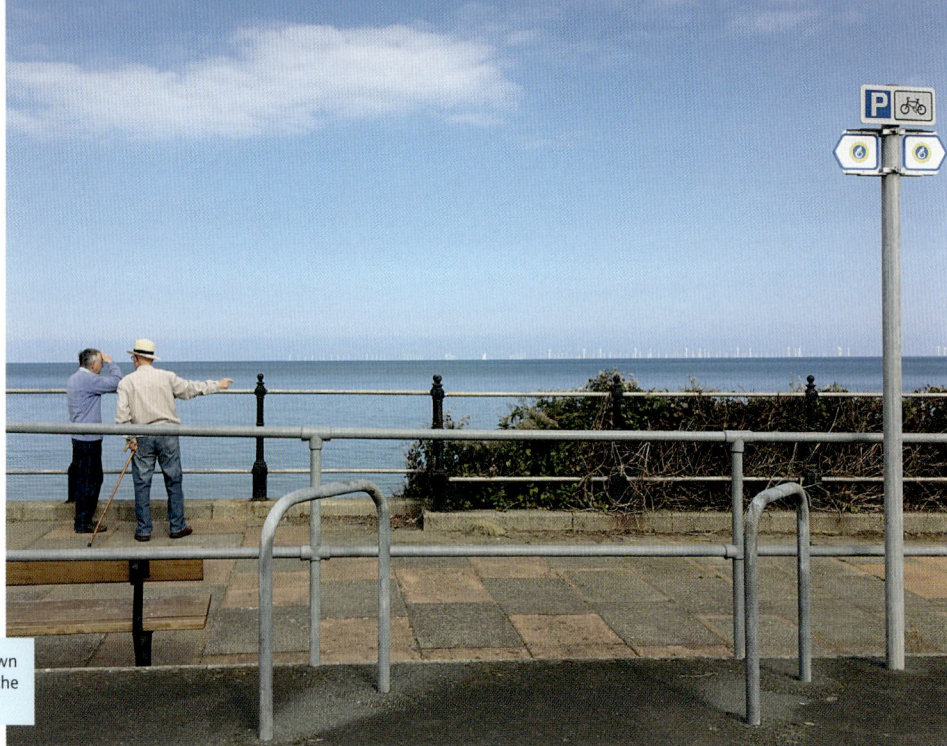

The Editor at Rhos on Sea being shown the location of the wreck by one of the local residents. [Photo: R.J.Hale].

158   *10. The Paddle Steamer 'Rhos Neigr'*

Wreck of Rhos Neigr July 1908. Photograph printed with postcard back. Otherwise unmarked.

Paddle Steamer Rhos Colwyn, Rhos Neigr & Rhos Trevor in Lloyd's Shipping Register 1908-9.

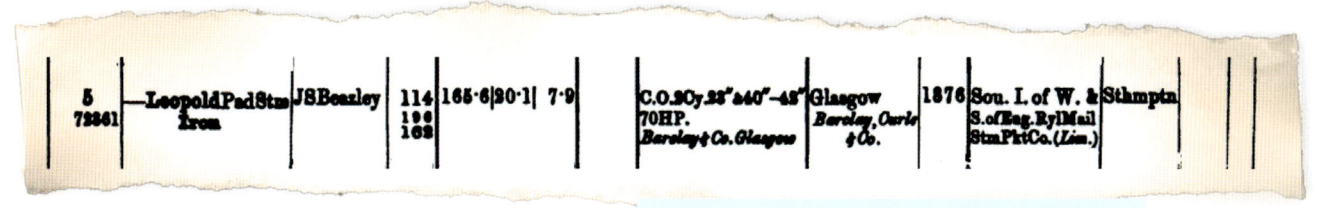

Paddle Steamer Prince Leopold in Lloyd's Shipping Register 1883.

10. The Paddle Steamer 'Rhos Neigr'   159

# Steamer Ashore Sensation for Blackpool excursionists.

Vessel sinks after rescue of passengers Much excitement was caused yesterday at Colwyn Bay and Llandudno by the sinking of a small pleasure steamer called the 'Rhos Neigr' belonging to the Mersey Trading Company and often advertised as the Red Funnel Line.

The Vessel, in command of Captain Smallman, called at Llandudno pier in the forenoon, and took on board some 50 passengers, some for Rhos-on-Sea and the others for Blackpool. It was intended to call at Rhos Pier where there were some 80 others waiting to proceed to Blackpool. At the time it was low tide.

The steamer, which is a paddle boat and the smallest of the company's fleet, passed the Little Orme going close inshore. From the Orme to Rhos Pier is about two miles distance. A little while after passing the Orme and while the vessel was cruising Penrhyn Bay, a grinding sound was heard and almost immediately the fireman from below ran onto the deck to report that water was rushing into the hull.

What had really happened has not been ascertained and a definite opinion will only be possible when the steamer has been properly surveyed. The captain and others of the crew believe that the Paddle wheel struck some floating object such as a heavy log of wood and that it then crashed into the side under the paddle box, striking some of the plates. In the opinion of a passenger however the vessel struck a sunken rock as the steamer was quite close to the shore.

Captain Smallman thought he would be able to reach the Pier but she took in water so rapidly that he thought it advisable when opposite the fishing weir, about 200 yards on the Little Orme side of the pierhead, to run ashore there and he grounded in shallow water. The boats were lowered and it was arranged to send the women and children off first. Up to this moment the passengers had displayed great coolness but when it came to taking to the boats there was a little alarm displayed. However terrafirma was not far off and the calls sounded by the captain on his siren had already summoned help from the crew of the 'Rhos Trevor' a steamer of the same line [which was not far away].

It was therefore seen that very little danger was to be apprehended and admirable order prevailed throughout.

The Rhos Neigr's boats were lowered and those of the 'Rhos Trevor' also arrived. These were sufficient to convey the shipwrecked holidaymakers to the pierhead whence the 'Rhos Trevor' took back to Llandudno those who wished to return to that resort. Fortunately the sea in Penryn Bay was very smooth although further out it was moderately disturbed by a brisk West wind.

The tide rose quickly after the rescue of the passengers and very soon the steamer floated again. Though waterlogged she had watertight compartments fore and aft and those suffice to keep her awash. During this time Captain Smallman and the crew, assisted by Captain Hawthorne[2] endeavoured to get off as much of the loose property on board as possible such as carpets, furniture and other chattels. Everything salvable was brought off in the boats. Gradually the vessel sat lower in the water.

At about 3 o'clock her deck was level with the water and even then there were three men on board including the two captains. Then suddenly, owing it is supposed to the forward watertight chamber giving way, the steamer dived bow first into the sea. Her stern then sank and nothing was visible of her but half her funnel and a little of her stern rail.

[Panel 10a]

Continued overpage

*[Panel 10a] continued*

Captain Hawthorne was thrown into the sea and drawn down by the suction, he came up on the opposite side of the boat. Crowds had by this time congregated on the beach and the electric Tramway brought car loads from Llandudno and Colwyn Bay anxious to see the wrecked vessel and when the men on board, as she sank, were thrown into the water there was great excitement but this was allayed when the signal was given that all were safe.

A gentleman staying in Llandudno who was one of the Passengers says he was seated in the stern when he heard the crash. His opinion, and the opinion of other passengers, is that they were too near the shore. After the shock the vessel's head was turned seawards but when the man came up from below, Captain Smallman steered straight for the shore and sounded his siren. If he had been in deep water it would not have taken the vessel 20 minutes to founder. Everybody on board - captain, crew and passengers - behaved splendidly.

[Liverpool Daily Post, 21 July 1908]

Photo taken in 2010 showing the Wreckage off Rhos Pier. [photo courtesy www.walesdirectory.co.uk].

**2.** Captain Hawthorne was Commodore of the Fleet and was on board that day by chance.

# Chapter 11
# Rhosneigr Then & Now

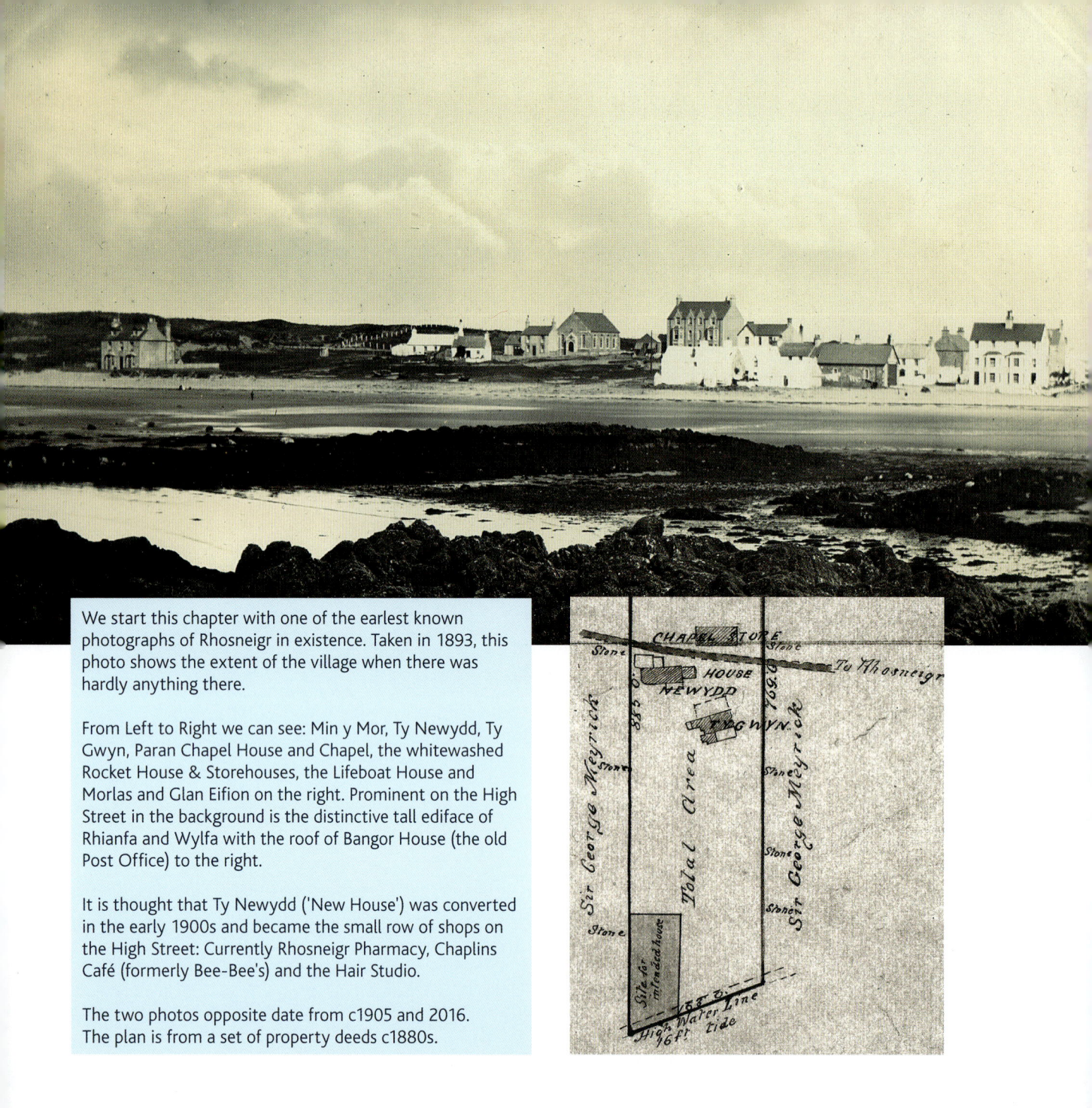

We start this chapter with one of the earlest known photographs of Rhosneigr in existence. Taken in 1893, this photo shows the extent of the village when there was hardly anything there.

From Left to Right we can see: Min y Mor, Ty Newydd, Ty Gwyn, Paran Chapel House and Chapel, the whitewashed Rocket House & Storehouses, the Lifeboat House and Morlas and Glan Eifion on the right. Prominent on the High Street in the background is the distinctive tall ediface of Rhianfa and Wylfa with the roof of Bangor House (the old Post Office) to the right.

It is thought that Ty Newydd ('New House') was converted in the early 1900s and became the small row of shops on the High Street: Currently Rhosneigr Pharmacy, Chaplins Café (formerly Bee-Bee's) and the Hair Studio.

The two photos opposite date from c1905 and 2016. The plan is from a set of property deeds c1880s.

11. Then & Now

# 11. *Then & Now*

Also from 1893, showing the Rocket House & Storehouse to the left of the Lifeboat House. Morlas and Glan Eifion with the old cottages Glan y Don, Glan Ivy, Drws Glas and Ty Plant behind.

Further to the right are Glan Dwr, the backs of Mona Cottage and Bryn Neigr, with Carreg Felan on the extreme right.

Five of the six square chimneys from the old row of buildings on page 182 can also be seen in this photo, helping to place them on the lower high street.

From Left to Right the houses are: Brodawel and Ynys Groes, Random, Dakota, Sandford and Sea View. (B/W photo from 1989).

Brodawel and Ynys Groes were built for R.W. 'Bob' Southern in about 1909 (it was Mr. Southern who lent his name to the latter half of the builders merchants 'Magnet Southern').

The old Random house was built in 1958 and demolished in 2014 to make way for the two new houses (Random and its neighbour Sain y Mor) built to a contemporary design. The project was the first major commission of architect Andy Wilde which has since earned him many new commissions in the area.

The granite stonework originated from the Trefor quarry near Nefyn. This particularly hard granite is also used for making curling stones, an offcut of which can be seen in the south wall. The precision and quality of the stonework has been commented on by many and it was single handedly carved by Niki Salter of Conwy over a period of 6 months.

Dakota, Sandford & Sea View were built in around 1902, on the site of the old Rocket House & Storehouses which can be seen in the top picture on page 166.

**The Bay Hotel - concise history.**

**1903** Built for Henry Smith Cole, son of J.H.Cole the artist.
**1904** Opened.
**1906** First small advert in a newspaper seen in March 1906.
**c1912** 4-storey extension built.
**1913** "Facing Sea. Unrivalled situation. Breezy, bracing climate. Bright, airy and comfortable rooms." Was Mr H.S.Cole's description of his own hotel in the 'Guide to Rhosneigr'.
**c1926** Single storey extension to bar built (licence transferred from Sheep Inn, Pencarnisiog).
**c1933** Henry Cole & his wife, Emily Bubier, ran hotel till appx. 1933 when it was sold to 3 man syndicate from Liverpool. 2 dropped out after a couple of years, leaving the hotel in the hands of the 3rd, Major Cockroft.
**1939** manager Norman Harrison, fined for selling beer in non-permitted hours - on a Sunday.
**11th July 1990** Bay Hotel Auctioned for £120k + vat.
**Feb 1992** - "fire broke out in derelict hotel" - it had been empty over 2 years.
**March 1994** - "derelict building unsafe for children" newspaper article. "possibly convert into flats, or use a WDA grant to demolish and make safe".
**June 1994** - old hotel to be 20 flats
**Aug 1994**, Architect C.Beretta (with his 'starfish' design), £2m complex.
**Feb 1996** permission granted for new design hotel & leisure complex.
**May 1996** petition to demolish the derelict old hotel handed to Anglesey MP Ieuan Wyn Jones.
**Feb 1997** collapse of planning application to demolish. Proposal to build 15 houses + tennis court on site.
**Apr 1997** new eco design - 15 dwellings 'houses for the millennium'.
**May 1997** 16 year-old fell from 3rd to 2 storey of derelict hotel. Trapped & hospitalised.
**Aug 1997** outline planning for 15 dwellings by Stockport based Mixsure ltd (2 brothers) now approved.
**Aug 1997** old Bay Hotel demolished by Mixsure Ltd. (It was dropped into the cellars and the voids underneath became known by teenagers who ventured there as 'The Caves'.)
**2003** outline planning for 15 dwellings renewed.
**2004** Site sold by Mixsure to Rural Space Ltd who started work on site the foslowing year.
**2007** Porth Crigyll development completed. 14 houses built on site, based on New England style Beach Houses.

168  *11. Then & Now*

The architect Clement 'Smiler' Beretta, inspecting the Bay Hotel demolition site. August 1997.

11. Then & Now   169

The continued expansion, then disappearance, of the Bay Hotel is seen in the pictures on this page, with the appearance of the Porth Crigyll development, from the start of its construction in 2005.

The prominent white house Trewyn Isaf (Lower Trewyn) was built by John William Marshall in late 1889 and the early 1890s. He was a housemaster at Charterhouse School and a keen fly fisherman.

According to family history, he came to stay at the Maelog Lake Hotel one summer to fish in the lake, not long after the railway to Holyhead was completed. Rhosneigr was then a small fishing and farming village. The story goes that he and his wife Jessie, went for a walk and came to the site of the house as the sun set across the bay. Jessie said, "Wouldn't this be a wonderful spot for a house!" He thought about what she said and eventually bought the plot of land with Trewyn Bach, the cottage, from the local Bodorgan estate.

Trewyn Isaf is still in the same family today and is a popular seaside let (www.holidayhousewales.co.uk).

The name Trewyn is said to derive from Tref Owain (Owain's Home) which is what the large expanse of sand dunes on the other side of the Crigyll river are called.

170    11. Then & Now

The Waterfront "Luxury Beachside Development" by Russell Homes, consists of twelve high specification properties on a linear, one acre site. It comprises three, four storey townhouses and nine, three-bedroom apartments. (www.russellhomes.co.uk).

It replaced the small row of 3 houses (one a D.I.Y shop for several years), facing Station Road and 'Bryn' which was in front of them, facing the sea. Vaenor, to the right and Nodded and Noddfa still remain. The Porth Crigyll development is on the left.

11. Then & Now 171

Beach Road in the early 1920s.

The land on the left of Beach Road was Henry Jones' builders yard from the early 1920's right up until the mid 1970's but it is now completely covered by the Norman Court development of houses, named after the famous shipwreck in the bay.

# HENRY JONES & SONS,

*Builders, Contractors and Coal Merchants*

Dealers in all kinds of Building Materials

Repairs promptly attended to.

ESTIMATES GIVEN.

Deliveries of Coal at Shortest Notice.

**Builders' Yard, Beach Rd., Rhosneigr**

172  11. Then & Now

The Folland Gnat T1 Reg XP512, crashed in the bay just in front of Beach Terrace on 23rd August 1967 following problems with the pitch control system. Official reports note that it was 'abandoned over sea following hydraulic failure, and landed on the beach at Rhosneigr, Anglesey.'

Both crew members (Pilot Officer P. S. G. Adams and Flight Lieutenant Gordon Allin) ejected at 3000 feet. It was recovered to hangar but deemed damaged beyond repair. Aircraft was officially Struck off as Category 5 (Scrap) on 1 September 1967. XP512 was later moved to the fire pits at RAF Valley for crash rescue/fire fighting training. [Photo: Dilys Moore collection].

The superb collection of automobiles parked in front of the Wave Crest Hotel on Beach Terrace c1940s. [photo: Nancy Davies collection.]

11. Then & Now   173

Uwch y Don ('Above the Wave') on the left and Broad Beach on the right with White Cottage and Parlwr just visible in between. Photos date from c1954 [© The Francis Frith Collection], 1989 and 2016.

174    11. Then & Now

It doesn't take long for changes to take place in Rhosneigr. Top photo taken 2006 showing Anglesey Leisure Ltd, being the 'Power Boat Centre of Anglesey'. Bottom photo taken in 2015 showing the completed Tides Reach development. Only the War Memorial clock tower - and the bus shelter - remain unchanged.

Tides Reach was built by R.L.Davies & Son Ltd of Colwyn Bay and completed in c2010. The site had previously been the Premier Garage (since around 1925).

11. Then & Now   175

Harold Hilton was a Cheshire born amateur golfer who won several championships in his heyday around the turn of the century, including the Open Championship, twice, in 1892 and in 1897. He was the first editor of Golf Monthly magazine, and also the editor of Golf Illustrated.

Created at the instigation of several local businessmen (including C. H. Palethorpe of Surf Point, C. .A. Mills of Cefn Dref, J.Ravenscroft of Trwst y Don and Dr. H. S. Lowe of Penrallt), the golf course was laid out during 1914 by Harold Horsfall Hilton. In October of the same year the Anglesey Golf Club was formed.

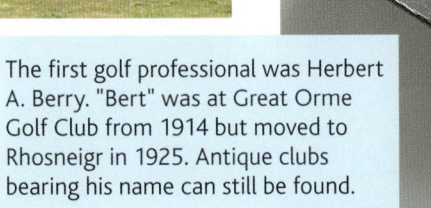

The first golf professional was Herbert A. Berry. "Bert" was at Great Orme Golf Club from 1914 but moved to Rhosneigr in 1925. Antique clubs bearing his name can still be found.

This amazing photograph from 1893 shows the house at the bottom right of Harrison Drive, known as Min y Mor (previously Acton).

The house can also be seen on the extreme left of the view from the boating pool on page 164.

11. Then & Now   177

Postcard by an unknown publisher and postmarked 1926, from a photo probably taken at least a decade earlier. James Roddick (subsequently H.Roddick & Son) Butchers on the left corner, later became the National Westminster Bank.

The smartly kept row of brick-built houses on the right, known as Marine Terrace, were originally built as coastguard's cottages in about 1895.

178   11. Then & Now

The 1933 Austin 12/4 Harley UJ1966 was already a 'classic' car in 1956, being first registered in Shewsbury (Shropshire).

Perhaps it is not entirely surprising to note that this car is still on the road. According to its last sale documentation (from the Classic and Sportscar Centre, Malton, North Yorkshire):

This very charming Austin 12/4 Harley has been with its last owner for the past nine years. The Austin has been part of a small private museum collection and has arrived with us in delightful condition. The car retains its original registration mark UJ 1966 and comes to us with MOT certificates dating back to 1991 showing us that the car has spent the majority of the past 24 years on the road.

The Austin comes with various receipts to include an engine strip down in 2003 that included re-grinding the crankshaft, re-metalling main and big end bearings and replacing pistons. UJ 1966 has been treated to new quarter bumpers, front bumper, full exhaust system and regularly servicing. The car has arrived with us in very good mechanical order with a strong engine, very good gearbox and the car feels reliable and comfortable on the road. It was on offer in 2015 at £13,995.

[Photos - 1956: John Ingle collection; 2016: Lisa Hale. Description courtesy the Classic and Sportscar Centre.]

11. Then & Now   179

180   *11. Then & Now*

### The Pavilion Cinema

Tel. No.: RHOSNEIGR 246

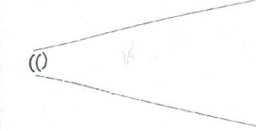

The small cinema which is proud of its Sound & Vision second to none in North Wales

**Why not make sure of your seat! We will reserve it for you at a nominal booking fee**

Box office open for booking 10.0 to 12.0 a.m. each day
HOURS OF SHOWING MON. TO FRI. 7.30 p.m., SAT. 5.0 & 8.0 p.m.

---

The Pavilion Picture House opened in 1920 when films were still silent and by the 1940s was holding frequent after dinner dances. There was also a badminton court for hire. In the mid 1940s it claimed to have "sound and vision second to none in North Wales". By the 1950s, this time advertising under the name of The Pavilion Cinema it boasted of "the latest projection system and the comfort you are accustomed to at home."

By the end of the 1960s it was sold to the Rhosneigr Village Hall Committee, and eventually became in such poor condition that it needed rebuilding. After £5000 of Lottery support for roof repairs in 1995, the entire building eventually needed renovating. EU funding became available in 2007 and the new Rhosneigr Village Hall opened in September 2008 as a registered charity. [2016 Photo: Lisa Hale].

"J. O. Lloyd. Family Butcher. Welsh Meat." This corrugated-iron clad establishment was located on the lower main street, believed to be approximately where Rose Cottage, Fern Cottage and Ivy Cottage are now located.

The photo is believed to date from the late 1890's and the cottages (known as Stryd Uchaf which simply means 'High Street') were demolished in about 1905. The sign on the cottage wall on the right, reads: "Ishmael Jones, Butcher, Shop, Tea & Coffee" and records show that Ishmael Jones had a new shop built during this year which would seem to confirm this date.

182    11. Then & Now

Mona Cottage on the lower High Street, from a photo believed to have been taken in the late 1890s. The name dates from at least 1922 as it was previously called Ty Main when sold in 1891. Next door (to the left) is the wall of Bryn Neigr.

The more modern B/W photo dates from 1951.

[Both photos courtesy Mrs Jean Crawford].

184    *11. Then & Now*

One of the earliest buildings in Rhosneigr was Tyddyn Leci ('Slate Cottage') which was recorded in the old Tithe record books as early as 1830. Shown here in a photo from 1936. (Leci, later mutated to Llechi.)

The cottage eventually became empty and at one point was used to store waste paper for the war effort. During the Second World War, the field became an army training ground and the cottage gradually fell into disrepair, possibly because it was regularly used as a target!

In the early 1960s, Llechi Field, as it was then known, began to be used for housing.

Photos shown here clockwise from top left: 1959 Harvey Barton postcard; 1989; 2016; 1936; 2016; 1956 [John Ingle collection].

11. Then & Now

The Queen's Head Livery Stables and Motor Garage on Maelog Road were also Parcels Agents for the London & North Western Railway. The proprietor was Richard Jones in 1913 and the building is now simply known as London House. [2016 Photo: Lisa Hale].

Unusually for a black & white photo, we know what the colours of the vehicles were, because the advertisement tells us: "Look out for the Blue and Red Motor Cars driven by thoroughly experienced drivers." (Taken from the 1913 'Guide to Rhosneigr').

'Maison Gordon' on Station Road, now known as Rhosyr. Originally the Rhosneigr-based photographer Stephen Feather's Bay Studio. The advert dates from the Guide to Rhosneigr, c1938. The top photograph is thought to be from a slightly later date. [Photo: V.Clancy Collection].

In the early 1930s, Eileen Gordon carried out Ladies' hairdressing at the Bryn Garage, but by 1939 had set up Maison Gordon in these premises.

'Phone 259.

## LADIES' AND CHILDREN'S HAIRDRESSING

## MAISON GORDON

HAIR TINTING, MASSAGE, SHAMPOO, MARCEL WAVING, MANICURE, EYE-BROW ARCHING, Etc., Etc.

HOURS: 9.30 a.m. to 6.30 p.m.
Wednesday, 1 p.m.

TOILET REQUISITES, CHOCOLATES AND CIGARETTES IN STOCK.

11. Then & Now

The cottage 'Y Bonc' ('The Bank' or 'The Hillock' ) stood on Station Road almost opposite the top of the lane down to Porth Crigyll (previously the Bay Hotel). Originally built around 1888, It was converted into 'The Minstrel Lodge' restaurant in the mid-1980s and ran as a restaurant for over twenty years. The property was demolished in 2007 and converted again into the Minstrel Lodge development of nine "mews-style houses" by the Alcamay Group.

The Bryn Garage was built by Captain J. W. Huws in 1931 for his son Glyn, who ran it until the Second World War when it was commandeered by the army. In 1945 Glyn was joined by John Shelby-James from Aberdare and the garage re-opened as a partnership. (Glyn on the left, John on the right, in the photo). [photo: Alf Moore]

The partnership flourished for 24 years until in 1969 Glyn retired and John secured a 10 year lease to continue trading. John continued alone until his retirement in May 1979 when the garage closed and the building was sold to Mr. Albert Williams, then the owner of the Premier Garage by the clock. After a degree of bitterness, the equipment was auctioned off and the petrol tanks filled with concrete.

'The Rhosneigr Motor Show' dates to around 1990 when the garage had been put on the market and the old vehicles had been put there to prevent fly-tipping.

11. Then & Now

LAKESIDE, RHOSNEIGR                                                        W 7015

Precisely dating from 1958, this array of parked cars is on the land adjacent to the stream outflow from the Maelog Lake to Broad Beach. Lakeside Bungalow is on the right. The only registrations visible are FTM123, LBK285 and PWE669 (the 4th car to the right of the footbridge).

Valentine's of Dundee - a prolific publisher of postcards - ceased publishing cards in the 1960s and the major part of their archive now resides in the Special Collections Dept. of the University of St. Andrews in Scotland. [2016 Photo: Lisa Hale].

190   11. Then & Now

This view over the Storehouse and cottages around the old Lifeboat House is dated 1893.

Repeating the photo is difficult, due to the modern houses now in place such as Ty Newydd (L), Sibrwd y Don and Magna Cottage (R). The newly rebuilt pair of houses, Random and Sain y Mor are also just visible with Ynys Groes and Crimble on the extreme right. [2016 photo: Huwmedia].

11. Then & Now

Panoramic view of Rhosneigr from the old (now demolished) water tower, which used to be at the top of Fford y Wylan, with the modern picture showing 'Cartref' in the foreground. Cae Cloc still unbuilt, as are Tides Reach and the Norman Court houses - to name but a few.

Photo taken by local photographer Stephen Feather whose shop & Bay Studio can clearly be seen on the right of the photo.

The Bay Studio later became Maison Gordon and is now converted to a house.
(See page 187).
[2016 Photo: Huwmedia].

192    11. Then & Now

View over Sandy Lane towards the Maelog Lake, with Fford y Wylan junction on the left of the modern photo. Another shot taken from the top of the now demolished Water Tower. [Photo: © The Francis Frith Collection, postmarked 1960].

The houses on the left of the modern photo, are some of those built by Hurstwell Developments of Manchester c2006. Also visible in this picture are Y Fron, Fronegar and Fronallt with red-roofed Longacre behind. The white walls of Rolleston, and Semmering further to the right, are just about distinguishable.
[2016 Photo: Huwmedia].

11. Then & Now   193

The castellated white house in the centre of these photos was built in around 1909 for Charles Palethorpe, who came to Rhosneigr from the Black Country, where the family name has long been associated with the manufacture and processing of pork. It is therefore hardly surprising that despite its official title of Surf Point, the building has always been affectionately known as 'Sausage Castle'.

The land on which it stood was purchased from Sir George Meyrick and tradition tells us that it was built to resemble a sandcastle on the beach - perfect for a holiday house. However the family did not live there at first -the April 1911 census shows only Ada Stride (housekeeper) and Kate Roberts (temporary cook) in residence.

After many years in Palethorpe ownership, the property was sold in 2005, and over the next two years was completely renovated from top to bottom. [Photo: © The Francis Frith Collection; 2016 Photo: Huwmedia].

In the foreground are the beginnings of Overstrand Avenue. The houses under construction are (from left to right) Romany Cottage, Swn-y-Mor and Bryn Glas. [2016 Photo: Huwmedia].

View from the Fire Station tower over the roofs of the Minstrel Lodge development, towards Station Road and the village centre. The 1989 photo shows Trewyn Uchaf at the corner of Sandy Lane but the 2015 picture just shows Ynys Hir (L) and Swyn Llyr (R).

The first view, looking West over the Bay Hotel towards the Crigyll and Cymyran Sands, also takes in the Bryn Colyn flats, which were built in around 1963, behind the cottage Bryn Gwyn and the Bryn Garage.

By 2016 the Porth Crigyll houses have replaced the Bay Hotel, and the Waterfront development by Russell Homes, on the left, is also completed.

Looking North over Station Road, Trem-y-Mor and the old Christ Church towards the links of Anglesey Golf Club in the distance.

198    11. Then & Now

Believed to have been taken in the mid 1960s, when roads such as Sisial y Mor and Ger y Mor had not yet been built, although some of the houses on Fford Llechi still seem to be in the course of construction.

[Photo: Committee for Aerial Photography, University of Cambridge]

# Bibliography & Index

# Bibliography

*"A Dictionary of Sea Terms"* by A. Ansted
James Brown & Son
1st Edition, 1919

*"A Universal Dictionary of the Marine"* by William Falconer.
1st edition, 1780

*"China Tea Clippers"* by George F. Campbell
International Marine Publishing Co.
2nd edition, 1990

*"Crime and Punishment - A Welsh Perspective"* by Mary Aris, Andrew Wynne & Jo Pott.
Gwynedd Archives & Museums Service
published 1987

*"Dictionary of National Biography"* (online)

*"Dictionary of Welsh Biography"* (online)

*"Elementary Manual for the Deviations of the Compass in Iron Ships."*
By Captain F.J.Evans
Published by J.D.Potter, 1875.

*"Hanes Methodistiaeth, Bryn Du, Mon"*, (The History of Methodism in, Bryn Du, Anglesey). by John Watkin Hughes.
Published 1912

*"Lie in the Dark and Listen"* by Wing Commander Ken Rees & Karen Arrandale
Grub Street, London
1st Edition, 2004

*"Liverpool and North Wales Pleasure-Steamers"* by John Cowell
S.B. Publications, 1990

*"Llwynogod Mon ac Ysgrifau Eraill"* (The Foxes of Anglesey and other Essays) by Rev. Dr. Dafydd Wyn Wiliam
Cyhoeddiadau Mei
1st edition 2003

*"Margrave of The Marshes"* by John Peel & Sheila Ravenscroft
Bantam Press
1st Edition, 2005

*"Max Horton and the Western Approaches"* by Rear-Admiral W.S.Chalmers
Hodder & Stoughton
2nd Edition, 1954

*"On The Stowage of Ships and Their Cargoes"* by Robert White Stevens.
Longmans London
3rd Edition. 1863

*"Saga of the Norman Court"* by P.J.Salmon
Sea Breezes, May 1965 page 346-351

*"Ships and Seamen of Anglesey"* by Aled Eames
Anglesey Antiquarian Society
1st Edition, 1973

*"Shipwreck Index of the British Isles"* by Richard & Bridget Larn
Lloyd's Register of Shipping
1st edition, 2000

*"Shipwrecks of North Wales"* by Ivor Wynne Jones
David & Charles
1st Edition, 1973

*"Steamers of North Wales - Past and Present"* by F.C.Thornley
Stephenson & Sons, Lancs.
1st Edition, 1952

*"The China Clippers"* by Basil Lubbock
James Brown & Son
3rd Edition, 1916

*"The Clipper Ship Era"* by Arthur H. Clark
G.P.Putnam's Sons
4th Edition, 1911

*"The Great Days of Sail"* by Andrew Shewan
("Some reminiscences of a Tea-Clipper Captain")
Heath Cranton ltd, 2nd Edition, 1927
also, Naval Institute Press, USA, 2nd Edition 1973

*"The Great War"*, Vol VI, March 1916.
Amalgamated Press Ltd, London

"The Place Names of Anglesey" by Gwilym T. Jones & Tomos Roberts
Isle of Anglesey County Council
1st Edition, 1996

"The Royal Academy of Arts, Dictionary of Contributors 1769-1904"
(Vol II) by Algernon Graves.
Henry Graves & Co Ltd, 1905

*"The Sailor's Word Book"* by Admiral W.H.Smyth.1867.

*"The Tea Clippers"* by David R. MacGregor
Conway Maritime Press
2nd Edition, 1973

**By the same Author**

"Rhosneigr Then & Now" – Published 1990, ISBN 1872710006, Now out of print.

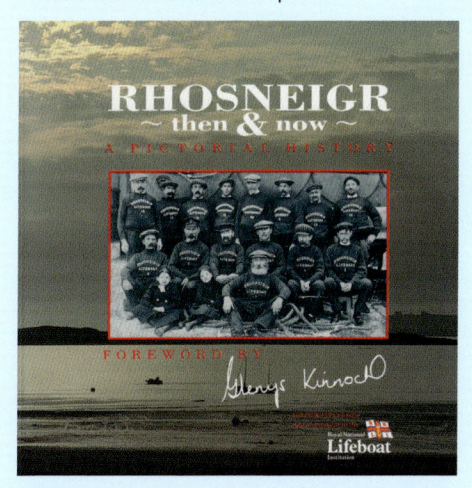

"The Rhosneigr Romanticist"– Published 2009, ISBN9780956296207. Still available.

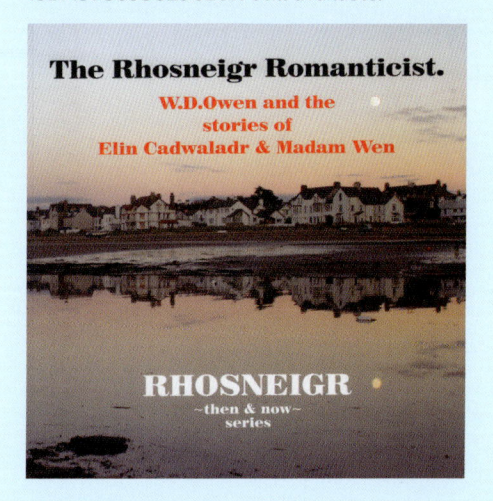

# Index

## A
Aberdare, 189
Aberdeen, 133, 148
Aberffraw, 15, 46
Aberystwyth, 16, 34
Acton, 177
Adams, S.G., 173
Admiral Dert, 128
Admiral Edward Vernon, 16
Admiral Grant, 120
Admiral Karl Donitz, 39
Admiral Mackenzie, 128
Admiral Sir Arthur Wilson VC, 35
Admiral Sir Max Kennedy Horton GCB, 32, 37, 39
aircraft, 36, 53, 55, 57, 60, 173
aircraft carriers, 36
aircrew, 53, 57–58, 60
Air Observers' School, 53
Air Training Corps, 37
Alcamay Group, 188
Alfred Basil Lubbock, 109
Aline, 116–17
Ambrose, Joseph, 119
Ambrose, Owen John, 15–16
Anemones, 82–83
Anglesey coast, 7, 109
Anglesey Court of Great Sessions, 16
Anglesey Golf Club, 176, 198
Anglesey legend, 26, 91
Anglesey Leisure Ltd, 175
Anglesey magistrates, 20
Anglesey MP, 168
Anglesey quarter session, 12
Anjer Point, 134
Annandale, Charles, 130
Ann Park, 61
antiques, 79
Antiques Roadshow, 67–70
anti-submarine warfare, 36
Arbroath, 119
Archibald Carter, 119
Architect C.Beretta, 168–69
Ariel, 136, 145
Arkwright, 61
army, 46–48, 54, 61, 189
army of innocents, 47
Arnold, J.R., 40
Art Galleries, 68
Arthur John Owen, 53, 60
Ashton, 89–90, 152
Asia, 111
assizes, 20–21
Atalanta, 123, 126
Athenia, British liner, 31
Atlantic, Battle of, 5, 29–41, 116
auction, 25, 41
Austin Harley UJ1966, 179
Australia, 74, 94, 142
Avro, 6
Aymar, Benjamin, 146

## B
Balkin, 3
ballast, 114, 135–36
Ballycotton, 120, 124–25
Baltic, 35
Baltimore Clippers, 114
Banca, 134
Bancroft Turner, 75
Bangkok, 146
Bangor, 89, 101
Bangor House, 164
Bangor-on-Dee, 103
Bannister D.W., 53
Barclay Curle, 153
Baring Archive, 123
Baring Bros, 116, 136–38, 148
barque, 17, 22, 109, 116–17, 120
Bartley & McBride connection, 126
Bartley family, 123, 126–27
Bath Chronicle, 21
Battery Sgt Major Alfred W.Moger, 53
Bay Hotel, 48, 66, 70, 168, 170, 188, 197
Bay Hotel demolition, 169
Baynham, Derrick, 54–55, 60–61
Baynham, Hubert, 61
Bay Studio, 187, 192
BBC, 47, 70
Beach Houses, 168
Beach Road, 172
Beach Terrace, 173
Beattie,T.G.K., 156
Beaufighters, 53
Beaumaris, 13, 15–16, 18
Bee-Bee's, 164
Belan, 127
Belfast, 24
bells, 123, 138
Benyon, Valerie, 40
Beretta, 169
Berry, Bert, 176
Berry, Herbert A., 176
Berry, John, 24
Betws-y-Coed, 75, 82
bicycle pump, 102
Big Pebble, 78
Billiton, 134
Bingham, Sandy, 105
birdwatching, 61
Birkenhead, 25, 72, 85, 101, 103
Biscay, 36
Bistro, 105
Blackadder, 140
Blackhill, 14
Blackburn Botha, 5, 51–61
Black Country, 194
Blackhill, 14
Blackpool, 160
Black Prince, 116, 136, 145, 147
Blackwall, 133, 140
Bletchley Park, 36
Bloomsbury Publishing, 111, 133
Bluebells, 75
boarding house, 61, 99
boarding schools, 34
Bob & Betty Heaps, 99
Bodawen, 85
bodies, 22–25
Boer war, 109
bomber, 53, 101, 103
bone-setters, 40
Bon Marche, 3, 81
Bookless, Betty, 61
Booth & Co, 157
Bootle, 152, 156
Borcaston, 157
Borneo Sumatra, 134
Boston, 24, 111
Botha, 53, 55
Bournemouth, 82, 85
Bowen, George, 24
Bowling, 134
brasswork, 146
bravery, 53, 60, 120, 129
Brian Gerald, 100
bridge, 9, 47, 74–75, 102
Brigadier, 61
Brigands, 13
Bristol Pegasus, 101
Britain, 13, 31–33, 101, 111
British Calendar Act, 16
British Empire Medal, 54
British ensign, 136
British Navy, 32, 37
British Submariners, 32, 35
British Tea Clipper, 112
British Underwater Skin Diving Team, 61
Broad Beach, 22, 46, 100, 174, 190
Brockell, Henry, 22, 24
Brodawel, 167
Bronant, 93, 95
Bronant Bach, 61
Brown, Adam, 126
Brown, James, 145
Brown, Jean, 40
Brummell, 138
Bryan, Dan, 37
Brychan, 2
Bryn, 7, 171, 202
Bryn Colyn, 197
Brynddu, 14–15
Bryn Garage, 187, 189, 197
Bryn Glas, 195
Bryngolen, 128
Bryngwran, 89, 93
Bryn Neigr, 166, 183
Bryn Siriol, 90
Bubier, Emily, 168
Buckingham Palace, 60
Bulkeley, William, 13–15
bulwarks, 146, 148
Bungalow, 5, 43–49, 81
Burgoyne, 145
Burrow & Co Ltd, 9
Butchers, 178, 182

## C
Cable Bay, 26
Cadrod Calchfynydd, 2
Cadwaladr, Elin, 90, 92
Cae Cloc, 192
Caernarvon Bay, 66
Callister, Leonie, 103
Calvinistic Methodist Chapel, 88
Cambridge, 35, 109, 199
Campbell, George F., 113, 132
Campbell, John, 24
Camping Coaches, 9
Canada, 26–37, 109
Canton, 111, 146
Cape of Good Hope, 116, 140
Captain Andrew Shewan, 110, 114, 116, 133, 145–46, 148
Captain Basil Lubbock, 109, 145
Captain Beazley, 120, 153–54
Captain Cayin, 129
Captain Chilcot's wife, 20
Captain Chrisholme, 23
Captain Delano, 146
Captain Hawthorne, 160–61
Captain Hight, 120
Captaining Tea Clippers, 110
Captain James Lawrence, 116
Captain Jones, 22, 47
captain London Welsh, 101
Captain McBride, 117–20, 123–24, 126
Captain Moodie, 140
Captain Nancollis, 22, 25
Captain Smallman, 160–61
Captain Stevens, 133
Cardiff, 88
cargo junks, 147
Carisbrooke, 155–56
Carnarvon, 66, 120, 124
Carreg Felan, 166
Carter, A.M., 119, 121
Cartref, 192
cattle, 26, 90
cave, 91–92, 168
Cefn Dref, 127, 176
Cefndu, 23
Ceirchiog Parish, 14
Cerrig y Defaid, 22
C.Evans, 81
C.Glockler, Sergeant, 53
Chalmers, Rear Admiral, 33–37
Chantrey Bequest, 72
chapel, 73, 89, 164
Chapel House, 88
Chaplins Café, 164
Chapple
 honest Judge, 16, 18–19
 William, 13, 16
Charles Baring Wall, 127
Charlie & Heather Parsons, 99, 101
Charming Jenny, 5, 20
Charterhouse School, 170
ChA-sze, 133
Chateau Rhianfa hotel, 93
Chef's Training Academy, 40–41
Chemical Warfare, 38
Cheshire, 48, 61, 84–85, 101, 103, 176
Chester, 22–25, 59–61
Chilcot, 20
Chilkoot trail, 109
China, 111–12, 116, 133–35, 142, 146–47
China tea trade, 112, 142
Chinese pilot, 146
Chinese Pirate Junk, 134
Chinese ports, 115
Chinese stevedores, 139
Chinese style rigging, 147
Chops, 135
Christ Church, old, 198
Churchill, Winston, 31, 36
cigarettes, 59, 102
Clark, Arthur H., 114, 147

Clay Cross, 89
Clements, Rex, 133
climate, 66, 168
Clipper Anglais, 149
clipper racing, 112, 116
Clipper Ship Era, 114, 147
Clive Stuart Mayall, 40
Clwyd, 100
Clyde, 114–15, 118, 120, 140
Coal Boat, 81
Coastal policing, 20
coast guard, 22, 25, 60, 82, 124–25, 129
Coastguard Officer Evan Jones, 53
coat, precious, 58–59
Cockram, Edna, 81
Cockram, George, 5, 63–85
Cockram, Mary Doris, 73
Cockram, Stephen, 72
Cockram, William, 72
Cockram's studio, 70, 79, 81
coffee, 55, 59, 117
coffee houses, 111
Cole, 66, 70, 85
  Hal, 66, 70
  Henry, 64, 168
  Lucy Mary, 85
Colwyn Bay, 34, 160–61, 175
Colwyn Bay & Liverpool Steam Ship Co, 155
Commander Max Horton, 38
Commodore Jamie Millar R, 37
Compton-Hall, Richard, 35
concert, 128–29
Conway, 72–73, 85, 167
Conway Valley, 73, 84
cook, 24, 45, 94–95, 119, 194
Cookham, 75
copper, 109, 139, 146
Corisande, 116
Cork, 24
Coromandel coast, 116
coroner, 23–25
corpse, plundered, 20
Cottage, Fern, 182
Cottage, Ivy, 182
Cottage, Mona, 183
Cottell, W.B., 119
cotton merchant, 45
court
  badminton, 181
  tennis, 168
courtesy, 22, 40, 108
Court of Enquiry, 59
Court of Great Sessions in Beaumaris, 15
Cowries, 46
coxswain, 119, 124–25, 127–29
Coxswain William Morris, 127
Crack Tea Clippers, 145
Craigside, 99
Crawford, 183
Cribb & West S'sea, 36
Crigyll, 7, 13, 16, 18–19, 22, 25
Crigyll and Cymyran reefs, 143
Crigyll and Cymyran Sands, 197
Crigyll river, 13, 170
Crigyll Robbers, 7, 13, 16, 19, 22, 26
Crimble, 191

Crompton, Stephen, 104
Cross, James, 24
Cruelty, 117
Cumberland Training Ship, 119
curator, 68, 73
curling stones, 167
currents, 109, 124, 134
Customs, 25
Cutty Sark, 109, 140–42, 145, 147–49
Cwmerran, 25
Cymyran, 7, 13, 109, 118, 129, 143, 197
Cymyran Bay, 7, 83, 118, 124, 126, 129

D
Dafydd Wyn Wiliam, 13–14, 16
Daily Telegraph, 61
Dakota, 167
D'Arcy Horton, 33
Dartmouth, 138
David S Turner, 40
Davies, Josephine, 40
Dean, John, 24
deck, half, 109
deck fittings, 146, 148
Deganwy, 45
Dennis George Clutton, 40
Derby House, Liverpool, 32
Derby Mercury, 20
Derbyshire, 89
derelict hotel, 168
deviation, magnetic, 127
Devil's Kitchen, 74
Devizes & Wiltshire Gazette, 127
Digweed, G, 155
Dinas Dinlle, 66
Dinglewood School, 34
Dixon,T.A., 53
Dönitz, 31–32, 36
Dorothy Warner, 110
Dorset, 61
Drive, Harrison, 55, 177
Drws Glas, 166
Dublin, 23–25
Dudley, 85
Dundee, 119, 190
dunes, 13, 78, 80–81
Dunes, The, 66
Dunn, Dandy, 116
Dunn, Susan, 116
Durham, 61
Dutch East Indies, 117
Dutton, 137

E
Earl of Chester, 22
early on, 66
East India Docks, 112
Edinburgh, 24–25
Edna Cockram, 73, 81
Edwards, 128–29
  Clare, 105
eggs, 59, 73, 90
Einir Wyn, 91
Elin Cadwaladr stories, 92
Elizabeth Bookless, 61
Elizabeth Ravenscroft, 46, 123, 126

Elliott, 129
Ellis, Edward, 15
English aristocracy, 111
English Channel, 102, 116
English parliament, 111
English Presbyterian Churches, 88
English visitors, 143
ensign, 136
Entwistle, Brian, 80, 144
Esplanade Pier, 154
Essex, 6
Esther Maud Horton, 33
Eton, 109
Europe, 102
European pilots, 146
Evan Hughes, 25
Evans, 55, 128
Evening Sunset, 74
exposure, 110, 119, 121
Eyre, 128–29

F
Fagan, Thomas and Sarah, 40
Fairweather, Margaret, 6
Falcon, 136
Falklands Conflict, 35
false lights, 18
Fanning Evans, Mrs, 129
Farquhar, W, 119
fathoms, 14, 121, 139, 146
Feather, Stephen, 192
Fern Cottage, 182
Fford Llechi, 199
Fford y Wylan, 192–93
Fielden, Thomas, 119
Fiery Cross, 145, 147
Finland, 24
First World War, 31, 89
Firth of Forth, 35, 118
fishing, 7, 33, 61, 79, 109, 170
fishing boats, 66–67, 70
fishing weir, 160
Fitz, Henry, 119
F.Jenson, 119
flat-bottomed barge, 135, 147
Fleming, Emmeline, 99
Fleming, Frank, 99
Flight Lieutenant Gordon Allin, 173
Flintshire, 38
Florence Nightingale, 95
Florence's cook, 93
Flower Paintings, 82
Flying Instructor, 101
Flying Spur, 136
Folland Gnat, 173
Foochow, 116, 135, 139, 146
Ford, Leslie A., 53
Foreland, 142
Foreman, William, 24
Formosa Straits, 146
Fort, Victoria, 154
fossil, perfect, 74
Fou-Chow-Foo, 135
Frank & Emmeline Fleming, 99
Fransisco, San, 109
Fraser, W., 119
Frederick B. Turner, 73, 75
Fronallt, 193
Frondeg, 80

Fronegar, 193
Frongogh, 80
FTM123, 190
Furnis, John, 72

G
gale force winds, 53, 110
gallantry, 53–54, 60, 129
Gathering Dusk, 84
Genedl Gymreig, 89
General Belgrano, 35
General Sikorski, 53
Geoffrey & Kathleen Wood, 61
George Alfred Davies, 40
George Cledwyn Arthur, 60
George Edward Jones, 40
George Frederick Campbell, 113
George's sketchbooks, 67
German invasion, 35
German Navy, 31, 39
Germans, 100–102
German submarines, 31, 36–37
German U-Boats, 31
Germany, 31, 35, 102
Ger y Mor, 199
Glandwr, 127
Glan Dwr, 166
Glan Eifion, 164, 166
Glan Ivy, 166
Glan y Don, 166, 174, 176, 191
Glasgow, 116
Glen Sugar Refining Co, 118
Gloucestershire, 89
gold cigarette cases, 53
Gold Rush, 109
Goldsmith, Raymond, 56
golf, 32, 40, 89, 176
Golf Illustrated, 176
Golf Monthly, 176
Goodard, E., 119
Good Hope, 116
Gordon, Eileen, 187
Gorringe's, 100
Gorse Banks, 83
Gough, John, 119
grass, marram, 7, 58
Grass Island, 143
grave, 19, 126, 143
Great Escape, 100–101
Great Orme Golf Club, 176
Great Sessions, 15–16
Green, James, 120
Green, Jamie, 142
Greenock, 117–20, 123–24, 126
Greenwich, 140
Griffiths, 6
G.Rollos map, 143
ground chop, 135–36
guard, 14, 102
guard's bicycle, 102
Guernsey, 24
Guide to Rhosneigr, 46, 95, 99
gunboat Moorhen, 146
Gunner Clarence H.Thornton, 53
Gunner Reginald Eaton, 53
Gunner R.K.Simons, 54
Gunner S.Wilkins RA, 53
Gwellt, 143
Gwent, 18
Gwrgon, 2

Gwyllt, 143
Gwyndraeth beach, 18

H
Hair Studio, 164
Hale, Lisa, 98, 179, 181, 186, 190
Hale Cemetery, 84
hall, Rhosneigr Village, 181
Hall, Samuel, 24
Hallett, William, 119
Hallowe'en, 116, 140
Hamble River Sailing Club, 110
Hampshire, 114, 127, 153–54
Hankow, 146, 148
Hanover, 24
Hanrich Mathies, 24
harbour rocks, 56
Harrison, George, 85
Harvey, Thomas, 24
Hay Williams, 93
H.Cole, 168
Heaps, Betty, 101
Hela, 34
Heligoland, 35
Henry Cole R.A, 66, 70
Henry Smith Cole, 168
Henry William Hall, 24
Heswall, 45
Hibernia Terrace, 25
High Sheriff, 128
High Street, 61, 164, 182
  lower, 54, 79, 166
Hill, James D., 94
Hilton, Harold, 176
Himalayan provinces, 112
hinges, 79
Hirfon, 90
HMS Clyde, 36
HMS Conqueror, 35
HMS Spearfish, 36
HMS St. Albans, 37
Holder, Anthony, 48
Holland, 24
Holyhead, 7, 9, 23, 25, 37, 109, 119, 122–23, 125–26, 142, 170
Holyhead Coxswain, 119–20
Holyhead Lifeboat, 5, 22, 119, 121, 124–25, 127–29, 142
hong, 135
Hong Kong, 138, 146
Horn, 133
Horrocks & Co, 152
Horton, 33, 35–37
  Esther, 34
  Max, 33–35, 37, 40, 202
  Robert, 33
Horton's parents, 34, 36
Horton's residence, 34
Horton's submarines, 36
Hotel and Golf Links, 32
household management, 95
housekeeper, 126–27, 194
housemaster, 170
H.Roddick & Son, 178
Huf Haus, 41
Hughes, Hugh, 25, 127
Hughes, Jane, 105
Hughes, John, 126–27
Hughes, Peter, 15
Hughes, William, 14, 85

Bibliography & Index  205

Hughes Butcher, 55
Hugh Jones, Trewyn Bach, 127, 170
Hurstwell Developments, 193

**I**
Idwal, 74
Illustrated London News, 112
India, 22, 67, 112
Indian Ocean, 116
Indigo, 117
Indonesia, 117
Inglis Ltd, 114
Ireland, 26, 37, 120
Irish Sea, 53
iron frames, 122, 127, 142, 147
Ishmael Jones, 182
Italian Prisoner, 61
Ivy Cottage, 182

**J**
jacket, good sports, 59
Jackson, George, 12, 14–15
James Grieve Jnr, 116
Japan, 146
J.Archer, 143
Java, 117–18, 134, 140
Java sugar, 116–17
J.Cotterell, 40
Jessie Marshall, 170
Johannesburg, 72
John Henry Cole R.A, 73
John Hughes, Ty Main, 127, 183
John Ingle, 179, 185
John Joseph Norwood Thompson, 40
John Leslie Stewart Wood, 60
John Morris, 16, 45–48, 55, 189
John Richard Prichard, 126
John Robert, Ty Gwyn, 127, 164
John Robert Parker Ravenscroft, 45
Johnson, John, 24
John Watkin Hughes, 7, 202
John William Marshall, 170
Jolly Roger, 35
Jones, 25
  Evan, 60
  Henry, 172
  Owen, 24
  Richard, 186
  William, 24
Joy's Green, 89
J.Ravenscroft, 176
judge, 15–16, 18–19
  drunken, 16
Julian calendar, 16
Jung, Peter, 55
Justice Thomas Martyn, 13
J.W.Lees brewery, 40

**K**
Kaisow, 136
Keay, 145
Kedge, 132
Kemball of Thermopylae, 145
Kensington, 73, 94
Kentish Gazette, 20
Kew, 75
King George VI, 60
King's Schoool, 61
Kinnerton, 61
kitchen, 45, 93
Klondyke, 109

**L**
Ladies' hairdressing, 187
Lady Barker, 94
Lady Day, 94
Lady of the Lake, 154
Lahloo, 136, 145
Lakeside Bungalow, 44–45, 190
Lake Traffwll, 89
Lammermuir, 110
Lancaster, 12, 101
land, common, 41
Larne, 36
Larry & Jane Hughes, 99, 105
LBK285, 190
Leading Aircraftman, 53
Leander, 136, 142, 145
Leave Land, 18
Leci, 185
Leece, William, 72
Lees Brewery, 41
Leicester, 72, 85
Leopold, Prince, 152–56
Lewis, William, 15
Lewis Morris, 18
lifeboat, 22–23, 26–27, 118–21, 124, 129, 154
lifeboat crew, 128–29
lifeboat house, 119, 164, 166, 191
life-saving apparatus, 125
Light Anti-Aircraft Training Regiment, 54
Lighters, 135, 147
lighthouses, 26, 120
Lingham, Thomas, 22, 27, 119, 127
Little Orme, 160
Liverpool, 12, 14, 18, 22–25, 32, 40, 72, 78, 120, 168, 202
Liverpool Academy, 72
Liverpool Art Gallery, 85
Liverpool Cathedral, 37
Liverpool Daily Post, 85, 161
Liverpool Mercury, 117, 125
Lladron Crigyll, 13, 19, 22
Llanallgo, 25
Llanbadrig, 24
Llanbeulan, 14
Llanbeuno, 23
Llanddulas, 126
Llandrillo, 126
Llandudno, 66, 73, 160–61
Llanfaelog, 13–15, 22–25, 45, 54, 90
Llanfaelog churchyard, 25
Llanfaelog parish, 2, 22
Llanfaelog school log, 22
Llanfair Bach, 123, 126
Llanfechell Parish, 14
Llanfihangel-yn-Nhowyn, 15
Llangwyfan, 24
Llanwrst, 73
Llechi, 185
Lloyd J.O (Butcher), 182
Lloyd's agent, 22
Lloyd's Register, 116, 126, 145, 156, 159
Llyn Idwal, 74
Llyn Maelog, 2
Llyn Ogwen, 70, 74
Lombok, 134
London & North Western Railway, 186
London Dock, 138
London Docklands, 110
London Gazette, 54, 60
London House, 186

London Stock Exchange, 33
London-Sydney trade, 140
London Welsh, 103
the Lonely Shore, 78, 85
Longacre, 193
Long March, 102
Lorcha, 147
Lord, Vernon, 40
Lord Dundonald, 38
Lothair, 142, 145
Loveday and Betty, 5, 12–15, 61
Lowe H.S., 176
Lower Norwood, 27
Lowry, Marlene, 40
Lubbock, Basil, 109–10, 113–14, 116, 137, 140
Lucy Mary Bolongaro Cole, 73
Lyons, 25

**M**
Macao, 146, 148
Macdonald, James, 24
Macgravy, John, 24
Madam Wen, 26, 89, 91–92
Maelog, 29, 32, 40–41, 46, 76, 84, 190, 193
Maelog Lake Hotel, 5, 29–41, 47, 170
Maelog Road, 186
Maelog Villa, 167
Magna Cottage, 191
magnetic field, 127
Magnet Southern, 167
Maison Gordon, 187, 192
Major Cockroft, 168
Malay, 134
Malcolm, A., 119
Malton, 179
Manager, 40
Manby, G.W., 119
Manchester, 6, 73, 75, 129, 193
Manchester bales, 115, 146, 148
maps, early, 143
Margrave of the Marshes, 46, 202
Maritime crime, 13
market, new teas, 135
Marshall, William, 119
Martin, Coastguard, 25
Martyn Rees & Charlie Parsons, 99
Mary & Ken Rees, 103
Mary Sinfield, 101
Mason, Barry, 108
Master Mariner, 110, 140
Master of steam ships, 126
mate, chief, 119, 136, 138
Maudslay Sons and Field, 140
Max K Horton, 31, 36
McBride, Charles, 117, 120–21, 123, 126
McBride confusion, 126
McBride story, 123
McDonald, James, 25
McKinnon, 145
McQueen, Steve, 100
Medal, George, 5, 53, 60
Medici Society, 82
Melbourne, 146
Menai Bridge, 24, 100, 102, 155–56
Menai Straits, 93
Mercantile Houses, 135
Mercantile Marine, 53
Merchant Navy, 60
Mersey Trading Company, 155, 157, 160

Mesopotamia, 7
Messrs Bateson & Co, 120
Meteorology, 100
Methodism, 7, 26, 202
Meyrick's Island, 109, 143
M'Fadden James, 119
Middle Temple, 89
Midland Railway, 9
Military Cross, 110
Mills, C.A., 176
Mincing-lane, 112
Minstrel Lodge, 188
Minstrel Lodge development, 188, 196
Miss Adeane, 129
Miss Nightingale, 95
Miss Paget, 94
Mixsure Ltd, 168
mob, 5, 13, 16, 18, 40
Moelfre, 109
Môn, 18
Mona, 166
money, 48, 67, 76, 112, 129
Moore, Anthony, 40
Morfa, 105
Morlas, 164, 166
Morris, Lewis, 13, 16
Morris, Owen, 119
Morristown, 90
Morus, 16, 18–19
Morys Williams, 91
Moses, Thomas, 119
Mummery, Stephen, 24
Mundella, 35
Muswell Hill, 89

**N**
Nahum, 68–70
name McBride, 117
Nancollis, 23–24
Napoleon, 36
Nason, John, 119
National Lifeboat Institution, 128–29
National Provincial Bank, 99
National Schoolroom of Llanfaelog, 23, 25
National Service, 47
National Training School, 94
National Westminster Bank, 178
Nautical Photo Agency, 141
Naval Architects, 113
navigation, 121, 125, 149
navy, 36, 136
Nazis, 31, 36, 100
Nefyn, 167
Nelly & Sarah Owen, 93–95
Nelsen, P., 119
Neville, H., 119
New Season Teas, 112
New York and Boston, 111
New York tea trade, 142
New Zealand, 74
Nigel Bruce, 101
Nightingale, Florence, 92–95
Nimrod, 109
Noddfa, 78, 80, 171
Norman, Roger, 127
Norman Court, 5, 22, 107–33, 136–38, 142–49, 192
Norman Court houses, 172
Normandy, 61
Norman Harrison, 168

North America, 123
Northern Ireland, 36–37
North Richmond Street, 23–24
North Wales Chronicle, 7, 25, 120–21
Norway, 35, 101
Nugent collection, 69

**O**
Oakland, 25
oars, 55–57, 134
Observer newspaper, 48
Octavia, 116
Officer Training, 48
O'Gaunt, John, 109
Ogwen Cottage, 74
Oldham, 68, 73, 85
Oliver, Jamie, 41
Onslow Gardens, 94
Open Championship, 176
Orchard, 145
Oregon, 123
Orme, 160
Ormerod, Winifred, 65–66, 68
Outward Cargo, 115, 146
Overstrand Avenue, 195
Owain's Home, 170
Owen, 25, 89–92, 143
 Evan, 14
 Harry, 127
 John, 127
 Lizzie, 104
 Morris, 16
 Nelly, 93–95
Oxo cubes, 59
Oystercatcher Restaurant, 40–41

**P**
Paddle Steamer, 151–61
Paddle Steamer Prince Leopold, 159
Paddle Steamer Rhos Colwyn, 159
Pagoda Anchorage, 135–36, 147
paintings, postage-size, 73
Palethorpe, 176, 194
 Charles, 194
 Henry, 80
Pant y Gloch, 126
parachuting, 102
Paran, 88
Paran Chapel House, 164
Paris, 103
parish, 15, 23–25, 90
Parliament, 36
Parlwr, 174
Parry, John, 21
Parsons, Charlie, 99
passage, best, 133
passages, fast, 139, 149
Pavilion Picture House, 181
Paxton, 120–21
PC George Cledwyn Arthur, 53
Peel, John, 5, 43–49, 202
Pencarnisiog, 168
Penkey, Frank, 119
Penny, Mrs, 25
Penrallt, 176
Penrhos, 126
Penryn Bay, 160
Pentowyn, 127
Peterhead, 110, 133
Peter M Hannigan, 40
Philadelphia Museums, 117

Phillips, Kevin, 122
pictures, flower, 82
pier, 133, 152, 154, 156, 160
Pier, Victoria, 154
pier, Yarmouth, 153
pilots, 100, 137–38, 146
piracy, 13, 20
pirates, 13, 35, 37, 109, 114, 134, 146
plane, 53, 55–57, 59, 102
plaque, 37, 54
Plas Club, 3, 46
Plas Mawr, 73, 85
Plas Rhianfa, 93
Plas Rhoscolyn, 93
plundering, 7, 13–14, 20, 22
Plunkett, Sergeant John James, 54
Pointhouse, 114
Poland, 53
 refugees traversing, 102
police-officer, 23–24, 60
poppies, 82–83
popularity, tea's, 111
port bow, 121, 124–25
Porth Crigyll, 168, 170–71, 188, 197
Porth Trecastell, 26
Portobello, 16
Post Office, 82, 101, 103, 164
POW camps, 100
Power Boat Centre, 175
Premier Garage, 175, 189
premium, 116, 139, 147
Presbyterian Church, 88
Prichard family, 126
Prime Minister, 53
Prince William, 104–5
Pringle, James, 24–25
Pritchard, Elizabeth, 126
Pritchard, John, 15
Pritchard, Richard, 123, 127
Proas, 134
Prowse, William, 23
pubs, 46, 103, 105
PWE669, 190

**Q**
Queen, 129, 154
Queen Mary's Doll House, 72–74
Queen's Head Livery Stables, 186
Queenstown, 120, 124

**R**
racing, 110, 116, 145–47
Radar Operator, 47
RAF, 53, 100–101, 103–4
Raffles, 120, 124, 128
RAF Rhosneigr, 53
RAF Valley, 41, 104, 173
Railway Caravans, 9
Random house, old, 167
Rangoon, 146
Ravenscroft, Bob, 45
Ravenscroft, Douglas, 46
Ravenscroft, John, 48
Ravenscroft, Leslie, 45
Ravenscroft, Sheila, 47–48
RBA, 48, 61
Rear-Admiral Chalmers, 33, 37
Rear Admiral Karl Dönitz, 31
Red Funnel Line, 160
Red House, 45
reefs, 13, 60, 134

Rees, Ken, 5, 97–105
Rees, Ken and Mary, 99, 101, 103
Rees, Martyn, 99, 101
Rees, Mary, 19, 101, 103
Rees, Suzanne, 101
Rees, Tony, 18
Renfrew, 6
Rennie, William, 114, 145, 147
Rhianfa, 93, 164
Rhos, 2, 157–58
Rhoscolyn, 22–23, 41, 93, 118
Rhoscolyn life-boat, 24
Rhosneiger Lifeboat, 121, 125
Rhosneigr bay, 111
Rhosneigr Boatowners' Association, 61
Rhosneigr Coxswain, 119
Rhosneigr Library, 37
Rhosneigr Lifeboat, 27, 109, 119, 124–25
Rhos Neigr paddle steamer, 151–61
Rhosneigr Pharmacy, 164
Rhosneigr Romanticist, the, 92, 203
Rhosneigr's William David Owen, 26, 89
Rhosneigr Village Hall Committee, 181
Rhos-on-Sea, 160
Rhos Pier, 158, 160–61
Rhos Point, 157
Rhos Trevor, 156, 159–60
Rhosyr, 187
Rhyl, 152
Richard Jones Pentowyn, 127
Richard Prichard, 126
Riddiford, 129
River Crigyll, 7, 14
River Llifon, 7
RNLI, 53, 61, 127
RNLI Silver Medal, 120
robbers, 13–16, 18–19, 91
Robert, Thomas. Maelog Villa, 127
Robert Fields, 24
Robert J.A.Horton, 33–34, 40
Roberts, Gabriel, 14–16
Roberts, Kate, 194
Roberts, Richard, 24
Roberts, Samuel, 14–15
Roberts, Thomas, 14–16, 119, 125, 127
Roberts, William, 14, 21
Robinson. Alexander, 119, 145
Rochdale, 66, 75
rocket apparatus, 119, 121
Rocket House & Storehouse, 164, 166–67
rocks, pinnacle, 146
Rocks, Lion, 45
Rocks of Crigyll, 7, 19
Roddick, James, 178
Rolleston, 193
Romany Cottage, 195
ropes, 14–15, 56, 119, 145
Rose Cottage, 182
Rosemount, 129
Rosiewicz K.S., 53
Ross-shire, 109
Rowland Humphrey, 15
rowlocks, 55, 119
Royal Academy, 72–73, 85, 203
Royal Air Force, 102
Royal Artillery, 47
Royal Australian Air Force, 54
Royal Cambrian Academy (RCA), 64, 72, 85
Royal Cambrian Society, 72

Royal Canadian Navy, 37
Royal Charter, 25, 109
Royal collection, 74
Royal Institute of Painters in Watercolours, 72, 85
Royal Navy, 35, 37
Royal Yacht Squadron, 110
Ruabon, 100
rugby, 100–103
Rural Space Ltd, 168
Russell Homes, 171, 197
Russian-born Carl Balkin, 79

**S**
Saigon, 146
sailing ships, 22, 109–10, 113, 116
Saint Eneigr, 2
Sain y Mor, 167, 191
Salford, 73
Salisbury, 127
Salter, Niki, 167
salvage, lawful, 21
sampans, 147
Sandford, 167
Sandy Lane, 193, 196
Sandymount Club, 5, 97–105
Sandy's Bar & Bistro, 105
The Sarah, 25, 61, 95
Sausage Castle, 194
schooners, 25, 110, 114
Scilly, 142
Scotland, 53, 61, 190
Scully, Hugh, 70
sea
 heavy, 60, 119, 121
 treacherous, 119
Sea Cadets, 37
Seacome, Samuel, 14
Seaforth, 89
Sea King, 25
Sea View, 167
Second World War, 31, 37, 53, 100, 103, 185, 189
Seed, Matilda, 126
Semmering, 193
Serica, 136
Service, Malcolm, 24
Shanghai, 115–16, 145–46, 148
Sheep Inn, 168
Sheep Rocks, 22
Shelby-James, John, 189
Shewan, 113, 115–16, 133
 Andrew, 109–11, 133, 145, 203
Shewsbury, 179
Shields Daily Gazette, 118
shipbuilding, 140
ships, fastest, 140, 145
ship's compass, 127
shipwrecks, 13–14, 20, 25–26, 130, 172
shop, antique, 15
Shrewsbury, 20
Shrewsbury Chronicle, 21
Shrewsbury Public School, 45
Shropshire, 179
Sibrwd y Don, 191
silk, 111, 147
Simons, 53
Singapore, 146
sinking, 34–35, 109, 111, 157, 160
Sir George Meyrick, 80, 143, 194
Sir James Paget, 94

Bibliography & Index  **207**

Sir Joseph Causton, 117
Sir Julian Goldsmid, 36
Sir Lancelot, 133, 136, 145
Sir Percy Noble, 36
Sisial y Mor, 199
Slate Cottage, 185
Smiler Beretta, 169
Smith, John, 14, 145
smugglers, 13, 26, 91
Snapshots, 45
Sourabaya, 117, 120
South Africa, 109, 116
Southampton, 153–54
South Cape, 148
South China Sea, 146
South Kensington, 94
South Stack, 121
South Street, 93, 95
South West, 7, 13
Speed, John, 143
Spindrift, 136
sprue, 136
squadrons, 53–54, 136
Stalag Luft, 100–102
St. Andrews, 136, 190
Stanley, William O., 128–29
Stanley Wood MA, 34
Star, Harold, 102
Starvation Island, 55, 109, 118, 143
station, 2, 27, 36, 53–54, 74, 90, 125, 187
   coastguard, 121
   police, 59
station master, 129
Station Medical Officer, 59
Station Road, 89, 171, 188, 196, 198
steam, 94, 142
Steamer Ashore Sensation, 5, 160
steamer George Eliott, 119
steamers, 126, 136, 149, 154–55, 157, 160
steam tug Challenger, 119
Steele clippers, 140, 145, 148
Stepney, 110, 133
Stevenson, A., 119
Stewart Wood's Story, 53–55, 61
St. George, 136
St. George's Hall, 120
St John, 110
St Luke's Chelsea, 126
St Maelog's Church, 22, 54
Stockport, 168
storehouses, 7, 191
storm, 7, 14, 92, 154
Stowage, 153, 202
straw, 143, 147
stream, 9, 46, 190
Stretford, 85
Stride, Ada, 194
Stryd Uchaf, 182
Studio Gate, 81
Submarine A1, 34
Submarine E9, 36
submarines, 31, 35–37
Suez Canal, 116, 142, 149
Suffolk, 47
sugar, 116–19
Sullivans, 104
Sumatra, 134
Sunda, 134
Sunderland, 116
sunset, 67, 77–78
Surabaya, 118
Surf Point, 176, 194
Surrey, 61
Sutcliffe, Lester, 85

Sweden, 35
Sweeney, 25
Swn-y-Mor, 195
Swyn Llyr, 196
Sydney, 133, 148

T
Table Bay, 109
Taeping, 136, 145
Tan-y-Fron, 80
Tasmania, 148
Tate Gallery, 72
Tate's Sugar, 117
Taylor, W.B., 23
tea, 47–48, 73, 111–13, 116, 133, 135, 142, 146–47
   chests of, 114, 135
   first, 135–36, 139, 146, 149
   load, 127
   new season's, 116
Tea Caddy cafe, 54–55
tea chest storage, 113
tea clipper activity, 110
Tea-Clipper Captain, 133, 203
Tea Clipper Crews, 145
tea clipper Norman Court, 136
Tea Clipper Races, 116
Tea Clippers, 5, 107–31, 133, 135–36, 138–40, 142, 145–49
   first British, 111
tea fleet, 139, 142
tea-gardens, 135
Tea Ports, 146
Tea Race, 115, 147
tea ships, 111–12, 116
tea smuggling, 111
tea trade, 116, 149
Tenants of The Maelog, 40
Terrace, Marine, 178
Tetbury, 157
Thames, 61, 75, 140
Thermopylae, 108, 116, 136, 140, 142, 145, 148
Thermopylae and Cutty Sark, 145, 149
Thomas, Evan, 40
Thomas, William, 15
Thomas & Sarah Fagan, 40
Thomas Baring, 114, 127
Thomas Fanning Evans, 128
Thomas Lingham Lifeboat, 119
Thompson, John, 24, 116
Thomson, Jane, 110
Thrilling Lifeboat Story, a, 120
Thundersley, 6
Tides Reach, 175, 192
Timpson family, 41
Titania, 145
Towyn Llyn, 40
Towyn Trewan, 2
Trac Mon, 49
Traffwll, 91
train, 41, 78, 101, 119, 125
Trearddur Bay, 46, 48, 61, 109
Trefor quarry, 167
Tref Owain, 170
Tre-Iago, 80
Trem-y-Mor, 198
Trewyn Bach, 127, 170
Trewyn Isaf, 170
Trewyn Uchaf, 196
trial, 5, 13, 15–16, 18, 101
Trwst y Don, 176
Tryfan, 66, 70–71, 74
tuberculosis, 90, 92
Turner C.E., 33, 81
Turner Dunette, 72

Tuskar, 120–21, 124–25
Ty Croes, 25, 46–49
Tyddyn Leci, 185
Ty Gwyn, 127, 164
Ty Main, 127, 183
Ty'n Cerrig, 127
Tyn Cerrig, 119
Ty Newydd, 164, 191
Tyn-y-Cai Pool, 82
Tyn-y-llan, 24
Ty Plant, 6, 166

U
U-boats, 31–32, 36–37
UJ1966, 179
underwater images, 122
United States, 111
Universities Royal Naval Unit in Wales, 37
University, 190, 199
Uttley, Winifred, 65
Uwch y Don, 174

V
Vaenor, 171
Valley, 53–54, 59, 101
Vancouver, 109
Vectis, 154
Venice, 66–67, 69–71
Ventnor, 154–55
Verney family, 93–95
Vernon, 16, 18
vessel
   stranded, 20, 121
   wrecked, 119, 125, 161
vessel struck, 121, 160
village policeman, 53
Volunteer Reserve Officers, 100
voyage, first, 25, 133, 139–40
V.Roe & Co, 6

W
Walker, Johnnie, 36
Walker Art Gallery, 78
Wall, Charles, 127
Wallroth, Louisa, 109
Walton-on-Thames, 60–61
War Memorial, 175
Warr, 120
Warren Road, 89
Washington, Thomas, 14
watch, gold, 23–24
water, shallow, 132, 134, 160
Waterfront development, 171, 197
water tower, 58, 192–93
Watt, A.W., 156
Wave Crest Hotel, 173
Waymouth, Bernard, 145
weapons, 35, 101
Webb, John, 55
Wellington bomber, 101–2
Welsh, 13, 16, 92, 182
Welsh farmers, 73
Welsh mountains, 78
Welsh Presbyterian Churches, 88
Wembley Exhibition, 73
Wessex Brigade Royal Field Artillery, 110
West Blackhall Street, 123
Western Approaches, 32–37, 202
West Freugh, 53
Westminster Estate, 61
West Tytherley, 127
Wexford, 120
Weybrdge, 61
Whaite, Clarence, 85
Whampoa, 146

White Cottage, 174
White Dogs, 146
White Eagle, 41
White Gables, 46
White Lady, 26
Whitley, 101
Whitworth Art Gallery, 73, 75
Whysall, Peter T., 53
Wickens, 78
Wight, Isle of, 153–54
Wight Steam Packet Co, 154
Wilde, Andy, 167
Wild Island, 109, 143
Wiliam, Dafydd Wyn, 16
William, Prince, 5, 41, 104–5
William David Owen, 26, 89, 92
William Griffith Hughes, 14–15
William Henry Baring, 127
William Henry Fooman, 24
William Henry Jones, 40
William Lewis Esq, 12
William Robert, Glandwr, 127
Williams, Albert, 189
Williams, David, 40
Williams, Edward, 24
Williams, John, 23
Williams, Robert, 24
Williams, Thomas, 127
Williams, William, 21
Williams R. rector of Llanfaelog, 23
Willis, John, 140
Wilson, Dr., 85
Windhover, 136
Wing Commander Oliver, 59
Wingett, Frank, 101
Winston S Churchill, 31–32, 36
winter, 67, 75, 82, 102, 118
Wirral, 45
Withens, Samuel, 40
women, 34, 61, 102, 160
Wood, Judith, 61
Wood, Kathleen, 53
Wood, Rachel, 61
Wood, Sarah, 61
Wood, Stanley, 34
Wood, Stewart, 5, 51–61
Woodhead R., 40
Woodlands boarding school, 45
Worcester, 27
   John R., 145
Work Box, 55
World War, 32, 35, 70, 73, 110
wreckers, 13, 22, 25–26, 109
wrecking, 13, 26, 146
Wreck of Rhos Neigr, 159
wreck site, 122
Wright & Co, 156
Wylfa, 164
Wyllie, Alick, 119
Wylo, 140
Wynaud, 134

Y
Yankee clipper Golden State, 146
Yarmouth, 153–54
y Bonc, 188
y Fron, 193
Ynys Feirig, 109, 118, 143
Ynys Groes, 167, 191
Ynys Hir, 196
Ynys Wealt, 143
Ynys Wellt, 109, 143

Z
Ziba, 136

**208** *Bibliography & Index*